Trotsky



A CIP catalogue record for this book is available at the British Library

ISBN 978-1-7398276-1-8

First Edition

# PREFACE

My world, like everyone else's paused in March 2020. At the delicate age of 57 I and my family felt very vulnerable to the coronavirus pandemic that was sweeping the globe, and through a subsequent period of self-isolation, and a surplus of time, I looked around for something constructive to do within the confines of my home.

A month into Lockdown, I received a request from my Walking Football Club, Chelmsford City, to write a personal player profile. I had retired from playing football seven years before but had found a new lease of football life in this very gentlemanly pursuit. It was to be a short piece about my life focusing on football, family and work, and any funny stories that might amuse my colleagues. Every player was being asked to do this in turn while living in our Groundhog Day existence of lockdown.

At first, I struggled to write anything, being very conscious of any bad impressions I might give. I didn't want to come across as arrogant, or worst still, boring. As I started to compile a few things that might be of interest to my football team colleagues I then found it exceedingly difficult to cram so much into a short piece to make it sufficiently concise and interesting. How should I prioritise? What should be included, or had better be left out?

Like most people's journeys I had enjoyed the highs and endured the lows that life unfolds before us. As I sketched out the framework of my story so far, I wondered if my tale may be of wider interest. I had helped facilitate the birth and then watched from within the onset of the Housemartins pop group, performed or appeared in numerous TV Programmes, music videos, Feature Films, TV Commercials, and fronted international advertising campaigns. I had endured being crushed in the Lepping Lane end of Hillsborough a few years before the infamous tragedy. I had been elected to the national party council of the Ecology Party, now Green Party and I later understood that I had consequently become a person of interest to MI5 with my phone tapped, letters opened and was frequently followed by the state due to our anti-nuclear policy. I later uncovered that I had narrowly escaped the clutches of a serial killer at the naive age of eighteen.

Once I sent off my short profile, I was hungry for more, I continued to write and expand my story, as I hoped that at the very least this might become of interest to my children or any grandchildren one day. With the Coronavirus Pandemic at its peak, the concept of my life ending prematurely had already started to make me reflect on my journey so far, the memories of which had started to be re-written, fade, or completely forgotten.

The process of accounting for one's life is not easy, our memories are great at recollecting joyful or humorous times, but also for burying trauma and suffering which inevitably is brought to the fore during this process. With every journey you do not know what you will find, and retracing one becomes its own journey. You do not know what you may discover, what you will do with it, or what it will do to you.

I have painstakingly researched gaps in my memory and dug out and corrected my own myths that had been inaccurately cemented in my time. I hope that my flaws exposed will be understood within the context of age and time, but also as the necessary compliment to any virtues or accomplishments. At times it was hard to fully grasp my reasoning and decision making, but with the benefit of hindsight you start to fully understand the mistakes made and the consequences that ensued. I now comprehend how sometimes the most ostensibly innocuous decision can have life or death outcomes, or decisions that you struggled and stressed over for an age had in time little or no importance. Looking back, you see the missed opportunities, and what life could have been, but understand that other wonderful things might not have consequently taken place, so I try to have no regrets. Had I not had the terrifying Mr Moore as my primary school music teacher, who was wholly responsible for delaying my interest in music in my formative years and the ability to learn to play an instrument, who knows how things might have turned out given who I grew up with. In contrast, losing my driving licence and so my job, I chose to move to Hull which unfolded whole new opportunities for me and others.

With so much time on my hands this became a full-time project, and in time developed into an autobiography of the first forty odd years of my life. I have referenced the milestone events of the world, social attitudes of the time and the musical accompaniment of my journey that shaped the person I was, I am and who I might become. My life has always been accompanied by music, and I felt it fitting to label each chapter of my account with a song that is pertinent to that time or resonates as a trigger for events in my life.

Before finalising the content of my self-indulgent project, I learned that my dearest friend Alfred Wirth passed away on 5th August 2021. He was a significant and perhaps the greatest inspiration on my outlook, politics, and positively influenced me in so many areas of life. I owe him so much and he's passing has broken my heart, especially as I was looking forward to sharing my memoirs with him. There is a little of Alfred in me, and I hope I can successfully pass on his values and joy of life on before I pass. I have therefore dedicated this book to him. This is my journey so far.

Alfred Wirth
18th September 1953 – 5th August 2021

I Wonderful Land. *The Shadows*
1962 – 1972
II Space Oddity *David Bowie*
1969 – 1973
III Annie's Song *James Galway*
1973-1978
IV Oh' What a Circus *David Essex*
1978-1979
V I Don't Like Mondays *Boomtown Rats* 1979-1982
VI Suicide is Painless. *The M*A*S*H*
1980
VII Tainted Love *Soft Cell*
1981-1982
VIII All the Madmen *David Bowie*
1982
IX Come on Eileen *Dexy's Midnight Runners* 1982
X Wherever I Lay my Hat *Paul Young*
1983
XI One in Ten *UB40*
1983 -1984
XII Hello. *Lionel Ritchie*
1984 - 1986.
XIII Two Tribes *Frankie Goes to Hollywood* 1984 -1985
XIV Chain Reaction *Donna Summer*
1986 -1987
XV Never Gonna' Give You Up *Rick Astley* 1987 - 1990
XVI Wonderwall *Oasis*
1990 -1996
XVII Missing *Everything but the Girl*
1996
XVIII Don't Marry Her *The Beautiful South*
1996 -1999
XIX Seasons in the Sun *Terry Jacks*
1999 – 2000
XX Fallin' *Gabrielle*
2001
XXI Thursday's Child. *David Bowie*
2001-2002

**Spotify Link**

https://open.spotify.com/playlist/2qJMsrXPM4u06YCZ66GxnT?si=1ILpTuHyQOq_EJX2VwpmbA&utm_source=copy-link&dl_branch=1

Paul Heaton and I in Dietkirchen 2002.

# CHAPTER I WONDERFUL LAND

It was relatively common at the time to deliver babies in the home, but unlike my three predecessors I was delivered in Redhill General Hospital in Surrey, in the early hours of Monday 9th April 1962. My first action on this earth was to inconvenience the family traditional Sunday Roast the day before, by inexcusably pushing my mother Josie into labour after she had taken all morning preparing, cooking, and serving up the family meal. Possibly the smell of roasting rosemary seasoned lamb and crisp roasted parboiled potatoes prompted me to leave the warm and safe confines of her womb, fed up with the regurgitated offerings of the last few months.

My mum, Josephine Barry, but Josie to her friends, had many talents, but Sunday Roast was her speciality, and no one in else in the world has ever come close to creating this epicurean heaven, which is evidently why my mother remained seated during her narrowing contractions until she had cleaned her plate, causing probable deep anxiety in my father Dessie.

Redhill General Hospital was not the closest, however due to capacity issues it was the only possibility on this Sunday afternoon, and the two of us were whisked away in haste down the A23 towards Earlsfield. The Hospital grounds are now a housing estate with only the Porter's Lodge and Sherwood House buildings still standing after the rest was finally demolished in 1995.

Having already supplied two sisters, Denise and Vivien, and my brother Desmond, my parents were keen to round up the numbers equally being superstitious and from a traditional Irish Catholic background renowned for large families.

Following family tradition my Auntie Patsy Sheehan named me Raymond, as it rhymed with my dad’s and my brother’s name Desmond. My Grandfather, a well-known boxer supplied the inspiration for my middle name William. William “Billy” Barry was now retired some 27 years, after 80 professional bouts. If I ever were to have become a professional boxer, I would have chosen the catchy Ray Bill Barry as my designation.

The world was vastly different in 1962, The Beat Brothers had only charted in still divided Germany as a backing band for Tony Sheridan, dropping their Beatles name as it sounded too like the Hamburgisch dialect for penis's. Pidles pronounced peedles.

Back in London the BBC had yet to design its first Dalek, and Harold Macmillan lived in 10 Downing Street. John F. Kennedy was the President of the USA and the first anniversary of Yuri Alekseyevich Gagarin becoming the first man in space, was just a few days away.

Same-sex acts between men were punished with imprisonment, although not between women, but they had to contend with the illegality and therefore criminality of abortion. There were just two black and white television channels, BBC, or ITV. Average pay was just over £15 a week, and an average house would cost you £2'670. There were no anti-discriminatory laws in place. You could legally turn someone down for accommodation or a job or pay them less because of their ethnicity or gender. All this under the dark clouds of a four-minute warning of nuclear extermination as the world was at the height of cold war tensions, with the means of mutually assured annihilation.

My parents were raised in the old London Metropolitan Borough of Marylebone and had both been evacuated as children to Nottinghamshire during the second world war, where friendship pathed the way for future romance, which blossomed once back in war damaged Paddington.

Children then were placed with families who had no vetting, and I learned much later in life that both were subjected to a level of sexual abuse whilst in the care of these families. Josie plucked up the courage to inform her mother Nancy on a visit and she responded by whisking her two daughters across the Irish sea to the safety of neutral Ireland, only returning to London after the fall of Berlin.

The years between the war and my parents formally getting together are a mystery, and I think these teenage years of teddy boys and the new found freedoms of young people, must have been exhilarating, but my parents' role is forever undisclosed. There was a new hope in the Country, the war was won, a radical Labour Government was swept into power on a landslide, created the NHS, and brought many industries under public control.

Back in Paddington, being a romantic, my dad Desmond Reginald Barry, was keen to get married in a rush. So, they legally married before the financial new year, to cash in on a reduction in income tax payable through marriage allowance. The next month, he succumbed to the practical aspects of married life by giving his wife the church wedding she deserved on Old Marylebone Road.

Mr & Mrs Barry

After getting duly hitched twice my father moved his new family out of central London to Kenley Surrey on very edge of the London's expanding suburbia.

I recall my mother often complaining about living out of central London, as she was missing the affinity of having the extended family in our lives, but it was fair to say that her parents, Nancy, and Valentine Sheehan had already moved out to Carpenters Park Hertfordshire, and the Barry's of Paddington had something of a reputation that my dad was keen to shrug off or at least be a good arm's length from our new home in leafy Surrey.

The decision to have me in Hospital was made after my parents fourth planned child did not make it into this world. I only learned about this tragedy in adulthood when I was considered more emotionally intelligent to understand these things, however, the news was a devastating revelation to me. I did feel detached in my early years of life but had never understood why. I could only try and imagine how painful that was for my doting mother.

I could not help feeling that I was a replacement, a substitute, an afterthought by my family, and although I know beyond any doubt that I was completely loved by all my family, I did perceive that I was not always equally embraced. Always following me was the shadow of the lost one that everyone could see, but me.

Obviously, the family would have been traumatised by the death, and it was never spoken about, certainly not in my ear shot, but my life begun due to this tragedy, and it still feels like a borrowed life even now in the Equinox of my years. Had my lost brother been born, I doubt I would have existed. Now born, I appeared into a dangerous and volatile world.

It was just 17 years since nuclear weapons had been dropped on civilian targets in Japan, and tensions between the Communist East and the Capitalist West could not have been more stretched and dangerous with escalating levels of nuclear weapon proliferation. At 6 months of age, I was of course oblivious to the very real danger of all out nuclear war. On October 27th, an American U-2F reconnaissance plane provocatively flew over Communist Cuban airspace and was shot down, and Soviet Captain Savitsky B-59 Submarine with Nuclear tipped Torpedo's was depth charged in response. Far away, Russian MiG fighters scrambled after an American spy plane encroached Soviet air space, and in turn the US F-102 fighters were scrambled in response.

Out of radio contact in the depths of the Gulf of Mexico, Vasily Arkhipov convinced Captain Valentin Grigorievitch Savitsky not to launch a nuclear attack on the USA from their submerged submarine, in retaliation for being depth charged by US war planes.

I was only a few weeks old when Soviet Premier Nikita Khrushev secretly started the process of planning the deployment of short-range Nuclear Missiles to Cuba, as the USSR still did not have the reciprocal ability of the USA in striking the mainland. They understood they needed to re-dress the imbalance, which historians now suggest the Soviet Union only had 300 Nuclear War Heads, to the USA's 5000.

As the world held its breath in October 1962, Nuclear armed US B-52's remained on permanent stand by. All out Nuclear War was a very real threat as both sides considered military action, which if escalated would have eradicated the world before it had really begun for me.

Only one person was killed in this short skirmish, but the Americans agreed to withdraw their Nuclear Missiles from Turkey and Italy, in exchange for the Russians withdrawing theirs from Cuba. However, the threat of a Nuclear War sustained a Cold War across the globe and would continue for the first twenty-eight years of my life.

It is difficult to understand how close our world came to eradication; I was fortunately wrapped in my swaddling oblivious of the perilous journey I had survived.

My first home was in a small block of three-bedroom flats called Betts Mead Parade on Old Lodge Lane Kenley Surrey, down a Country Lane just out of site of the metropolis of suburban London. As kids we had the run of an adjacent field, a recreation ground, and small woodlands to the rear. We were also within walking distance of the abandoned Kenley Aerodrome a significant site in the Battle of Britain 22 years earlier. The Shadows were number one in the charts and provided the musical backdrop on the radio with *Wonderful Land,* as my senses started to appreciate the wonders of my post war new world.

My first memories were being wheeled dangerously down a small narrow windy Country Lane with no pavement. The sound of a distant car engine squeezed the air out of my lungs, strapped into a rambling push chair with my head just a couple of feet off the ground, eyes fixed on the next bend for any warning of the oncoming terror of an expected full-on collision. Cars usually slowed down when they could, but with a 60mph speed limit in place you could never feel safe.

My mother did not have any choice. She had to make this trip every School Day to take and pick up my Brother and Sisters from Hayes Lane Primary School, something I came to understand caused her more anxiety than it did me. She also had to do this for many years before my initiation. We were, as were most families a one car family, with my father the only one with a driving licence, which he secured during his enforced national service.

He once explained to me that he was lucky to pass, as one of the surprise tests involved driving an HGV over very bumpy ground, and then down an embankment with enough speed to get back up the other side. If you hesitated and put the brakes on you would never make it up the other side and need an embarrassing tow out of the ditch, while enduring the wrath of the commanding officer in your ear and the failing the entire test.

Fortunately for my father he explained that he panicked completely, but with no half measures causing any hesitation. In the bouncing cabin he hit the accelerator instead of the break as intended and flew down and up the other side to his and everyone's surprise. Many years later I would too be issued with a Class II Heavy Goods Licence, and often thought of my dad's ordeal while learning, although my test was quite different.

We were not poor, but things were very tight as my dad supplemented his income by washing wealthy neighbours' car, Albert Hill lived just a stone throw away in exceptionally large house with extensive grounds along with his subservient wife and young child Kevin. He also gave me my first taste of Beer in the local pub, the Wattenden Arms, at the tender age of four.

I hated the bitter taste, and it took me longer than usual to get a taste for Bitter which was not necessarily a terrible thing.

Albert was a director at Lesney who made the famous matchbox car toys, and one Christmas we were presented with a large box of the full collection of their matchbox model cars. Given the prudent requirements of my childhood, being the youngest I rarely got anything new. Once the squabbles about who should have which cars, or should they all be shared had eased off, the fact that the size of my toy collection had simply exploded overnight was still exhilarating to a 4-year-old.

This feeling very much overcame an innate fear I had of Albert due to his deformed eye, caused by the family dog jumping up at him, a beautiful well-mannered Golden Labrador called Sandy. It was revealed to me later in life that his toddler son Kevin, had accidentally stuck a fork in his eye, and poor innocent Sandy had been saddled with the crime to protect the sensibilities of his son. Little did I know that the cementing of this friendship with our neighbour through this generous act would lead me down a path that still torments me over fifty years later.

However, it was 1966 and my interest in Football was still formulating, but not enough to watch the World Cup Final all the way through on a tiny fuzzy black and white TV in a holiday caravan in Cornwall. My Nan, Nancy Sheehan taking the troublesome toddler outside to teach him the words to the children's song "Puff the Magic Dragon."

It was around this time my father announced we were planning on moving into a proper house, and I was introduced to house hunting, and remember being taken to the set of a haunted house. Here the deceased had obviously not had sufficient time to do the housework for many months, the gloomy interior had antique furniture garnished with thick flowing cobwebs, and sinister looking portraits and photos which followed your every move. Even with my light frame, I treaded very carefully not to creek the floorboards and disturb the spirits.

Fortunately, my Parents imagination would not stretch to make this our family home, and shortly afterwards, despite having already attended a "get to know you" session at Hayes Lane Primary School, we were whisked off to Coulsdon on the Chipstead Valley Road. Overlooking the valley was the sinister looking water tower of an asylum called Cane Hill Hospital, where my Mum and Brother would in time know very well working there for many years.

I was provided with the greatest bedroom in the known world, or at least according to my perceived world to date, and one that I would never have to share. My Brothers new room was twice the size however, mine had a sky light window over the bed, and I was close to touching heaven and the stars every night. Standing on a chair I could also see my new Primary School playground across the road.

We had a narrow garden that went on forever or at least to the railway line, with a small courtyard, lawn and then a vegetable patch and rear garage a coal bunker and behind that the railway embankment. It was still the days of having an open fire, and I used to delight at being asked to count the coal sack delivery. Later, in the winter of 1972 I was concerned because the coal miners had gone on strike and we might not receive our regular delivery of coal, not realising that coal was mainly required to generate electricity which during the many subsequent power cuts the open fire became the only source of light and the source where we would light the necessary candles to overcome the remaining darkness. I loved the miners as I found this all extremely exciting, and my dad without a TV to watch taught me to play chess most nights lit only by flickering candlelight which added to the magic.

This was my very first political position, I supported the Miners because they gave me priceless time with my dad, I learned how to play chess, and when my Nan explained they wanted fair wages for their families as the work was dangerous and unpleasant. I became a Socialist at the age of five.

Opposite our house on the Chipstead Valley Road, and I mean within a few meters, was an entrance to my new Primary

School, so I and my mother would no longer risk life and limb, in fact my mum could see me off to School without leaving the front Garden as the lollipop lady stood by our gate on School days every morning and evening.

I would say the first few years of life had been very lonely, my brother and sisters rarely had time for me, referring to me as “Trollop” which I understood to be derisory even then, but my siblings obviously did not comprehend the correct meaning as I was not a woman, and was obviously still a virgin. Nevertheless, I was wildly excited about making new friends at School as well as anxious and a little afraid as most children would be.

Scouring the playground desperately looking for a friend. I could feel my mother’s eyes observing my every move, which is why I learned in time to mostly play around the back of the shed out of sight. On my first day I spotted Vincent Bond who was sitting on the back rest of a bench kicking everyone who came close to him, and I approached him to ask why he was doing this in a naïve and innocent manner, becoming of a child over protected by the standards of the 1960’s he kicked me in the mouth. This was my first memory of Chipstead Valley Primary School.

As became a pattern in my life I befriended the perpetrator, and we played together a little, developing into good friends as both our mums became School cleaners which meant we had the run of the School while they were busy after school, usually playing football on the field. We also joined the chess club and enjoyed a friendly rivalry.

I toughened up under the guidance of Vince, and he provided the first opportunity to kick around with a friend, as back at Kenley in the adjacent field, it was always “three and in” with tackling rather than passing rules and being half the age of the other kids rarely got a touch, and this infrequent possession of the ball was often triggered by crying in desperation and threatening to tell. I phased this tactic out because the humiliation and looks of pity from my peers countered any enjoyment of getting an unchallenged kick of the ball.

I was bright at School and was proud to be the first in my class to learn their times tables, although that is not strictly true. In a test where we had to write in a grid the answers to each of the 1-12 times tables I learned to simply add up from the previous answer, which was highly effective until I was rumbled by close observation, and Mrs Durie had to change her testing technique. However, she was impressed in how I had devised a process to get to the desired answers.

I never quite grasped the importance of the Duck and Cover drill we practiced, but it was fun to hide under our desks when instructed to, and I did love the sound of the air raid siren situated at the end of our football field that would be tested every now and then. The assassination of Martin Luther King five days before my sixth birthday did not get a mention at school, or at home. I lived in an exclusively white world, oblivious, privileged, and protected.

I remember spending many anxious hours trying to learn how to convert money into the new decimalisation currency. A shilling would soon be 5p, but a penny was to be a half a penny, and a ha'penny no longer existed. However, a pound was still a pound, but it occurred to me one day in class to ask the obvious question. As we do not have any money yet, and by the time we do have some, decimalisation will be in place, so why don't we just learn the new currency?

The other thing I leaned at primary School was Crochet. This obviously proved invaluable in later life along with Duck and Cover and understanding Old Money. If I found some old money in an air raid shelter, while crocheting during a four-minute warning I was well prepared indeed for Armageddon.

I liked dance drama, and one year I was selected to be Joseph in the School Nativity Play, escorting my virgin bride Barbara Lumb with her tiny tears doll around the assembly hall in front of cooing parents, and I showed genuine Christian pity for the seven lads who had to wear tights to mimic seven swans are swimming. At the end of our performance someone's embarrassing mum grabbed my cheeks, overwhelmed by my obvious cuteness, but none the less I was frightened, dreading she was close to kissing me.

I loved sports day, with all the mums lined up as we progressed to our race, moving up a bench at a time until it was our go, with the excitement of winning a coloured card star for coming in the top three of four, which we had cut out ourselves the day before. I was good at rounders, and loved being on 3rd base, which was the best place to be to catch people out.

I also learned that I had not inherited my father's singing ability, as I could not sing. During assembly, the Head teacher complained that some pupils were simply groaning the words and decided to do an experiment to find out who were responsible for spoiling the overall tone. As we all sang, the teachers paraded around telling those who were singing properly to fall silent and eventually I and a handful of renegades were exposed as the groaners. Many years later my Cousin Darren had an operation on his nose as he was born with a defect which obstructed his breathing, and it became clear to me that my Brother and I had both had this problem without realising it, and this may account for my complete inability to get close to any recognisable pitch. Had I had a reasonable singing voice my life may have turned out very differently, and perhaps this experience stopped any exploration or development of a singing voice. Ironically for me, my daughter Jessica inherited a fabulous singing voice from her grandfather.

Dessie Barry on the microphone

Breathing issues may well have accounted for the fact I was one of the last of my peers to learn to swim. My family had been involved in several fund-raising events to help the school build a swimming pool, however it remained unbuilt throughout my five years. It would be many decades later those pupils did not have to travel by bus to nearby Reedham to learn to swim.

I visited Chipstead Valley Primary School again when my first-born Sean attended in 1998, and during the tour of the School I saw the new swimming pool for the first time but as we walked past the Goal Post where Vince and I hung out many years before, a sense of foreboding soaked into my previously relaxed body, and I actually felt a real sense of fear and anxiety. I realised that behind the goal was the prefab music class, where as a child I was terrorised along with all my classmates by the disciplinarian Music Teacher Mr Moore.

These were the school days where teachers rule was absolute, with no restraint of modern standards, and coaching consisted of a whack with a ruler across your knuckles for not holding your pencil correctly. Music was classical music, and at Chipstead Valley primary School there was no other music.

A quarter of a century had passed, as had Mr Moore due to a heart attack, but the trepidation and fear of seeing the classroom again triggered a physical and psychological response I was ill-prepared for. I never received a physical chastisement from Mr Moore, but the fear of attending weekly classes for five years had taken its toll.

My Brother Des had preceded me at Chipstead Valley and had taken up the Trumpet and performed under Mr Moore in the well renowned CVPS Orchestra, once performing proudly at Fairfield Halls in Croydon. I loved music and was desperate to play the Clarinet but with the family having to fork out for an expensive Trumpet there was no budget for my Clarinet, however the only way to learn was to attend additional lessons with Mr Moore and that was seriously out of the question.

This early experience never soured my love of listening to music. None the less the concept of trying to produce any was as dead as a violin without strings for many years to come. Especially given my vocal inability, something which closed numerous life changing opportunities that presented themselves to me in time to come. My life would have been significantly different if I had not been so terrified of Mr Moore or had recognised, I had a genetic breathing difficulty and been able to do something about it.

In my final year two new children joined my class, who were very curious because they were black. I was close to ten years old and had never interacted with anyone other than white British or Irish people. However, my heroes were Muhammad Ali and Pele, and I was excited to meet children who I naively hoped could be related somehow. Racism and racist attitudes were mainstream in the early 1970's and I was a product of my time.

I lost touch with Vince after leaving Primary School, but years later he struck up a friendship with my Brother Des which he sadly betrayed, but that is my Brother's story and that's for him to tell.

# CHAPTER II SPACE ODDITY

I had followed the Apollo Moon Missions on TV and had built my own Saturn Rocket out of the family Lego set, but this was in the days when you would only buy the basic bricks and the rest relied on your own imagination. I had begun its development from the wreckage of Thunderbird Two that my sister Denise had designed and built for me. It had recently crashed, slipping out my control while traveling downstairs on an unplanned unassisted flight.

When the first human moon landings were publicised in 1969, I stripped down my Saturn Rocket to include a landing module and considered trying to reproduce the lunar surface at home in the way that Vince Bond and I had done so successfully during Art lessons, using Polyfilla and an egg cup to pull out the craters.

I was into anything to do with space and was overwhelmed with excitement when I heard David Bowies *Space Oddity* on the radio for the first time. Denise my sister bought the cassette tape version of the album, and that was the first album I listened too. I would have been intrigued to know that this astronaut had a half-brother living in the scary hospital across the valley, but this remained a closely guarded secret at the time.

Live TV was exceedingly rare in 1969, I had been off sick from School when I watched the live coverage of the Investiture of Prince Charles at Caernarfon Castle, but the excitement of someone landing on and then walking on the moon live on TV was incredible to a seven-year-old and something that still amazes me half a century later. Watching a very fuzzy picture I vividly still remember that moment when Neal Armstrong uttered those immortal lines, however I have no fixed image of the historic event as I had to take the commentators word for what was happening, as it was like watching a ghost in a snowstorm.

I was taken to my very first football match at Selhurst Park on 7th February 1970 to see Chelsea beat Crystal Palace 4-1 in the

FA Cup 5th round tie and followed that up by a trip to White Hart Lane in March for the Semi-Final against Watford. Dad was a Chelsea match day steward and these matches really ignited my passion for football. In those days there was an agreement between London stewards at each club to let each other in, and to pass their kids over the turnstiles.

Chelsea won the Semi-final 5-1 and the next day my dad showed us a picture in the London Evening Standard in which my brother was clearly visible in the front row of the standing crowd wearing our home-made knitted balaclavas. I was hidden behind the leg of a stretcher bearer, whom I cursed for denying me my moment of fame.

It was not however, possible for us to attend either the Wembley or the Old Trafford Replay Final as dad had been invited onto the Stewards coach which was no place for children. However, draped in blue and white we watched both Cup finals at Wembley and Old Trafford against Leeds United at home on a black and white TV. It has been ranked among the greatest ever FA Cup finals and named as the "most brutal game" in the history of English football, due to the animosity between the two teams. Chelsea won their very first FA Cup in such a dramatic style coming from behind for a third time, inspired me with hope and a desire to become a footballer.

Later in the year I was delighted to be woken up in the middle of the night to watch England, the current World Champions, defending our title in Mexico in the ninth World Cup.

Starting with the opening match it became clear that Mexico and the Soviet Union were wearing identical grey and white strips, the only difference being the CCCP logo of the Soviet Union, but our neighbour invited us around at half time to watch on their Colour TV. I had never seen a Colour TV before and became fascinated by the stark red and green colours.

These games were live, and I cannot thank our neighbours enough for allowing the three of us to come around to their house in the early hours of the morning to watch their TV.

Obviously as World Champions I understood that England were the best team despite narrowly losing to Brazil in a game that included Gordan Banks's miraculous save from Pele. During the early hours, with two families arranged around a small TV focused on the quarter final I helped myself to apple juice from my neighbour's kitchen, and unforgivably fell asleep with England 2-0 up against West Germany, fortunately, unsupervised the difference between Cider and apple juice was not obvious to an 8-year-old.

As I was passed over the rear garden fence in the early hours, I learned that the Germans had beaten us, and I felt devastated and cheated but completely responsible, which I still do. Although my Chelsea goalkeeping hero Peter Bonetti should have taken some of the blame for his performance during the German fightback.

By Christmas that year I was well settled into school and it was decided that my brother and I would share our main Christmas present, a Subbuteo version of the recent World Cup in Mexico, a new football game that was head and shoulders above any other tabletop football game. I had already saved up for the England Team, but no one realised that they were included as one of the three teams in the box set, so my mum negotiated a replacement. Obviously, the shop assistant was savvy enough to fob her off with Peru of all countries.

As a child I started to collect 00 scale soldiers, tanks, field guns, and Airfix model war planes, and delighted in designing my own war games on the green cloth usually used for Subbuteo. I am not sure what it says about me, but my Nazi German army grew to be the largest.

My brother inspired my love of Muhammed Ali in his attempt to regain the title stripped from him for refusing the draft for the Vietnam war, we loved his cheeky antics out of the ring, and we counted down the days before each live broadcast of his fights in the early hours with Jerry Quarry, Oscar Ringo Bonavena and then the fight of the century against Joe Smoking Frazier when he regained his world title.

In the Spring of 1971, we went on our very first foreign package holiday to Majorca, with my Sister Denise bringing her hippy boyfriend Phil Crosby. I delighted in tormenting him by constantly asking "Phil, Phil up my glass," and always being present when they wanted to be alone. Holidaying abroad had been a past time for the wealthy. This was a very new trend and none of my friends had been abroad yet as foreign travel had been beyond the average pay packet, but prices had become affordable at the beginning of this decade. I still could not swim so the Pool was a place of fear even with my inflated ring but eating out in candlelight and spending hours on the beach digging complex moats and sandcastles was a dream, crowned by watching Chelsea win the European Cup Winners Cup in Athens against Real Madrid in the Spanish Hotel bar.

Riding a Spanish donkey 1971

I had forgiven our parents for leaving us with our grandparents in Carpenters Park while they flew off to Ibiza a couple of years prior, but I understand much better now that the cost of taking four children on holiday was just not doable, but my dad seemed to be becoming more relaxed about money, as I believe he was becoming more and more successful in his work.

I never grasped exactly what my dad did for a living, except he worked in Croydon in an office for an engineering Company and seemed to spend a great deal of time entertaining clients on Golf days, and when my mother was duty bound to attend functions accompanying him, she persistently complained about having to pander to his client's needs and watch in her view her husband belittle himself on a charm offensive that was infrequently bestowed upon herself. However, she understood that holidays abroad would become normal and it was a sacrifice worth making.

The family were uprooted once more, but this time just a few roads up the side of the valley, as we moved into a larger house on Nutfield Road which had a small fishpond, but the Garden was smaller than Chipstead Valley Road. We had our own rooms and in time a new Colour TV arrived. Val my grandad diabetes had gotten the better of him a few years prior and he had had to have some toes amputated, and then the lower part of his leg.

They had moved to a remote cottage near Launceston in Cornwall, and a decision was made that he would stay with us after a third amputation above the knee, and my brother gave up his bedroom to accommodate him, so we were back sharing again. Our household was a busy one, and this proud man found it hard to be so disabled, reliant on a monstrosity of an artificial leg that was extremely cumbersome, took an age to strap on, and looked like something the plastic model children wore in the St. Bernardo begging stations in which you could post your spare change.

I enjoyed playing cards with him most days, but he could sense I was getting bored with so many competing interests I was developing, and I now feel a deep sense of regret that I did not cherish these moments at the time, rather than after he passed. I certainly appreciated learning how to card count giving me a distinctive advantage playing anyone at cards, but it must have been so difficult for him to be so helpless and be apart from his wife who remained with her adult son Terry who had crashed and burned with his extravagant lifestyle and ended back at his Mums.

I had fond memories of playing Cowboys and Indians in our garden with my Uncle Terry, armed with cap guns and home-made bow and stick, and then tying him up with my mums knitting equipment so that I could set him on fire. He also had a cool Jaguar with all the leather trim.

Terry was by some accounts close to being alcoholic, or at least drank to excess especially after departure of his partner Bjorn and children to Sweden.

One of his endearing qualities was his willingness to take risks. Unfortunately, this led to his demise when he apparently fell from the cottage roof when trying to fix the ariel. If he was drunk nobody knows and it was unclear if he survived the fall only to be hit be passing cars down the thin country lane that ran beside the cottage entrance.

At the time I was told he fell out of the cottage front door, which opened very dangerously directly onto the lane, but either way he passed away that day in tragic circumstances.

I learned in retrospect that when my sister Denise was visiting, he allegedly tried it on with her and she had had to fight him off, I guess he may have been too drunk to recognise his niece, but my grief for his loss waned significantly.

When Nancy passed on, we assumed she had passed the Cottage and all the land to my mum and her sister Patsy who was doing very well, having married a professor, Brian Bell who resembled Roger Delgado, the actor who played the Master in the early 1970's BBC Doctor Who series. However, the news broke that the estate was worthless because essentially it had been mortgaged up to the hilt to pay for Terry Sheehan's lifestyle.

My mother took a job at a garage of all places drilling into all box sections of a car and injecting a thick wax, and then an equally messy substance was sprayed over exposed panels. All this aimed at preventing corrosion. Unfortunately, although the process did extend the life of cars, it had a corrosive impact on my mother lungs, and almost certainly contributed to shortening her life.

However, like my father she smoked excessively throughout her life, long before the Tobacco industry owned up to the cancer link, but with my mum continuing surreptitiously long after the family Doctor warned her to stop, and it is obvious that this is the main reason neither are around in 2020.

Both my Parents were Catholic and sent us to Church at St. Aiden's Coulsdon every Sunday morning, however they stopped attending but dropped us of with Denise the eldest being in charge. It was here that I received my first communion, confession, and confirmation from the bishop. It was also here that I was initially put off smoking because whatever you say burning Creeper behind the Church and inhaling the smoke is not pleasurable in any context. When I got the chance to smoke real cigarettes the outcome was similar.

I was grateful that I was going to miss the nauseating Queen Silver Jubilee celebrations at home as our School summer French learning trip to Dieppe clashed and in time as my fate as a non-smoker was sealed when my mum had insufficient last-minute money on her to supply enough pocket money for the trip.

To hide my embarrassment at having only a few pounds to exchange for Francs I informed my peers that I had given up smoking, which in hindsight was one of the best decisions I ever made, saving tens of thousands of pounds over time, and undoubtedly extending my borrowed life. This was a time when there were no warnings on cigarette packets, and the Tobacco industry spent millions convincing most people how cool it was to inhale the smoke of their burning death sticks and pay excessively for the privilege due to the excessive value added tax imposed to compensate the NHS left with rising smoking related illnesses.

However, this opened the way for me to concentrate on another vice, alcohol which developed into a dangerous habit in years to come.

I was never told the real reason my Parents stopped going to Church but when I had my own children the reason became clearer. I never caught on at the time as to why my parents were so happy on a Sunday afternoon.

In early life I never questioned anything I was taught by my parents, School, Church or Sunday school in relation to God. The first time I questioned things was watching the brilliant comedian Dave Allen who mixed delightful storying, jokes, and questions about people's faith that was both very entertaining but also very thought provoking.

As soon as I could, I stopped going to boring Church Services, even though they had modernised by bringing in a "happy clappy" band to raise the spirits of the falling congregation. In time my faith would completely dissolve into the reality of science and facts, but I do miss my invisible loving companion who would always be there for me if only I believed hard enough. I would only now attend Church for Weddings and Funerals, but still feel compelled to undertake the rituals of the holy water, taking the knee, and sign of the cross when I enter a catholic church, after years of conditioning.

Having moved a few roads up the valley before I left primary school, and settled into life in Nutfield Road, which would be the last family home before its four fledglings would fly the nest, Denise to Australia, Vivien to Purley, Desmond remaining in Coulsdon, and I left for East Yorkshire.

I have fond memories of playing football in the street with other friends and neighbours, as most cars were parked off street in their drives. Keith Bingley who shared my birthday, his older brother Clifford, Adrian Price, Nigel Hussey and Phillip Leg, and anyone else who was around to devalue the neighbourhood.

Clifford started a local army so that he could recreate his experience in the Territorial Army up in the woods, only this time he would be promoted to Captain, but I would never rise above the rank of Lance Corporal. Armed with a single air rifle to share, we were taught everything Clifford was learning, skills that later in life brought many benefits such as being good at hiding in the woods when playing hide and seek.

Nigel persuaded me to join the local Boys Brigade at nearby Church of England St. Peters, who had a football team I would defiantly get picked for, even being the only Catholic, which was emphasised during the entrance interview. The Youth leader was the first person in my life who made me feel different for being a Catholic.

The Boys Brigade had a militaristic uniform, which looked super cool to my young impressionable head. Thunderbirds style side cap, white sash, and belt with a brightly polished brass buckle, all on a navy-blue background. There was also the chance to march in a parade and do drills. I started to have bugle lessons but found the mouthing the correct five notes exceedingly difficult, and therefore invented some new ones, and the ensemble of the bugle section of the 1st Woodmansterne Brigade could have given Mr Moore a seizure, or perhaps a seizure of our instruments to protect the musical purity he demanded of this world.

In my first and last football match for the Brigade we lost thirteen nil, and it was obvious why I had eased into the team so easily. I also had the disadvantage of wearing ill-fitting rugby boots Nancy, had got for me from the local jumble sale. The youth Leader made me extremely uncomfortable. I was a shy kid and initially he befriended me in what I assumed was his way of drawing me out of my shell and boosting my confidence.

As time went on, I felt like he was doing the opposite, and isolating me, and fill me with self-doubt. He often referred to my Catholicism in a way that a racist might mention the colour of someone's skin, in that it is not what is said, but how it is said. There were times he asked me to pack up the football equipment in the Church Hall and I instinctively felt uncomfortable to be alone with him and got someone else to help.

One of the worst weeks of my life unfolded at the Boy's Brigades National Summer Camp in Swanage. Upon arrival we were split up and I was placed in a tent with two boys I had never met before. My social skills were limited and due to my unease, I started to brag and make things up to compensate which were easily rumbled and exacerbated my feeling of isolation and low self-esteem. I wanted to go home after just twenty-four hours and I still had four nights to endure.

It was true I was a good runner so I genuinely talked up my chances of winning the cross-country race, but at primary School we never ran very far, and when the race began, I led for the first quarter of a mile but it was not long before I was out of breath and moving very quickly to the rear made up of obese or indifferent kids. No one cared when I crossed the line, or even if I did cross the line.

That night, I realised I needed to go to the toilet, so slipped out of the tent and discreetly relieved myself.

When I woke in the morning there was a stench of urine, and then I felt a dampness throughout my sleeping bag. My embarrassed tent mates established that I had gone outside the tent but not far enough away, and due to the slope, it had returned to its rightful owner.

My confidence was so low that I declined to take part in the go-karting which I had particularly been excited about before leaving for Swanage but now sat spectating on my own, with no friends.

The Youth Leader from Woodmansterne seemed to lose interest in me but seemed partial to a few games with other young boys on the last night, which included soaking them with a hose pipe to an extent that their shorts and t-shirts were almost transparent. This had been a miserable experience but it could have been worse.

I returned my bugle and uniform without explanation when I returned for my last Football training night. I was called into the office to ask why I was leaving. These seemed to be more senior members of the Boy's Brigade, but I did not want to let them know about my humiliations. Despite this they probed asking me awfully specific questions about the Youth Leader, and if I felt comfortable with him, or had he said or asked me to do anything I felt uncomfortable with.

At that moment in time, I was too naive to understand they were investigating rather than conducting a simple exit interview. They then told me the Youth Leader had left and would that change my mind about leaving. I said no.

Looking back, I am sure I was obviously being groomed. My mum warned me about strangers after a man started chatting to me at the rear of our garden when I was four, but of course the danger rarely comes from strangers, but people we learn to trust.

It was my Parents faith that sent me away from all my hard-earned friends at Primary School to attend Catholic Secondary School at Thomas More in Purley, where my sisters had already left, and my Brother was in the third year. I had missed out in going to the posher John Fisher Catholic School by virtue of failing my 11 plus which I never understood at the time as I could not recall taking it.

Thomas More Roman Catholic School Purley

It was sometime later I realised that the teacher who facilitated the test decided to avoid children getting too nervous, so she underplayed the test to the point I did not understand its significance, with my concentration settled instead on Tina Furber who was keen to play with me her very innocent but rude games we were secretly performing under our desks, and the result was I didn't really try very hard while so distracted.

This is one of those episodes where something of seemingly little importance to me at the time was life changing. Had I taken the test seriously I feel sure I would have passed the test and then never gone to secondary school and then needed to go to college to get my o-levels. As my story unfolds you will realise how significant that was in determining future events.

So, I was destined to undertake CSE's rather that GCE's and my academic future meant that in any sixth year I would be taking O levels rather than A levels, but I would go on to choose to kick off my School Uniform and attend 6$^{th}$ form college instead where a new friendship would have a very positive life changing impact.

Settling down in Coulsdon, my father remained friends with Albert Hill, who had moved to Caterham on the Hill. I was taken sometimes to play with Kevin, in their much larger house, with extensive grounds that included a woodland area, swimming pool, and a maze of paths around shrubbery, and a view of Surrey that extended into Sussex. The only flaw was that the extensive grounds were on a very steep incline, which was great for tobogganing, and go carting, but useless for anything else, especially football.

Kevin was an only child, and had no friends, but whatever the intentions of our pairing he was a very dislikeable bratty narcissist who had fantastic toys and facilities at their disposal, and now at mine; but only if I could bear the subjugation. They also had a colour television which set them apart from the masses.

I did look forward to my Saturday visits just to see what he had been bought by his very wealthy parents that week. I agreed to visit for longer periods over the holidays sleeping over and started to feel conflicted in that part of me wanted to truly befriend this tyrant in short trousers, and coach him towards being a decent human being, and the sense that I was just a live toy delivered for his amusement to make his life better.

I was extremely uncomfortable with the sleeping arrangements, in such a large property we had to share a bed, and my sense of becoming a toy grew along with Kevin's libido as he tried to introduce sexual games when his Parents were out or asleep. I had never considered my sexuality at this point assuming to be straight, and this was only a few years after the 1967 Sexual Offences Act had made same sex acts legal but only from the age of 21. I was not even 14 yet, and neither was Kevin, but one-night Kevin tried something that went too far and in tears I told my mum and dad I did not want to go back there again.

This experience forged an innate contempt for wealthy people, and it only occurred to me some time after that I was the victim of an attempted rape, and I had a suspicion that his Parents may well have subconsciously ignored this. Their disturbed son had permanently disabled his father and tried to rape a child. Thankfully, I never saw or heard from Kevin Hill or his family again.

Sexual abuse of children has undoubtedly occurred through history. Nevertheless, it has only re-emerged from the shadows in recent decades, but I also feel that back in the 60' and 70's there was no information about sex available to growing adolescence except rumour and hearsay obscured in Catholic doctrine, and maturing children were left to work it out for themselves which undoubtedly led to a lot of low-key, but high impact child on child abuse. Perhaps this experience saved my life in summer of 1980 when by chance fate dealt me some potentially lethal cards.

# CHAPTER III ANNIE'S SONG

I usually had to catch a regular bus to School, unless my journey coincided with my dads who could drop me off on the way to his Office in Croydon. The walk-up Russell Hill to the School which sat on the peak, obscured by trees, was a long one, but as I got used to it, and it became the ideal place to hang out and meet up with friends.

On my first day as I approached the clearing at the top where the school's venetian gothic facade emerged like the opening scenes of a horror film, had the September weather not been so bright and cheerful, I might have curtailed my journey and played truant on the grounds that I did not want to be horribly murdered, or join the ranks of the un-dead.

The school at the time had very extensive grounds, gender segregated playgrounds, three football pitches, an indoor swimming pool, and in summer a painted grass athletics track, and two neatly mown Cricket Greens. Academically it also had a science laboratory, a language suite, a library, two assembly halls, one with a theatrical stage.

I was assigned St. Edmund as my house who traditionally had always come last in most sporting events and being a keen athlete and competitor, I sought advice on how to change houses. However, before working out who to approach my yellow kit had already been bought and I was not ready to approach my mum and dad again to fund a change of strip.

I developed two close friendships at school Clifford Cully and Andy Sex. Yes, that was really his name, and it was only a matter of hours before I got bored of ridiculing his name and stood firm in his defence from other who obviously could not resist every morning's register with "Yes Please." Cliff Cully did manage to change Houses, and he switched to mine on the basis that he would be involved in every sports team, due to the lack of competition, something that had not occurred to me, but paid dividends as I and Cliff captained most of the St. Edmunds inter house sports teams.

One of my first experiences in the playground was with a confrontation with the biggest child in our year, Andy Leonard. He would not let me near the water fountain to refill my hilarious water squirt joke ring I had gotten as a gift from a comic, so I threatened him despite that fact he was close to six-foot-tall at the age of 11. He was impressed with my guile and my reputation in the school was set, and I would not to be messed with.

One of the first after school clubs I signed up for was swimming, but my lack of attention to detail had nearly fatal consequences. I joined to learn to swim, but the club was designed for selection for forthcoming swimming competitions. I should have recognised the fact that there were no arm bands being worn, or floats in site indeed I do not think the school had any.

Thomas More Catholic School Purley Swimming Pool

I was lined up to do what I later understood were warm up sprints, and as I was instructed to dive in by the formidable Hungarian Sports Teacher Mr Emecz, something I had only ever seen on TV, but I compliantly threw myself in. My underdeveloped and skinny body slapping the surface and, in an instant, it felt like I had landed face down on concrete, and then the panic ensued as I drew in a mouth full of water into my lungs and sank. This was the first time I swam unaided as I scramble to the surface, and mimicking a cat thrown in water and splashed my way to the side and hung on for dear life.

It was fortunate that I had subconsciously chosen an outside lane, otherwise that may have been the end of my story. You would think you would learn from your mistakes, but a couple of months later when I had learned to swim a width of the pool with ease and was close to being able to swim a length, I was selected for St. Edmunds relay swimming team. Humiliating myself again, as my diving style had remained consistent and history repeated itself only on this occasion, I had three team mate's wrath to deal with who never managed to get into the water while I recovered from my flop.

I was a very enthusiastic footballer, but Chipstead Valley had only taught me to chase the ball around a field, but I was ok in goal and enjoyed the attention if I made a save. Thomas More School had a particularly good Football reputation. Coached by Mr Emecz, a retired football professional, and the charismatic and supportive Mr Layzell.

By the third year I had developed a reputation in school yard football as a decent stopper of the ball but was a little shy to play outfield very much, but I was developing and learning all the time, watching football and my dad taking me to Chelsea every home game.

Our year three School Keeper, Andy Leonard approached me and said he was unable to play on Saturday morning and based on my playground performances had suggested I went in Goal for the School Team away at St Andrews. After a sleepless night, I was overly excited on a bright Saturday morning waiting in the grounds of the school, until my dream was shattered when I spied Andy approaching the school. On the public bus journey to Duppas Lane recreation park in Croydon I consoled myself that I was now in the team, be it only as a non-playing reserve. These were the days when only one substitute was allowed.

At half time, with the scores level 1-1, I was aware that Andy had taken a knock, and when asked if he was ok to continue a brief flicker of hope ignited only to be extinguished on his *"I'm fine"* response.

Sometimes you listen to words, but you do not grasp at once what is being said as it is so unexpected. I was to come on and play left wing. Yes, left wing. I was right footed and had never played up front, and they were taking off a decent outfield player for me? I was grateful it was not my best friend Andy Sex who was playing on the right.

My sense of guilt only lasted a fraction of a second as I heard positive encouragement from the touchline. The logic made sense in hindsight, it was unfair to ask a child to give up their Saturday morning and not play at all, and the safest place was up front where I could do no damage to my own team except loose possession high up field.

I ran around a bit, understanding that it was important to stay on side, which was difficult as I was extremely fast, but most importantly the opposition had no idea I had never played up front before, and in my opinion was totally crap.

I was yet to touch the ball when on a counter attack a long ball was floated towards me and I realised I was going to have difficulty controlling it especially being tightly marked, so I opted for just heading it goal wards without any real concept of how far away the goal was. I made a good connection and the ball sailed just under the cross bar. There was no net, but I was shocked I had put us into the lead. I had taken the keeper by complete surprise. I turned in disbelief and was confronted by my teammates who were equally astonished and ecstatic as my substitution had obviously not been popular up to that point. I had scored with my first touch on my debut.

My confidence grew and grew, as did the confidence now bestowed upon me. A short time later we won a corner. I was talented at playing British Bulldog in the playground and had no trouble losing my marker at the near post and as I tried to flick the ball over to the far post, this time my connection was a little off. The ball instead deflected into the top right corner making the score 3-1.

This was a moment in my life that I will cherish forever, I discovered I was quite good at the sport I loved, and for the first time my peers agreed.

We went on to win 4-1, with me setting up the fourth goal for David Toal who had assisted my first goal, and we returned heroes back to Purley on the bus.

From that day I was part of the football set up, and Mr Layzell took his wingers under his own wing and gave individual coaching lessons to me and Andy Sex that would really develop our ability and confidence.

It was strange that I had to break through the confidence barrier with my favourite sport when I was at once considered good at Athletics, Cricket, Softball and Basketball, and was awfully close to being the best at many of the available athletic events with the 400m's being my speciality. I missed out on winning the prestigious Athletics Victor Ludorum by a single point in the 4th year to another pupil called Ricky, who was not remotely human but a machine in the mould of TV's bionic Steve Austin. I was made captain of the Cricket team and captained the House teams for hockey, basketball, and softball.

That summer I became interested in the news about the United Kingdom possibly leaving the European Economic Community it had just joined. Listening to the arguments I recognised even as a thirteen-year-old that Britain was in decline, its empire lost, in a deep recession and leaving this economic club would not be beneficial. Also, it occurred to me that the Soviet Eastern bloc benefited from economic and military cooperation then it would also be a good idea to supplement NATO with stronger links in western Europe. I felt I should have had a vote as this would affect my future more than pensioners who could vote, but I would have to wait until 1983 to vote in a national election and that didn't go very well. I recall going to bed on 5$^{th}$ June 1975 hoping sincerely that the referendum result, being counted through the night, would support staying in the EEC. I was delighted that over two thirds of people voted to remain.

My close friend Cliff Cully invited me to a party at his house in South Norwood and introduced me to his family. Cliff was wiser than me, because he must have understood my naïve benign racist attitude from our friendship for which I was totally oblivious, after all I had him as a black friend. Perhaps he was on a mission to facilitate my growth towards being anti-racist.

As a young teenager you are always nervous meeting friend's wider family, but they seemed painfully aware that I also felt awkward about being a racial minority for the first time in my life even for a few hours. Everyone was truly kind, and attentive and his hot sister even gave me a slow pity dance as she could see how uncomfortable I had become. I was also introduced to extremely hot Caribbean cuisine. When I left, I was a little angry at myself because although ideologically against racism, I recognised I was far from being anti-racist. Five years at Thomas More School and yet it was Cliff who provided me the opportunity to learn more about myself than at any other time.

A School colleague had been reprimanded by the School for distributing anti-fascist leaflets, because the School took a neutral stance in politics, which in effect normalised the growing National Front Party. Looking back at my history text books which I kept for many years, the story of Africa and Ireland were written by the slavers. Not only had I been socialised as a racist, but my School also had contributed to it.

Being of Irish descent, I read up on its history and learned that the industrial slave trade started in Ireland, and the colonial atrocities committed there were a rehearsal for the exploitation and enslavement of much of the African continent.

I had always considered myself fair minded, but now I understood despite my Irish roots, I had a long way to go to unchain my shackles from a white supremacist socialisation, but I was determined to undertake that journey, because I wanted to be on the correct side of fighting injustice. Unfortunately, my next practical journey was into the former Nazi homelands.

My first time to venture into the European mainland seemed to take forever on a slow hot Coach, as we combined with another local School for an educational and sporting trip to Lake Mondsee in Austria. By the time we reached Luxembourg City we were all really fed up, cooped up on a Coach I had found the courage to talk to the girls from the other School, and learned a valuable lesson in exploitation, as my interest was converted into gifts for them, with no reciprocal intent on their part.

I loved Luxembourg City, standing at the confluence of the Alzette and Pétrusse rivers which were both crossed by a series of lit up bridges and viaducts in the evening sky. After making a brief stop at the Munich stadium which had hosted the 1972 Summer Olympics, we Arrived in Mondsee late at night we were distributed dormitories divided of course by gender. It was not until morning that we got our first views of the hills that were believably alive with the sound of music, and the beautiful lake reflecting the mountains and rich blue sky.

A visit to Salzburg and its famous salt mines did not really appeal, but after climbing up through the mountain we were treated to the longest slide back down, which was both exhilarating and  stressful, as it always appeared that you were about to crack your head on the out of reach overhanging rocks as you sped down the seemingly endless tunnels. We spent time in the town centre and I pretended to be out of Austrian Schillings and my love interests left to their next victims.

An indoor football match was organised in a tiny indoor stadium which belonged to our host school. It has never ceased to surprise me how European children have such better facilities than their British counterparts.

I agreed to go in goal as no one else wanted to, and the Austrian team looked twice as fast, and tall as us. I felt a real swell of pride that I was not only representing my School, but also my country and I was determined to play well.

The Austrian Team were far better than us, but every shot, or header was within reach and my confidence grew. Towards the end of the game, we had taken an unlikely lead, after which the Austrians essentially camped in our half and were piling on shot after shot, but each one within reach.

Towards the end of the game, I was left with two strikers completely free, closing the angle of the one in possession, he was undoubtedly put off by my performance so far, so he squared it to his friend for an open goal. In anticipation I flung myself across and managed to get a hand to it and parry it up and over the bar Gordan Banks style.

The English started chanting "*Raymond, Raymond, Raymond,*" and this was followed in appreciation by our German speaking hosts.

With seconds remaining, I exposed with another one-on-one situation and the lanky Austrian striker drove the ball at me with everything he had, opting for brute strength over placement, the ball struck me clean between my legs sending by balls up into the roof of my mouth and down again in a Warner Bros cartoon style carnage.

I was close to being forced over the line, balls in hands, but my clean sheet prevailed as I lay in agony in the goalmouth. The Austrian Referee had seen enough and called time in sympathy. As we left, we were treated by our hosts to a rendition of *edelweiss.* I was not a fan of musicals, however in time that changed. Forty years later my daughter Jessica played her part in a live television broadcast of *The Sound of Music*.

I was the hero of Mondsee. I had literally put my balls on the line for my School and Country, and upon our return to England I was selected to play in goal for the first eleven of the School almost made up exclusively by 5$^{th}$ year pupils, and I became the only 3rd year player ever to be selected. My dad came to watch me and that meant more to me than the chanting in Austria.

My official sex education at Thomas More School was simply biological and based on Catholic doctrine of no protection and no sex outside of marriage, and anyone who got pregnant would have to be a child mothering a child or face the eternal fires of hell.

This oppressive ideology was tolerated by me as I matured through my teens, because it could explain away my lack of success with girls, but I was only kidding myself. I was painfully shy, had my mother's enforced taste in clothes, and worse of all I had no comprehension of the opposite gender. I felt a sense of entitlement to befriend Anne Fuller as our Mums were friends at work, but I lacked the charisma, confidence, and the necessarily know how develop a relationship. When I was invited to a Party in Purley, with a plus one possibility, I plucked up the courage to ask Ann, and she miraculously said yes.

This was my first ever date, but it did not end well. I left the party early as I could not tolerate her snogging John Gilbert for hours while he groped her in a darkened front room. John Denver released *Annie's Song* that year deliberately to torment me, although he was kind enough to ensure it was purely an instrumental with no mocking lyrics. I held an unrequited flame for Anne throughout our last years at School. A year after leaving School a new friend from Sheffield taught me the lyrics used by Sheffield United fans for Annie's Song. When I occasionally attended games with him, the tune always brought a touch of sadness as I remembered Anne Fuller

*You fill up my senses,*
*Like a gallon of Magnet,*
*Like a packet of Woodbines,*
*Like a good pinch of snuff,*
*Like a night out in Sheffield,*
*Like a greasy chip butty,*
*Like Sheffield United,*
*Come fill me again*
*Na na na na na...Ooooohh*

My dad had been taking me to Chelsea for every home game, passing National Front paper sellers all the way down the Fulham Road. He had the best Stewards job at the club due to his friendship with the chief steward Ian Jenkins. A gift of bottle of malt whiskey every Christmas provided an influence that lasted many years, and I "supported" my dad's role of checking the Identification of all the TV technicians and Commentators before they entered the gantry in the West Stand along with the Police Binocular Team on the lookout for the wanted and to pin point people to arrest on the unruly terraces.

This was often more exciting than the match, watching the blue helmets of the Metropolitan Police float across the sea of skin heads, like guided torpedo's remotely controlled from the Sergeant in the gantry. It was sometimes hilarious as police on the terracing would grab a young fan up only to be told no not him it's the guy with a beard, and the innocent fan would be unapologetically returned to the ground startled and confused.

Our job was done well before the kick-off when we were both free to watch the game from the gantry, which is why I often suffer memory lapses if I was at the game or watched it on TV given the view was identical.

Chelsea drew the European champions Liverpool in the 3rd round of the FA Cup in 1975, and the 4-2 win was astonishing by any standards given Chelsea were still in the 2nd Division.

My Brother Des had now almost abandoned Chelsea for Crystal Palace and when Chelsea drew 3rd Division Crystal Palace in the 5th Round our family and my school were deeply divided. I arrogantly boasted how easy the game was going to be to all that listened.

It was a real torment to face my brother and School friends after the humiliation of the 3-2 defeat. I was deeply hurt as I could not understand how Chelsea could easily beat the best team in Europe and just a few weeks later the very same players on the same ground could lose to lowly Crystal Palace. Since that traumatic and emotionally draining catastrophe, I have never taken anything for granted.

At School I rashly volunteered to be in the school play as I understood rehearsals would take you out of lessons. Unfortunately, this was not true, a deliberate misunderstanding perpetrated by the school to encourage participation. I was cast for a two-liner part in The Government Inspector by Nikolay Gogol with numerous after school rehearsals. I was a little afraid of the drama teacher and although I plotted how to get out of this commitment, I never had the courage to execute my plans and one summer evening I sat about back stage for what seemed an eternity, with increasing anxiety as my que was moving ever closer. What seemed like a few seconds later I returned backstage trying to control the rush of adrenalin that had almost overwhelmed me moments earlier.

As it slowly subsided, I started to feel a little low. I had expected to feel substantial relief after the build-up of stress as performance day moved ever closer, and my rehearsal performances did not inspire any confidence from anyone involved, but now I felt an emptiness. I missed the stress and anxiety, and I wanted it back. I asked myself why had I not put myself forward for a bigger part, how could I get back on stage? I loved sport because I wanted to show off my skills and acting was not any different.

As I was leaving that evening the Drama Teacher said, "well done Barry, much better when it mattered."

The next year I had a small part in T.S.Eliots, Murder in the Cathedral, and got to kill a young Thomas Becket. It would be over twenty years before repeating this performance but that would be in front of a camera, where I would recreate this role for a TV docudrama and most importantly get paid for it.

Academically I was slightly above average in my School being placed in the second set of four, but this was secondary education, so I was below the national average. Like sport I was an all-rounder in the classroom but never brilliant at anything, but quite good at many things. My exam results supplied a long run of grade 2's just below O-Level standard, what I would have given to swap a few 2's for an equal amount of 3's and 1's which would have given me a handful of O-Levels to get a decent job.

However, the problem was that I had absolutely no idea what I wanted to do for a career. Being a professional footballer, an actor, or an astronaut were fantasies as I could see no pathway open to me in 1977. It was therefore essential to delay my life and attend 6th form college to get my O-Levels and then try and decide what I wanted to do with the rest of this borrowed life.

I had to choose between Carshalton or Redhill Colleges to take my O-Levels, a further year in uniform was out of the question. It was politely suggested that I take a summer job and ended up in the local Cooperative supermarket stacking shelves.

My social life was still very restricted due to lack of money and places to go, so my parents got me a membership at the local Comrades of the Great War Club which they frequented, a stifling conservative association, but they had four snooker tables. My mother was much happier in the Cane Hill or Victoria Social Club where my Brother had become a regular, a working man's club where people were people and no one was there just to be seen and brag about their success, just have a few beers and let your hair down over the weekend.

Now that I had a small income, £18 for my first full week, which was £13 after paying my keep which I was intently proud to do. £5 was a fair bit of money back in 1978, and it felt good to be eating food I may have funded. I was also earning £3 every two weeks or so at Chelsea becoming a Steward in my own right.

Monday nights were darts nights for my parents, and they invited me along to join the team where I could drink a couple of pints. I developed a love of beer and darts and I was bought a dart board for home to practice on, and I slowly developed into a decent player. To motivate practicing on my own I devised a football game, giving doubles and trebles to Football teams, drawing out a full fixture list, and for each game threw 5 sets of three darts, 2 in the first half and 3 in the second, with each strike obviously counting as a goal. This way it was possible to play a full fixture list with the scores developing like they did on Grandstand or World of Sport at the time. This really improved my darts and gave hours of entertainment. My interest in darts was destroyed a few years later when my brother challenged me to a game at his new house and absolutely humiliated me. I never recovered from this defeat and my darts started gathering dust from that point forward.

## CHAPTER IV   OH WHAT A CIRCUS

In September 1978 I walked into Coulsdon Town Centre and caught a bus to Gatton Point just north of Redhill where the Technology College sat across the road from the Gatton Point Pub. The only student I knew was attending was a fellow Chelsea fan David Jelley, who I had gone to Primary School with. He was a local star because apart from his silky football skills, his uncle was none other than Steve Kember who had been Captain of Crystal Palace before signing for Chelsea in 1971 but had just left for Crystal Palace again. I was very apprehensive about settling into another new educational establishment where I did not know anyone.

I had not taken an interest in fashion having always lived on hand me downs, but with the income from my Summer Job, and a £50 windfall from the premium Bonds my Grandparents bought for me when I was born, I was ready to shop. My only fashion link to college was from the American College Situation Comedy Happy Days. Dressed in black leather jacket, white T shirt, and blue denim, all I needed was to grease my hair back with my dad's Brylcreem and I was the Fonze, unless I took a reality check and looked in the mirror.

I was also behind musical trends, so I had to be secretive that I had just bought a David Essex single from the Evita musical "*Oh What a Circus*."

In the refectory David sort out and introduced me to Paul Heaton, a friend he had been playing football with who was from Sheffield. I was taken back by his spiky hair, and new wave clothes and thick Yorkshire accent.

David explained I was a fellow Chelsea to which this uncompromising alien spat out an obvious insult about my choice of team to support and my identity as a southerner. This hurt more than the kick to the teeth over a decade ago from Vincent Bond, but my reaction this time was to punch him as hard as I could.

He reminded me visually of Mork from the American Comedy show Mork and Mindy, played by an incredibly young Robin Williams which ironically was a spin off show from Happy Days.

I positioned myself accordingly but realised I might have to use my weaker left arm, and as I tried to position myself, whilst planning my retribution it occurred to me that Paul was sat with his back against a very large pane of glass, and although I was not in a position to assess its weakness I certainly did not want to punch someone through a window on my first day at College as this might be considered an overreaction when all I wanted was to give this Mork impersonator a slap to put him in his place.

This delay gave me time to re-assess the situation and realise that this was simply meant as banter. He had the gift of the gab, spoke irrelevantly but in a very sharp amusing manner reinforcing his Mork credentials.

There was something authentic about this son of Yorkshire that invited additional examination. He had a unique quality well beyond his 16 years. Quality is often misplaced in circumstance, or position, but something told me this teenage student, six weeks out of School was someone to befriend.

When I mentioned Chelsea's 4-0 recent drubbing of his team Sheffield United while getting promoted to the top flight and knocking them out of the league Cup, I was impressed that he said he was there and it was clear that we both recognised each other's passion for football, and like Vincent Bond I acquired a new friend, but could not resist nicknaming him Mork to his obvious irritation.

Many years later Paul did a photoshoot as Mrs Doubtfire illustrating his resemblance to Robin Williams once again. After hearing about my political views, he nicknamed me Trotsky due to my socialist beliefs, a name that still sticks today. That night I went home and looked at the Football Programme that featured photographs of the sparse Blades supporters on the North Terrace of Stamford Bridge and in the background of Ray Wilkins volleyed goal, I was able to find Paul sat crossed legged on the terracing.

As a child my dad and even his dad Bill Barry, had enjoyed providing me with very informal boxing lessons. My dad boxed during national Service, but Bill Barry was a professional boxer between 1920 and 1935. He boxed at welterweight; middleweight; heavyweight and took part in 80 professional contests. He also was head steward at Lords Cricket Ground for several years. Most of the Barry family lived in Marylebone London but they were collectively shrouded in a mystery by my dad who was reluctant to divulge much about his extended family. From his five sisters and one brother it was clear that they regarded my dad with love but considered him a little aloof and above himself.

He had decided to whisk away his bride and first born to the suburbs looking for a better life because behind the tight knit family community mostly located around Church Street Market, was an underbelly of low-level organised crime and I now appreciate what a sacrifice this was for my mum and dad on behalf of their child and children to come.

Few of my dad's family had recognisable trades or jobs, but seemed to be rolling in cash, and when we, his four children, were provided with the latest fashion Budgie Jackets by Auntie Josie, each costing a few weeks adult wages, my dad was visibly angry not only of being undermined but probably in the knowledge that they had no doubt fallen off the back of lorry. As I grew older, I did a little research and recognised a few family names in the indices of the flourishing memoirs circulating about organised crime that were appearing in book shops.

My Grandfather ran a boxing Gymnasium in Paddington and it was alleged that those who could not make the grade as a professional boxer could be offered work in the enforcement business.

My Brother had taken a job in Coulsdon as a Taxi Radio Controller in the 1980's, given he could not drive it was a fairly ironic role for him, but Des was a popular man across his peers, and was well suited to the role. However, it was clear to him that a gang were harassing the firm out of business in an effort of a very hostile takeover. This would involve false call outs to the East and West End, Drivers being increasingly attacked and robbed, with specific threats. Taxi firms were becoming notorious in moving drugs around London and organised crime were looking to take over local firms to control their distribution.

During a wider family event my brother just mentioned this to one of our Aunties and after finding out more information told Des not to worry about it anymore. The problem vanished overnight. This was both reassuring and simultaneously frightening.

In the Pool room of Redhill College, it was customary to pay your extortionate 50p fee to release the balls but then to block the pockets to stop the balls fully descending so everyone could play during an entire session for a much-reduced fee.

When an old Thomas More school acquaintance arrived with an oversized gorilla impersonating a student arrived in the Pool Room, they demanded to take over the table but would not offer any contribution towards my 50p investment. So, for the sake of 10p I took on the gorilla outside in a public fight that due to the physical mis match, generated significant interest of those who wanted to see a massacre and they appeared in an impromptu ring holding their soft drinks and lunch in hand to enjoy the free entertainment. Realising I had perhaps bitten off more than I could chew and there was no obvious honourable withdrawal available now, I realised the only hope I had was that the gorilla would be incredibly overconfident and might be a slow mover. He did not use his huge advantage of reach and weight, and grabbed my head in a wrestling move, providing me with the unprotected target of his fat face and the freedom to strike a rally of blows which were delivered with such speed and ferocity it was over in less than 20 seconds.

Ray Barry, grandson of the great Bill Barry had won his first public fight, and instantly became a face at the college, whilst destroying his opponents. Paul went to spy on the other camp and reported his face had swelled up beyond recognition, and many who were not present but knew us both found it hard to believe the stories outcome. Paul was no coward, but he suddenly felt very safe in my company. His broad Yorkshire accent was very much out of place in a Surrey College but references to his heritage declined shortly after and our friendship became ever closer.

A week later my acquaintance from Thomas More who laughed at me when I offered his friend out asked me if I was trained in martial arts. I gave a vague response hoping to mystify my reputation as someone who was not to be messed with.

I managed to get a place in the college football team along with David Jelley, Paul Heaton, and Andy Sex. I really enjoyed our home pitch which was called Battlefield, and it felt very professional with a running track around it, and a raised bank for spectators, not that any would come. However, our first game on 27th September 1978 was in the college grounds against an adult factory side called Locomotive who seemed visually ill matched. It was men versus boys. I was in goal, Paul sweeper, Dave in midfield, and Andy Sex up front, but my personal performance could hardly be judged as all I had to do was field a few back passes and kick the ball aimlessly up field and pluck one out of the air from a rare corner as we ran out 8-0 winners.

During the game I became an uncle, my brother became a dad, and our Parents became grandparents, as Darren Barry was delivered into this world by my relatively new sister-in-law Lynn.

Just two weeks after my sixteenth Birthday, I was still not old enough to drink when I was invited to my brother's wedding. He was only nineteen himself. His bride to be Lynn Foster was expecting, and along with traditional Catholic thinking that meant marriage. Des brought the extremely nervous Lynn up to meet our parents for the first time, with strict instructions from my brother, "Do Not Swear in front of my parents."

After polite introductions, with Lynn trying hard to suppress her working-class roots as well as my parents had managed to do so well over recent years in leafy Surrey, my mother remarked that Lynn was wet from the rain. Lynn's unforgettable nervous reply was "yeah, it's fucking pissing down."

I shared my dad's scepticism that this could not last, and my dad was far from impressed by Lynn's inability not to swear, replacing obscenities for almost every adjective.

But my parents stood by them, and as they got to know Lynn, they warmed to her, then they really respected her, and then loved her dearly. The Barry's and Fosters descended on an Old Coulsdon Church; two very exceptionally large families united in a way through history would have been a mechanism for peace between warring clans. So far, my prediction of it will not last is out by over four decades and counting. There first born, Darren was provided with a sister Natasha shortly afterwards, and when a relative asked Des and Lynn to look after young Billy they ended up adopting him. When he found his bride to be a few decades later he emotionally changed his surname to Barry, announcing it just before the ceremony. What better accolade could Des and Lynn have been afforded, apart from the stream of grandchildren that have been delivered to all three of their children.

Back at Redhill Technical College, my confidence in Goal took a nosedive after a few mistakes in the following games and I was unceremoniously replaced which ended my short student playing career and any competitive football for a few years more.

Realising that Paul lived reasonably close to me in Chipstead, I started to hang out there, his dad Horace was an ex-professional footballer with Tranmere Rovers and is one of the nicest people I have ever met. Paul was very much into music and introduced me to new wave, which had gone largely unnoticed by me with my only musical reference being Top of The Pops on a Thursday night. My record collection consisted with only a handful of 45's that I could call my own, but the family had accumulated a small truck load of vinyl from Frank Sinatra, Barry White, Stevie Wonder, Teddy Pendergrass, Rod Stewart, and David Bowie each being the individual favourite of my family in age order.

Paul and his brother Adrian were into the Clash, the Damned, Stiff Little Fingers, the Jam, Sham 69, the Members, Elvis Costello, the Buzzcocks, and so on, while I was still stuck in 70's soul music and a disco trench and had not really grasped how exciting this new wave was revolutionising teenage tastes, as although I was very amused by the antics of the Sex Pistols towards Bill Grundy, and the punk attitude, I didn't appreciate the screeching hard rock guitars, but slowly Paul's influence guided me into a new genre of musical taste.

We looked old enough to buy drinks in a pub, and I believe I bought Paul his first ever drink in the Gatton Point Pub, something I was immensely proud off at the time, but in later years was tinged with elements of guilt as later life he developed a drink problem, far more severe than the one I was about to develop.

Paul had started to hang out in Reigate, at a pub called the Railway Hotel adjacent to the station and level crossing, where a local music scene was developing. However, it was a long time before I attended, not being particularly cool enough. Instead, our friendship developed over a few pints at the White Hart in Chipstead on a Monday night to compensate for the end of the weekend.

We would also occasionally meet up to kick a ball around with others or play cricket in his back garden.

College days were a time of discovery, but it was Paul who got the girlfriends, as I was still to understand the mating game, and was too painfully shy, and unaware of any positive signals I may have got from girls. Paul had shrugged off the Mork label only to start seeing a girl could Lindy, and he very quickly tired of my resurgent and consistent Mork and Lindy jibes.

We befriended two other local kids who we nicknamed Snorkel and Bingo and became the gang of four anarchists and sort to disrupt student life as far as we could.

This included stealing the Student Union cash tin in protest at their naff ideas about discos and campaigns. I still have not forgiven Paul for not sharing out the loot, I should have got a quarter share of the 50p found in the tin we had broken into. The tin itself was probably worth a few pounds, or it was before we smashed it up to open it.

Listening to Paul's lyrics for *You Keep It All In* penned many years later for The Beautiful South *"Just like that robbery in '62, with all these things that have happened to me, I kept it all in."* I often wondered if this small change robbery was the inspiration, with the year changed to our birth year to protect the guilty?

However, this theory does fall on the words *Just like that murder in '73* that proceeds, because as far as I was aware Paul never killed anyone, especially not at eleven years of age.

The Gatton Point Pub had very rudely replaced their fruit machine, probably on account of it losing money to those who spotted its fatal flaw. If you leaned on the plastic transparent cover you could physically force a winning line to stay in place. There was an understanding to milk this cash machine gently, but as word spread the Proprietor got suspicious about its unique popularity when people starting to queue up to play. The new machine which beckoned people to play at every opportunity with flashing lights stood idly by as guests shunned it for its inability to be manipulated.

The next main stunt was to make 50p bets with other students that the four of us would jump individually out of a second story window, cushioned only by a four-foot-high bush below. It was all for charity, in the hope that we could supply a small amount of alcohol for the underprivilege students aka the gang of Four; in the Gatton Point Pub at lunch time, now deprived of our illicit winnings.

After several successful leaps from the window, Paul seriously hurt himself as we had not factored in the destruction of the bush, and it ceased to supply a soft enough landing after a couple of jumps each.

I believe there was an investigation undertaken but there was insufficient evidence to take any action against us, but of course if this type of unruly behaviour is not dealt with of course it leads to the inevitable stunt too far.

This came close to the end of year when realising that the sun was slowly but surely setting on our academic career, and we were not going to achieve much due to the distractions of our attempts of a rock and roll lifestyle. Paul was not in college when we decided it would be fun to distract the more diligent and consciences students during their vital revision in the library.

I do not remember whose idea it was, or who supplied the fireworks but we immediately raised suspicion by just being in the library probably for the first time in months, and we were acting very suspiciously as we huddled in various isles placing a small group of Swiss style bangers between books with the plan to do a quick circuit setting each group off in sequence.

Once set, we lit the first bunch, but Bingo lost his nerve and panicked rushing back to try and stop the flaming fuse, hotly pursued by the remainder of the gang and a tussle ensued which ended with the first crack and explosion of the first fire work, followed quickly by the rest, and as we ran out in some ridiculous effort to distance ourselves from our arsonist tendencies, we paradoxically ensured that our guilt was displayed for all to see.

This was profoundly serious, and we should have been given a criminal record as we had not considered that the ground floor library had four floors of classes and offices above it. We were summoned for an explanation and summarily expelled with immediate effect, only we could sit our exams which they considered leniency, but we considered further punishment.

After Redhill College I never heard from or saw Bingo or Snorkel again, but Paul and I would remain friends to this day.

My musical tastes had improved under Paul's and others influence, and I had discovered the Boomtown Rats as a soft punk pastime when *I Don't Like Mondays* reinforced their credentials to me after *Rat Trap*. Just the anthems one needs to start a full-time job.

# CHAPTER V I DON'T LIKE MONDAYS

It was 1979, I only had 3 O-Levels at pass level, and few prospects. In those days' jobs were a plenty, but I had no idea what I wanted to do. I perused the Croydon Advertiser and spotted a job in Mayfair. Being the most expensive property on a Monopoly Board, and with their business being commercial property sales and lets, it did have potential at least in my eyes. I thought with £30 a week I could really develop a great social life. Please note the complete absence of any career plan except to work in the posh part of town, and the only motivation was being able to go out and buy a few drinks.

Even with the deductions of £5 for my keep, and a weekly travel ticket of just under £10, I would still have three good nights out with a pint costing between 25p and 33p. So, in September 1979, wearing an ill-fitting cheap suit for the first time, I commuted into London for my first job as an Office Junior at 11 Bruton Street between Berkeley Square and New Bond Street, and just a few doors along from number 17 where our current monarch was born in 1926.

The previous Officer Junior John Gordan had in effect become a trainee negotiator and he was very keen to emulate the legendry Ray Cottington who had risen from Office Junior to one of the most significant and successful property negotiators in London. He was a stereotypical east ender, a real geezer who spoke in simple terms but had a real gift for communication and understood the deep psychology needed to achieve the best results and subsequent commission. He was a working man, who loved life, money, West Ham, and his wife possibly in that order.

John Gordan was a more complex character, he lived-in middle-class Wimbledon with just his Scottish dad, but just like the two Ray's he loved the social life and Friday lunchtimes in the Coach & Horses on Bruton Street, or occasionally other local pubs became a fixture of our life. The four stuffy partners often went home early Friday afternoon and my new gang of three would flash the cash we were provided with in a brown envelope handed to us by the unimpeachable Mrs Cohen the Financier for Dudley Samuel & Harrison. When going or returning to and from Rymans stationery store on Bond Street, she would examine the cash given, my receipt and the change provided to a level of scrutiny and re-examination that felt accusing, and belittling.

Being sixteen, I was naturally submissive, and did not know much about life. Looking back, it is hard to understand what I did except hide filling that I knew would never be needed again and respond to the Senior Partners buzzer summoning me to his Officer. Walter Freed was a gentleman but did not appreciate anyone outside his class, and he would rarely actually look up at me, and if he did it was only to check my understanding of his instruction. He only referred to me as Barry, or worst still the boy. My servant duties in the morning included fetching his mail and copies of the Times and the Financial Times from the delivery box downstairs, and placing them neatly on his desk, then re-filling his water jug with fresh water, and fill up his well with ink, although I was tempted to reverse the last two orders.

I did not even have to make the tea for everyone, as the firm employed a cleaner and tea maker Mrs Edwards. An exceptionally large sweaty woman who wobbled as she wheezed, all contained within her ill-fitting plastic piny, with each step circumnavigating the last in a Sumo Wrestling style dance as she progressed like a hippopotamus in a confined space to each desk in turn. This twice daily macabre show had the very unfortunate outcome that beads of her sweat visibly dripped often onto the tray of hot dinks she had assembled to distribute.

She was a ferocious woman who everyone in the office was afraid of including the partners. On my last day I generated the necessary courage to ask Mr Freed why he continued to employ Mrs Edwards, and to my surprise he did not respond by taking offence that this nobody had dared to ask the most senior partner about his personnel decisions and responded in a completely honest and self-deprecating manner that he was afraid of her, and then chuckled to himself. It was the first time in two years I saw him smile, or that he recognised me as a human being. Perhaps it was the guilt that he had made me redundant just before I would have been entitled to compensation, to install his son Timothy as my replacement.

It is understood that every employee at this company had a plant on their desk which had a regular diet of warm tea and coffee, and the sweat from the brow of Mrs Edwards.

While the punk rock revolution was very much anti-establishment through provocation, the wearing of swastikas by the Sex Pistols is repugnant to me now, but back then I sniggered at the reaction of the older generation to this outrage. Unbelievably swastika badges could be bought in any music shop, and I succumbed and I am ashamed that I wore one up to a Smirks gig at the Rock Garden.

When I arrived in Covent Garden Paul introduced me to some footballing friends, one of whom was black and who instantly shunned me. I took it off embarrassed, my target audience were meant to be middle class white suburban outraged of Surrey, looking back it is incredible that it had not occurred to me at that point that I would be perceived as a right-wing fascist thug.

On my way back home, I hid the badge in a crack between brickwork at Woodmansterne Station.

Back in the office, the three of us were full of banter, giving each other plenty of jip when things went wrong, but we were all particularly good friends.

In the basement was an Aston Martin DB5 and was probably from the first very year of production, with personalised number places. This treasure belonged to Walter Freed. However, the basement was my nemeses, as it had stacks and stacks of broken rotting wooden shelving holding cardboard files of previous property deals. Although well indexed, I had inherited a complete mess from John Gordan who had obviously over the preceding years just chucked things anywhere and finding anything became a real trauma.

Ray Cottington often needed information urgently and dispatched me on a trek through the cobwebs, grime and car exhaust smelling broken cupboards to find what should have been easy had each file been stored to correspond with the index and dates. Ray had taken me under his wing and became a mentor for me, and he understood the basement was a mess and my predecessors were mostly responsible for the basement chaos.

Having had two unsuccessful trips to find a file on a Friday morning, I was getting it in the neck from John Gordan as he bragged, he knew exactly where the file was. He bet me £5, a considerable sum then that he could find it in inside 5 minutes, where I had spent over an hour that morning to no avail.

He returned a couple of minutes later with file in hand giving it large. Ray suspected foul play and was angry with John for not helping in finding the file earlier when he had many opportunities, putting his property deal at risk as he desperately need comparison prices. There was no internet in these days and agents were solely reliant on filed data.

It was then that Ray decided that justice needed to be restored understanding that £5 was a third of my week's disposable income. We split the file in two and created two new files, dirtying them up and putting fresh dates on them, one was hidden in Ray's desk with the required paperwork for his deal, and other left on John's desk with a note "Wrong File."

When John came back to the Office, he was dumbstruck until he begged to be given another chance. We negotiated a new bet. He could still win his £5 if he could find the file by 5pm, giving him three hours to search for a file that was locked in Ray's desk while we went to the pub for an extended lunch without him.

We had planned to put him out of his misery, but unfortunately as he became more desperate, and his new suit was covered in dust and grime, it became funnier and funnier and we could not find it in ourselves to put him out of his misery.

Once he had calmed down and started to see the funny side of the prank, he realised it was well deserved and he graciously rejected my offer of £5 and I bought him a pint to settle the matter.

Apart from a class divide, there was also a gender divide. We had a typing pool of young girls and a telephone receptionist called Tracy Webb who sat opposite me. She was a very thin girl with curly hair from Woolwich and she became my second big crush. She worked a telephone exchange that needed leads to be manoeuvred and plugged in across a board to ensure incoming calls were directed to the appropriate desk and connect all outgoing calls. Our telephone number was 01-629-7111 but we often got accidental calls from people trying to reach the John Lewis store on Oxford Street nearby and their number was 01-629-7711.

On a handful of occasions when the Partners were not around and we had been drinking, Tracy would hold her hand over the phone and whisper to us "John Lewis." Whoever was free would take the call and wind up the caller as much as they could before declaring they were not speaking to the right department and offering to pass them on. This would prompt Tracy to apologise profusely and then pass the matter on to the next prankster who would take the matter as far as they dare before declaring they had the wrong number and should try again.

It was clear to everyone but John that Christine in the typing pool fancied him, and it was equally clear to everyone that I fancied the receptionist, Tracy. This did not matter until we started to socialise and eventually John and Christine got it together while Tracey kept a strict platonic approach to me which started to drain my confidence and made my working life increasingly miserable. How could I compete? She was bit older than me with an even older boyfriend who had a car. When she confided in me that she was no longer a virgin it sent me into a rage of jealousy and made the seating arrangements in the Office extremely uncomfortable for both of us as I was positioned facing her sideways on in full view of her entire frame seven hours a day five days a week. It was torture.

Ray tried to alleviate my inner turmoil, by taking me to Shepherds Market to window shop the high-class call girls in operation, he understood what I was going through but could nothing more than offer obvious advice.

I foolishly agreed to be a guest, along with John and Christine at a wedding reception for one of Tracey's girlfriends and we all travelled in John's car down to Woolwich. I do not remember the details very well, but my body language, fuelled by alcohol sent very unwelcome signals to Tracey's boyfriend and his mates, as I watched the couple dance and snog together. I had met her Asian friend Pramjit before, and I had a couple of drinks with him, but like me he was feeling uncomfortable as eyes were also on him but for distinct reasons. He was the only person of colour.

We decided to leave for a while and go to a pub, but as we approached one, he said he could not go in there, and then the next one, and so on until we had passed four pubs. Being Asian in Woolwich meant there were certain public places you would not be welcome at best. My instincts were to go home, but Pramjit wanted to go back and I felt a sense of duty to try and look after him.

Arriving back at the reception it did not take long, with my eyes fixated on my lovelorn quest, I hardly saw the first blow arrive as someone punched my friend so hard and without warning he fell to the floor with blood streaming from his nose. I went to retaliate and sunk my head into the head of the assailant but I was overwhelmed by his friends and my face was pummelled from every angle forcing me backwards as I was dazzled by the disco lights and could not make out my assailants any more before being severely beaten to the ground.

A stranger drove me to A&E and it appeared my nose was broken for the second time in a matter of months. When I returned to the reception it was closing and when I asked

Tracy's boyfriend to pass a message to her that I was ok, he was silent and starred at me and I think he was considering lining me up for another hiding despite my obvious injuries.

It would be sixteen years later that these parts became well known for the murder of Stephen Lawrence, in an unprovoked racist attack. Perhaps we had got off lightly that night. I was truly shocked that someone could be targeted just because of their race. I would be returning to the safe white environment of Coulsdon, but could not imagine what being black or Asian was like living around here?

Tracy called in sick on the Monday morning, so I had to cover the switchboard all day. This gave me plenty of time to reflect. If this was her choice of boyfriend with his racist thugs as friends, who enjoyed beating up one of her friends because of his ethnicity, with no consideration for the bride and groom's special day, then I was better off without her. The other consideration was that to date her I would have to spend time in South East London.

Ray Cottington asked the obvious question, where was John? This was a rhetorical question as just before Christmas that year John and I were walking towards Green Park tube station late at night with Christmas presents in hand when John picked a verbal fight with a small group of young office workers, and when they became threatening, I turned to offer them out, believing two against four was reasonable odds given my fighting ability, but as they approached, John had run away and left me. I was fortunate that night as the four lads were impressed that I had stood my ground, and after a brief exchange of blows, one breaking my nose they felt justice was done.

In February 1981 images of Prince Charles and Lady Diana Spencer were everywhere as they had announced their engagement. I celebrated by collecting my Valentine's Day ticket for the Saturday away match at Upton Park. This was a frightening fixture for Chelsea fans and in the past, I would travel to Earls Court to be amongst Chelsea fans before getting close to the East End. Ray was a happy hammer, and he was going to the same game and invited me to his working man's club close to his home to play Crash. Crash is a gambling snooker game played by up to six players. Playing cards 2 to a 7 are shuffled and put beside the table and a single stake decided upon.

However, your stake would increase with every foul shot you committed. In order, you played an ordinary game of snooker with the exception that after potting your first red you would draw a playing card which remained secret which would correspond to a coloured ball value. Two yellow, three green etcetera and these balls would not be returned to the table if dispatched.

If you potted a red ball, you then had to go for the nearest Colour regardless of position, but if you potted your coloured ball, you won the pot. If your colour was potted you just kept quiet and hoped there would be no winner, and the pot would grow frame by frame.

This was an incredible game of skill and cunning, and it was hard not to reveal you were trying to get your colour when you went all around the table to get to it, your rest hand shook like a washing machine on full spin when the pot of money was just one pot away and was more than I earned in a week.

Whilst enjoying this game and I did not notice that I was drinking excessively, and the pints kept coming. When we reached Upton Park we separated to our respective ends and then as I waited in line to get into the away end, I realised I had lost my wallet and tickets or I had been pick-pocketed. I approached the turnstile hoping they would materialise, but they did not and suddenly I found myself severely drunk, no ticket home, and I was in very hostile territory. It was not long before I got into an argument with a seasoned police officer who was demanding I went into the ground and stop hanging about outside, when my temper got the best of me and I told him impolitely that I was a touch annoyed with him. I had heard of Black Marias but now I was going for an expensive ride in one and would not find out the fare until I attended Stratford Magistrates Court in a few weeks' time.

I was charged with being Drunk in a Public Place, designed with vagrants in mind. This distraction was almost welcome as Chelsea lost 4-0, but I was still faced with trying to jump trains barriers all the way home which was a little easier late at night having been held long after the game was over.

As I grew older my confidence grew, and the belittling Walter Freed became a sense of frustration, so sometimes I would not hear his buzzer, and when he gave me a dressing down, putting me very severely in my place, he made me feel worthless and angry.

The next morning as I was filling up his jug of water in the toilet, I realised I needed to go myself. Without really considering what I was doing I allowed a couple of drops of urine to somehow find their way into his daily supply. Every time he treated me badly, I would look into his eyes and think you have drunk my urine which made the humiliation bearable.

Two weeks after the St. Valentines massacre at West Ham, I set of to catch the supporters train to Deepdale, Preston North End. The 1980-81 season was unique for me in that I attended every Chelsea game, home, away, league and cup. However, this was helped by free travel and tickets to games outside London, or at Stamford Bridge on account of being a Steward. It was unpleasant, but also helpful to my 100% record that we lost in both the league and FA Cup at the first hurdle. One of the stalwarts of the Stewards was Brenda Lee, with her son Garry. They were related to the Chelsea striker of the time Colin who became famous after scoring 4 goals on his debut for Tottenham in 1977 in a 9-0 annihilation of Bristol Rovers.

It was tradition for the Stewards to find a pub near to our destination station and have a few drinks before walking to the Ground. Garry had a couple of youngsters with him and chose to go to the ground early with them. He had offers from others to go with him, including from me, but he said he was fine.

When we took our seats in the ground an hour later, news filtered through to Brenda that her son had been killed. There is nothing more heart wrenching than seeing the realisation on the face of a mother that her son is dead.

Apparently, Gary was chased by Preston Supporters and fell to his death over the side of a Bridge. In the away section a short row of empty seats betrayed the horror of that day, and losing 1-0 that day seemed meaningless, although I was pleased Preston North End were relegated at the end of the season.

However, I was shaken to the core that life could just end in the blink of an eye.

# CHAPTER V1  SUICIDE IS PAINLESS

I had grown up with the theme to one of my unmissable TV programmes, a bitter sweet comedy set during the Korean war called M*A*S*H. The summer of 1980 was a wonderful time for music, and the theme had charted with added Lyrics, and kind of summed up my melancholy mood.

The game of life is hard to play
I'm gonna lose it anyway
The losing card I'll someday lay
So this is all I have to say.

Suicide is painless
It brings on many changes
And I can take or leave it if I please.

While working in Mayfair we would occasionally go out drinking in the evening, which was perilously close to the infamous Soho. Now that I had my own funds, I was getting into the habit of drinking myself into a stupor to try and ease my natural shyness. If I stayed out in the West-End with my work colleagues, it was for me a waste of drinking time to try and hook up with friends in the Reigate area with a couple hours travel time. My obsession with Tracy had taken its toll, and I was an unhappy and sexually frustrated young man. I found the West End exciting and was drawn to the seedy elements of Soho, with the forlorn hope that I might get lucky.

I often stayed out drinking but never had the courage to approach any girls, and I could never afford to pay for it on £30 a week wage, or have the courage to go up the stairs of these makeshift brothels, but just walking around the area sometimes gave me a buzz, but this was short lived and a deep feeling of inadequacy emerged through the alcohol, and I would often make my way back to Victoria Station to get the last train home, feeling depressed and unloved.

It took me forty years to understand the significance of a chance meet I had in Brewer Street in the early hours of a summer morning that year. I do not recall what preceded this meeting except I was very drunk and had stayed out too long to get a train home. Trains ran to East Croydon all night but I had spent too much cash to get a taxi back from there. However, the milk train was only a few hours away so I sort out an all-night bar and wondered around Soho killing time.

I became aware of a short older man, who approached me from behind. He had a kind face behind his glasses which reflected the inviting Soho neon signs. It was plain he had noticed my aimless walk around the streets of Soho, and my lack of walking coordination which betrayed my obvious intoxication. He asked me in a soft Scottish accent what I was up to, and I told him I was looking for a place to get a drink and given he was Scottish he should know if there was anywhere still open. He quoted a few places I had never heard of and we chatted as we walked along Brewer Street. He told me his name, and I remember this because I told him he shared my brother's name. I cannot recall the incidental chatter as we walked, but we talked mainly about girls and drinking. I told him about my predicament getting home, and what I had done the last time this happened.

Having a weekly season ticket, I would catch a nap on the trains between Victoria and East Croydon until the first train back to Woomansterne Station was available, hoping I would wake up each time at East Croydon, otherwise the next stop was Gatwick Airport or even Brighton and a possible hefty excess fare.

I was naïve at the age of eighteen, but my defences were up, as I had recently learned that Soho also had a gay scene, and I was at this time unashamedly homophobic, given my experience with Kevin Hill, being raised a Catholic and still being unworldly. Had he not been so forward in suggesting going back to his place for a drink we might have gone onto the bars he suggested, and then possibly back to his place. There was something I found a  little creepy about him, and I suspected he was trying to pick me up, so I told him I was heading home. Although I was tempted believing my six-foot frame would easily overpower him if he became too familiar and spending the night in a flat seemed preferable to crashing out on trains. None the less when I declined, he seemed disproportionately disappointed, almost hurt.

My only suspicion at the time was that he was simply homosexual looking to score, so I walked away in haste towards St James Square back to the safety of Victoria Station, hazarding a quick glance over my shoulder when I approached an area that was not well lit and remote. Although the sun was now rising and its shining pure morning beams were extinguishing the darkness, I had been immersed in, I still felt ill at ease.

After bouncing around on trains for the rest of the early morning, when I got back to the safety of home in the late early hours, I was a little unnerved by my experience, and vowed to keep away from the area that had only ever worsened my feelings of sexual inadequacy and loneliness. I was insufficiently wise to realise it was drinking to excess that was only temporarily masking my shyness, feelings of inadequacy, and my mild depression caused by an unquenchable but unrequited hunger for sexual experience. It was also making me very vulnerable.

It was not until September 2020, forty years later, that I discovered how close I came to die that night. In 1983 I would move to Hull, and quickly got out of the habit of watching much TV, and I am not sure we had one in the shared house at the time, so my intake of current news was limited at this time. Therefore, I did not follow the dramatic news appearing about one of Britain's most notorious serial killers. Although over time I had heard of Dennis Nilsen, I had no idea or interest in what he looked like, so I did not associate him with this chance encounter until watching the 2020 TV drama and documentary which aired on ITV entitled "Des." I may not have considered watching it had I known the subject matter, but having my brother's name as a title, and liking the main actor David Tenant, I decided to give it a whirl. Up until this point, I was blissfully unaware that Dennis Nilsen was Scottish, referred to himself as Des, or when or where he was actively butchering young men.

As I watched and listened intently, I became aware that he's killing spree was in the area and time I worked in central London. One photograph cut through me like a winter chill, it was without doubt the man who approached me in the summer of 1980. I sat in horror when the realisation surfaced that I was undoubtedly targeted by him three years before he was identified as a mass murderer. It was also clear from a little subsequent research I undertook; I had met him at the peak of his killing spree and could easily have ended up dismembered under his floorboards.

Due to excess drinking, I had a terrible habit of falling asleep in public when out socialising and drinking too much. I would have been easy prey in the state I was in despite my physical advantage.

Had I not been homophobic there was probably a remarkably high chance I would have taken up his offer for a bed for the night, and for the sake of a £5 taxi fare my story would have ended that night.

His victims were lured to Muswell Hill by guile, and killed by strangulation, sometimes accompanied by drowning. Following each murder, Nilsen would observe a ritual in which he bathed, caressed, and then dressed the victim's body, which he kept for extended periods of time to keep him company, before decomposing set in. He then dissected the rotting corpses with chef's knives and disposed of the remains by burning on a bonfire in his garden and flushing small parts down the lavatory. When he was forced to move to a new flat in Muswell Hill he hid the body parts throughout his attic flat.

From what is known, he had already killed Stephen Holmes, and Kenneth Ockenden before the summer of 1980 when he murdered three more Martyn Duffy, William Sutherland, and one still unidentified to date. He would go on to kill a further nine young men, and cases appeared where he had been unsuccessful and the victims survived their encounter with Britain's deadliest serial killer.

Dennis Nilsen, passed away on 12th May 2018 at HMP Full Sutton. I was aware he was an inmate at the time, but oblivious to the fact I had already met him when I made a professional visit in the autumn of 1990 to assess the suitability of housing another prisoner at the Liberty Trust in Hull, although it would have been highly unlikely to have seen him given his enforced isolation within the Prison Service for his own protection.

# CHAPTER VII TAINTED LOVE

I had started to frequent a pub on a Friday night in Reigate Surrey called the Railway Hotel. To get there was complicated but the simplest method was to catch a train from Coulsdon South to Redhill, then a connection which took me to the doorstep of the pub which was next to Reigate Railway Station.

I was introduced by Paul Heaton to new batch of friends who were into New Wave music and fashion and it was something of a "music scene" with bands being formed and performing at several minor local venues. Paul had by now aligned himself as a Mod and had a very loud scooter that I could distinctly hear some miles away at his home across the valley.

Iris, the Landlady at the Railway Hotel was a sex crazed pensioner, and not a woman to cross, but she tolerated a great deal of unruly but good-natured behaviour.

A tradition developed where on the playing of Tainted Love by Soft Cell from the duke box, everybody would stand on chairs, tables, and benches to do a top of the pops dance shuffle and swing.

It must be said that without the support of Paul's dad neither of us would have been able to sustain this social life, as without fail, regardless of time or place, Horace Heaton would pick us up and return us home.

I had a much larger group of friends now, Gus Gregory, Quinten Cook, John Laurenson, Chris Lang, Steve Musham, Roger Dixon, Mathew Wyatt, Sandy Evans and Andrew Dillmot, as well as my compatriots Paul and Andy Sex. There were also girls on the scene, Susan "Silly" Lillywhite, Joanne Goff, Wendy Richards. Sandy and Wendy, and Paul and Silly were items now. Susan used to drive her moped home to Horley in a shiny white helmet, and long black shiny mac, her attire to me became iconic. A cross between a firewoman and a cute panda on wheels.

Every Boxing Day morning we descended onto Reigate Priory sports fields for an annual challenge football match against the Panther Inn. The general rules of football were observed accept the sides often exceeded eleven a side. The pitch was usually a mud bath and became known under the acronym PORAJ, which stood for Plenty of Rogers and Jobbing. Roger, after Roger Dixon who had a reputation for robust ill-informed tackling,  and jobbing, taking on a unique definition of doing a job on someone. However, the title betrayed the reality that these were very gentlemanly affairs harking back to the public-school domination of football era when the game was first developing.

Reigate Priory

Historically it was fitting in that Reigate Priory FC, were one of the original fifteen teams who entered the very first FA Cup competition in 1872 but withdrew before kicking a ball, giving a walk over to eventual finalists the Royal Engineers.

Even after I moved to Hull with Paul, we still returned to our parents for Christmas every year as an excuse to be in place for the Boxing Day porridge, as we started to refer to it.

I enjoyed a short family holiday with the Heaton's to Salcombe Bay in Devon but have vivid memories of Paul spending a lot of time in various phone boxes calling his new love, while I stood outside impatient to re-start the holiday. To gain attention I would sometimes climb up and sit on top dangling my legs to catch Paul's attention suggesting the love fest had run its course. I loved my dad with all my heart, but

Horace Heaton was a great kind of substitute. He was truly kind and attentive and made me feel exceedingly welcome all the time. Paul's mum Doris was by Paul's account a little eccentric, a Scouser who often lost her social filter saying the first thing that came into her head, which could by very charming, funny, or inadvertently offensive. I loved them both dearly.

We spent our time playing catch, football, and cricket on the sandy beaches, and had competitive putting competitions. We also went to see The Members who were playing in nearby Plymouth on tour. It was a small intimate venue and I started to widen my musical tastes, as *This is the Sound of the Suburbs* and *Offshore Banking Business* were strummed out to a pogoing excited audience.

Paul, and his brother Adrian, had musical ambitions to perform and both had electric guitars at home. Several relatively successful bands were forming such as the Escalators and playing low key venues and Paul had a driving ambition to be a performer. The accounting job he had secured was boring him to the extent that he like me was struggling with the conformity of Office life and the escapism of the weekends became increasingly important to us.

Quinton had the most successful band and were gigging a fair bit in Surrey, something that would be close to impossible post millennium as live music venues are now largely replaced by restaurants or Bingo halls. The new wave that appeared after the ground-breaking punk era had made it seemingly possible for anyone to form a band and just get on with it, hoping to be noticed by the many music scouts Record Companies sent out on speculation and rumour.

Paul came up with the idea of producing a satirical surreal fanzine, which we produced and collaborated on, which was printed courtesy of the Dudley Samuel & Harrison Rank Xerox Photocopier where I worked, stapled together on my commute back to Woodmansterne Station in Coulsdon. We decided on breaking convention by giving the "magazine" a different stupid title each month commencing with "Pet Goldfish in a Deckchair."

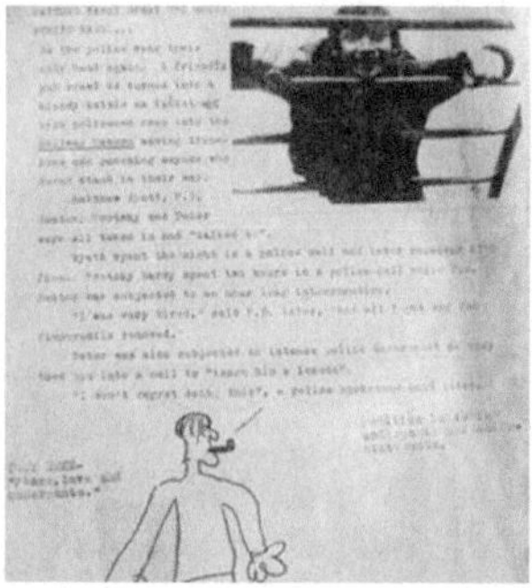

Our Fanzine

It was well received by our peers who honestly thought it was hilarious, but less well received by one of the Directors at my work who found an original page left in the photocopier on the Monday morning of something I was working on. This discovery went some way to the reason I was made redundant not so long after. It was a highly provocative image of the Pope threatening to turn people into a biscuit. At least for them I wasn't mocking Judaism which would have probably meant instant dismissal. With our printing press repossessed this edition never made it to our distribution centre at the Railway Hotel.

I did not expect them to be as offended as my catholic parents would have been, being a Company with a Jewish heritage, but they brought in measures to record every photocopy because of my indiscretion, and Mrs Cohen spent a lot of time auditing the stationery cupboard.

In July, with no football, and the nation getting ready for the Royal Wedding of Charles and Diana, the Railway Hotel was a shade boring all the action was up in London. A verbal fight ensued between Paul and Silly, as Susan wanted to go up to London to sample the atmosphere, but Paul being very much anti-royal would not go. I ended up escorting her in a very platonic way up to London with some others and enjoyed the night. Regardless of political views I do like to see first-hand historical events when you can, and my travel into London would not cost anything as I already had weekly tickets for work.

To improve my extravagant lifestyle, I had successfully negotiated a couple of £5 a week pay rises and had devised a well risk assessed scam to reduce my weekly ticket costs that had risen by over 50%. It started by deciding to walk from Victoria Station to Bruton Street to shave off the Underground element, then realising my ticket was never checked on route but only at end of my journey on a Monday morning I now purchased a weekly return to Purley three stops up the line, having already purchased on the Friday night before, a weekly return between Victoria and Clapham Junction. This saved me over £10 a week until I was caught by an inspector at East Croydon.

I explained that I had to go to our head office that morning and would pay the excess fare at Victoria, and the queue had been so long at Woodmansterne, I would have missed my train. However, I realised they were on to me when I bought my ticket the next week I was asked if I was going to my head office again with his tongue stuck tightly into his cheek. No wonder British Rail were struggling with the likes of me robbing them blind. I decided to stop my scam and request another pay rise, but this time it was refused.

To be fair, the company had shrunk in size in my two years, and the Country was in the middle of a recession and a property market collapse. However, the boss's son Timothy Freed had started recently, which I hoped would mean that I would soon be elevated from Office Junior to Trainee negotiator.

Mr Freed called me into his office one day and just announced I was being made redundant at the end of the month. The plan became obvious now, his son was replacing me, but not for my advancement.

Feeling hard done by, I contacted the local Citizens Advice Bureaux, and they told me that I was entitled to a letter confirming my redundancy, with the proper notice, and that I was unlucky not to have reached two years of service otherwise I would also have been entitled to statutory redundancy pay.

It was noticeably clear that the timing of my one months' notice was deliberate having worked there for twenty-two months. I drew on what courage I had and confronted the pompous old man, and he responded with alarm and said he would get advice. An hour later I got my two-line letter backdated a few weeks so as not to advance by contract any further.

Mr Freed's dosage of my recycled refreshments was increased substantially to the point he complained of a funny taste and that I was to replace the water at once.

Paul, his brother Adrian, and a guy called Stuart organised some band practices and after discarding many band name suggestions settled on a Trade Unions strike call Tools Down. It was difficult listening at first as the strumming guitars and Stuarts drums were not on speaking terms at first, and when they were, they were speaking different languages as they tried to etch out ideas and different riffs. Perhaps they were mimicking Employer Trade Union negotiations, but slowly something reminiscing of a pop song arrived, but only after the long-drawn out delivery pains of an extended labour.

Even though Paul had written the lyrics, he still needed to read them, and held them aloft as he performed, a habit he kept for some time.

Perhaps with too much haste they invested in an 8-track recording studio as they wanted to produce something to send to the BBC's John Peel show, which had built a reputation for giving new talent exposure.

Tools Down paved the way for incredible musical success to come for Paul, but these three amateurs, and their novice cheer leader had such high hopes in the first few hours of recording, but steadily things descended into chaos for the final fourth track, with the use of squeaky toys as a back drop did not amuse the sound engineer, Stuart, or Adrien.

Nevertheless, I thought it was hilarious, but that may have been partly inspired from the hopeless pleading expressions of the others. It was in hindsight awful, and I believe the only copy is hidden away with Paul never to be played again.

There were, however, elements to the song writing that were catchy, and the lyrics were good. Paul was very keen for me to help him develop things and asked me to buy New Musical Express each week, looking for venues for gigs, recording studios, musician adverts, and read the articles about new trends. I did start to buy it but found the journalists wrote in such an unnecessarily artistic way it was as if they were competing with, and jealous of the musicians they were writing about. I found it unreadable.

I was a disappointment and did not have the acumen or knowledge to provide much more than moral support, and at some stage I think Paul realised that if he was going to make it, he would have to do it alone, or at least find others who shared his ambition and talent.

Tools Down played some local gigs which I found exciting, but these were mostly in front of an audience made up of friends.

I took some temping jobs, including a fuel pump attendant in South Croydon where I was almost the victim of a robbery. Everything was cash, and my till was in the vulnerable open sentry box between the pumps. An open van pulled up carrying scrap metal and as I was filling up with my eye on the till, one of the occupants tried to distract me, and when I turned the other one was on his way to the till. Realising he had been rumbled he stopped and I added we have CCTV here you know. They left empty handed, but I was now on edge, and feeling very vulnerable.

I was embarrassed and somewhat humiliated when one of the Directors of Dudley Samuel & Harrison came for fuel, I was unaware that Ken Fogden lived in Croydon, and he was clearly uncomfortable that he had done nothing to counter the recent injustice of my redundancy.

I was meticulous with the cash. After a couple of days when taking the proceeds of the day to the office they told me it was £5 short and deducted it from my wages. I did not believe I had made a mistake but there was no way of checking as I did not have access to the data of how much petrol was sold.

Every now and then I would get the same accusation, once for £15 which was an exceptionally sizeable percentage of my weekly wage. I did not believe them; it was too much to be an error so something was going on. A manager took over from me for my lunch hour each day, but this was not taken into consideration.

I worked out that I could record the petrol use of each pump and takings and do my own reconciliation. I also counted the cash before and after lunch.

When they confronted me soon after with a shortfall of another £5, I supplied my accounts which showed the £5 went missing at lunch time. A huge argument ensued; they had obviously been rumbled because they would not verify my figures which should match theirs. I now understood why they were using temporary agency staff on a permanent basis. If that amount of money was going missing on my watch then surely, they would have involved the Police, or at the very least sacked me.

I left complaining to the recruitment agency, who did not seem incredibly surprised by events, and were undoubtedly earning from the constant turnaround of staff they were contracted to send.

Paul had freed himself from the constraints of his life dissolving book-keeping job and found real worth working as a support worker in a School for the Blind in Fetcham Leatherhead. Paul cycled 11 miles to work from Chipstead every workday and prided himself that he could make the journey without touching his handlebars. He was incredibly fit as some of the hills in the Chipstead Valley were brutal. Leatherhead was even further away.

On the other hand, a job in Croydon as a property negotiator was offered to me, after Ray Cottington had helped me compose a letter and supplied a reference to all the major agents seeking work. It was successful and I had several offers but settled with Best Gibson Holdsworth, and newly formed partnership fronted by George A. Best, who referred to himself as Alan to avoid being linked to the Irish superstar with a drink problem. He said they were an exciting company that were going places.

Going from £40 a week to £330 per month even before commissions was a real step up and became the highest paid young worker I knew in my small world, and they were paying for me to learn to drive. The deal between us was they provided  substantial earnings, driving lessons and travel costs, and my success would help them keep their heads above water during the recession.

It became clear that their recent merger had resulted in staff being laid off, and the selling of an office to economise, and the letter from a whiz kid from the West End provided them with an opportunity to turn their fortunes around.

The letter composed by my mentor and offer of a reference did not specifically lie. However, I did not recognise my characteristics anywhere in it, or anything about myself except when mentioned by name, and this deception was unfortunately matched by their own, and we deserved each other, and the inevitable outcome.

However, it was an opportunity to learn to drive on the company's expense, and due to being a passenger in my dad's car for many years, I was a very cautious learner, as my dad's style was that of a competitor with the sole object of getting to his destination faster than anyone else, which made any passenger feel like a crash test dummy at worst and at best car sick.

After a reasonable number of lessons, and as my confidence was building my instructor asked me to park down a back street in Croydon. As I patiently waited for my next instruction, proud of how easily I had manoeuvred the little dual control bright Orange Austen Metro so close to the kerb, he got out of the car and opened the back seat and started to place a child safety seat, with baby attached, into the back seat, and a woman got in the other side.

This is my wife and child he explained, and we are going to take them to Stafford Road to do our shopping, and don't worry she will get the bus back. My first reaction was what a cheek, then what a responsibility. Seeing my reaction, he said I have enough confidence in you to put the lives of my family in your hands. This wasn't completely true as he still retained dual control, but the impact was that after dropping them off we both agreed I was ready for my Test.

Obviously on a legal basis this was appalling conduct, however I took the view that this was designed to boost my confidence and make me a better driver under pressure.

On the day of the test, I was under intense pressure to pass as my Company were impatient that I could fulfil my role more efficiently than public transport. I was far more impatient as I needed a car to boost my social life and most importantly of all attract girls.

I entered the test centre in Croydon and sat as all the stuffy examiners appeared calling out each contestant in turn. Each name called ricocheted through my nervous system and I considered running out as I felt I was close to shaking.

Bearing in mind my adolescent and immature approach to girls and women, when my name was called by a soft female voice, I was thrown into confusion and then disbelief. All the other examiners were middle aged men in suits, but I had Miss World, or at least she would have been a contender if she ever considered entering. Although dressed respectfully, you could still see her mammary glands protruding through her low-cut dress, and her long legs from just above the knee.

I quickly dismissed my reaction to pretend I was someone else, to secure a change in examiners quickly realising this was futile, and the unwanted distraction was a handicap I would have to persevere with. Sitting side by side in the car, I realised I stood a chance as I now had to concentrate on the road and the array of controls before me, even with the distraction of her sweet perfume.

She asked politely if I could read the registration of the blue car on the right-hand side of the road, and I responded with confidence. My heart sank when she responded no that is not right. She reiterated the request adding a minor detail about the car and I realised with a huge sigh of relief that she was referring to a car much closer to the one I had identified, and as I explained the error, she was highly amused and said she could barely make out that car registration but would take my word for it. I had exceptional vision and this misunderstanding was a welcome distraction before I set of on my mirror signal manoeuvre odyssey.

When we arrived back at the test centre, I was exhausted, and when she said the test was not over until I parked, I barely had any strength left after strangling a steering wheel for the best part of an hour.

"Well, done". "Mr Barry you have passed." Suddenly all the excuses I had stored up during the test to explain why I had been forced to fail, to my new employers evaporated in a haze of joy. I was now a driver, ready to be extortionately ripped off by an insurance company, but I would now have the freedom to travel where I wanted and when I wanted.

# PLACES LIVED

2 Betts Mead Parade Old Lodge Lane Kenley,

470 & 472 Chipstead Valley Road

53 Nutfield Road Coulsdon

70 Grafton St,

375 Spring Bank West,

Flat 2 46 Grafton Street,

Flat 6 91 Westbourne Avenue Hull

Upper Flat 235 Brighton Road Purley,

166 Chipstead Valley Road Coulsdon,

Upper Flat 2 Old Lodge Lane Purley

# PLACES EDUCATED

Chipstead Valley Primary School Coulsdon,

Thomas More Catholic School Purley

Redhill Technical College, (Now East Surrey)

Bradford & Ilkley Community College.

# CHAPTER VIII ALL THE MADMEN

My first car, a white Austen1100 was secured by my Mum from a work colleague. where she was working in the catering department of the local Cane Hill Hospital. This Hospital, on the brow of one side of the Chipstead Valley had a water tower that menacingly oversaw everything in the valleys below.

Opened in 1883 as a Lunatic Asylum, it housed at times over two thousand "lunatics" and was a fearful place. Apart from the excellent staff facilities of a swimming pool, and social club, it was rumoured to house many famous people including David Bowies half-brother.

This was confirmed in 1985, when after many attempts on his own life, Terry Burns sadly succeeded when he threw himself under a train at one of my local stations Coulsdon South. I found out later that the American release of the 1970 David Bowie album "The Man Who Sold the World" featured an image of the Cane Hill Hospital administration block and the track "All the Madmen" was penned by Bowie with Terry in mind. For several years, I had listened to David Bowie albums including the man Who sold The World and all the Madmen, in my bedroom looking out over the Chipstead Valley with the prominent water tower featuring heavily on the horizon, oblivious that his half-brother lived there.

My mother also cooked for Michael Caine's "illegitimate" brother who was also resident there, his residence disclosed in 2002 by Caine during a Parkinson interview on the BBC. Occupancy of this institution were closely guarded secrets but Charlie Chaplin confirmed he visited his mother here as far back as 1912. The Hospital closed in 1992 but lay derelict until 2008. Patient's care was replaced by so-called care in the community. The area is now a housing estate and the remaining secrets of this refuge of insanity remain just that.

Having spent every New Year's Eve in English pubs or clubs, I found the experience somewhat underwhelming. Most people of my generation at least were out of it by ten o'clock, and everything closed shortly after midnight. Paul had spent the summer hitch hiking around Europe with John Laurenson when they decided to split up and go their separate ways. Alone in Germany Paul said he sort help in Limburg un der Lahn as he came across a Father's Day celebration in typical German style. It was here that he befriended Alfred Wirth an active member of the German Green Party Die Grunen. Alfred plied the young Paul with a few beers, not a difficult assignment and then invited him to stay with him until John could find him. This was a time before mobile phones, and so several international messages were passed around and Paul felt welcome enough for a prolonged stay. Before leaving Alfred invited him and any friends to come over for German New Year, because after discussion about traditions, it was clear the Germans had far better ways of seeing the new year in, especially in their picturesque and charming village.

With my new job, I had little holiday time available for the long journey, so while Paul, Silly and Joanne Goff caught the night train from Victoria Station via the Ferry Dover to Ostend and then the early morning train to Koln, I prepared to fly. Many others had dropped out due to affordability which was disappointing, and I barely knew Jo, so this was not a cosy foursome. I had more money in my pocket than sense having bought a flight from Gatwick to Koln Business Class. This would be the first time I ever travelled alone, and it cost £70 which back then was a week's wages. Being naïve I assumed being Business Class I should wear a suit which I did, which caused much hilarity when I was greeted at the airport. At the time there was no world wide web, or price comparison sights, so I am sure the travel agent saw me coming and sold me the most expensive tickets they could. Many decades later I would take a suit to Alfred's Wirth funeral, only to learn that his widowed wife Sabine had asked for no formal wear or black after I arrived. I was always one who would be inappropriately dressed for every occasion in Germany.

Greeted enthusiastically at the airport we were whisked away into the heart of Germany. I was used to the congestion of the M25, so I was stunned by the easy flowing autobahn and we arrived in no time at all in the small satellite village of Limburg un der Lahn called Dietkirchen.

I was a heavy binge drinker at this time, but one of the lessons I learned in Germany was patience brings its own rewards. I started to become agitated around 10pm on New Year's Eve, as although everyone was very gently drinking the occasional bottle of strong German Bier, this seemed something of an anti-climax, and my English obsession with getting drunk before closing time created anxiety and frustration.

There were only a couple of bars in the Village, but they both looked closed. My thoughts ran to the Railway Hotel where it was around 9pm and our friends would be well into the celebrations. Here, we were sitting down to watch TV at the behest of our German friends to watch a British Comedy. I was not very enthused but complied as our hosts had been so generous and were so incredibly friendly.

We were unaware that in 1963, the British 15-minute sketch show, "Dinner for One," was broadcast for the first time on German TV - and has been aired on December 31 every year, becoming the most often repeated German TV program ever. It was in English with no German subtitles and mildly funny. The story is of an aristocrat woman celebrating her 90th birthday, with her butler covering for her absent guests. They both get increasingly drunk. However, the reaction from the Germans was to howl with laughter to the point I might have considered calling an ambulance if I had known the emergency number. Laughter is contagious and this short film brought such joy, and the Germans were astonished that we had never seen it before as they assumed it was broadcast in England. It was eventual shown again by the BBC on New Year's Eve in 2018 after a break of over half a century.

As midnight approached, we left the confines of Alfred's house, and as the church bell chimed in the New Year suddenly the sky was filled with exploding fireworks from every direction silhouetting the lit-up church on the hill, and bangers were being thrown at everyone's feet. Fireworks were not much of a feature in England's New Year back in 1981 and this was an orchestrated thrill as they lit up the sky in a crackle and pop frenzy in accompaniment to the rhythmic Church bells that were ringing in 1982. Glasses of Sekt were passed around to Toast the New Year. Looking into the joyful eyes of my old and new friends their faces lit up in multicolour flashes, I felt an overwhelming sense of warmth and inner peace. Suddenly from all directions the villagers appeared in the street hugging kissing and shouting "Prost Neues Jahr."

These parties were just starting up as the party in Reigate and the rest of England had passed their peak. I was unaware that there were many houses that were hosting parties, and it was tradition to visit each one in turn. Every house had a rocking party but be it with a bizarre choice of music, although Alfred's love of the Pogue's brought some relief. In the village square a well-meaning banger fight was fought out and I remember glancing upwards and seeing the stuffy village elders looking on in that internationally famous parental look of disapproval. Many years later I would be too old to risk injury and debase myself in this game and remember the irony of standing in the very same place looking down on the German teenagers no doubt with the same look.

When it got close to 1am we reminded our hosts it was now English New Year and we counted down again.

Everyone wanted to hug you, and wish you a happy new year, and although I never danced at home, I felt comfortable here and threw myself into the night, losing all my usual English reserve and my innate shyness.

At some point things fizzled out, unlike England there were no last orders in the bars, it was when the last person left the proprietor would shut up shop and go to bed and prepare for Fraushopin.

I am not sure how widespread this tradition is in Germany, but it certainly was in Dietkirchen. Regardless of how you felt, or how late you turned in, we were rounded up and marched to the bar on the morning of 1st January 1982. I was under the illusion that New Year's Eve was the session to beat all sessions, but this was another step up in endurance. There was a tradition of in England called the hair of the dog which involved having a few drinks to cope with a hangover, but this was something else and lasted all day and all night. I often wonder how I was able to stand up, never mind roll a skittle down a narrow alleyway, but the Germans love to play while they drink. All kinds of drinking games ensued, that usually required the looser to get a round in.

Paying for drinks however was impossible, as the bar staff did not take any money, they just marked your beer matt on account. I could not imagine that working in England particularly where I lived, but here you were trusted. However, we could not trust our German friends not to sneak up and pay our bills before we were aware of what they were doing. Regardless most garages were well stocked with cases of various German beers.

I would return to Dietkirchen many times for New year, and once to be one of three best men for Paul Heaton's wedding to Linda many years later in the summer of 2016. Many of the Residents of Dietkirchen became lifelong friends. Sabine, Mario, Berndt, (Toast), Helmut, Tony, Manuel, George and Anna-Gried. My affection for Alfred was almost father like, he was something of a life mentor, introducing me to green politics, and although as a teacher in Germany he had a very serious side to him, he was in my company always a bundle of joy. His passing in August 2021 was simply heart wrenching

After Clifford Bingley left his family home in Nutfield Road, to join the regular army, I was distraught while watching news coverage of the Falklands War when I heard his name called out during a mass funeral at Goose Green. I had not heard from Keith Bingley's brother in a long time and did not want to compound their misery by calling. There was no internet in 1982, and so I assumed he was buried on this remote island in the South Atlantic, only to find many years later that it was Gary David Bingley from the Parachute Regiment who died that day in May, and I had obviously misheard the report. There was no rewind on TV's or internet back then, you only had one chance, but I was pleased that my old friend had not perished at Goose Green.

I was still attending Chelsea matches home and away in the second division, and as a Steward I had secured responsibility for the Home Dressing Room in the large East Stand Tunnel. My role put me on familiar terms with a lot of the first team players and coaching staff. Petar Borota Mike Fillery, Clive Walker, Gary Chivers, Joey Jones, Colin Pates, Gary Locke, Micky Droy, and Mike Nutton and manager John Neal who had just taken over from Geoff Hurst.

I suffered the humiliation of watching Chelsea lose 6-0 at Rotherham United aptly on Halloween, when the team were languishing mid table in the second division. Things had not really improved by the spring and I had low expectations when they faced Crystal Palace at Selhurst park on 12th April 1982. The National Front had become mainstream within the Chelsea fan base, and they felt free to sing songs promoting fascism and racism freely without rebuke or restraint from the authorities. It was hard supporting a club which my family had done for generations, which had slowly become the mouthpiece of overt and unashamedly racist ideology, and a recruitment ground for the far right.

With Chelsea winning 1-0 warming up on the touchline by our fans was our substitute, and there seemed to be something of a commotion. Paul Canoville was about to become Chelsea's first black man to play for the club at senior level. In his words

*"As I'm stretching and running, I hear loud individual voices through the noise: 'Sit down you black cunt! 'You fucking wog – fuck off!' Over and over again. Lots of different people. I hardly dared look around. They were right behind me. I snatched a glimpse. They were all wearing blue shirts and scarves – Chelsea fans, my side's fans, faces screwed with pure hatred and anger, all directed at me... I felt physically sick. I was absolutely terrified."*

Paul Canoville 11 goals in 79 Appearances for Chelsea FC

There were Chelsea fans who rallied around him, and that set Chelsea fans against Chelsea fans, and it looked like violence was about to break out within the confines of the designated away section. The Police looked on in bewilderment, with their only pre-match strategy to keep Crystal Palace and Chelsea fans apart.

He was a fast-skilful player, and I warmed to him at once, but part of me wanted to get him off the pitch to protect him from the barrage of abuse that was splitting my club in half. I was also desperate for him to score because surely that would shut up the bigots, or at least confuse their binary belief. Then it occurred to me, this may be a turning point, as more black players came through the ranks, the National Front, and all its splinter groups would surely lose their grip on the club. I was right but the process was a slow painful one.

We all owe so much to the brave Paul Canoville for his endurance, to break through against so much negativity and blind hatred. If anyone mocks PC (political correctness) I have frequently sited PC, Paul Canoville's experience to try and illustrate that there is no humour in hatred.

That summer, the Dietkirchen German Skittle Club arrived in Chipstead camping in Pauls large rear garden, and it was our task to entertain them, which was more of a challenge seeing we both still lived with our parents and were not flush with cash. We did the London tourist thing with them, but it heavily rained the entire day, and we spent most of the time taking shelter in pubs. We came close to being ejected from the National Gallery in Trafalgar Square because I decided to take a well-earned kip in one of the viewing rooms.

Inevitably we ended up at the Railway Hotel in the evening, all in high spirits after an entertaining and fun day out. Mathew Wyatt was propping up the bar with a South London friend who kept shouting across the bar at us "where are our bicycles," "give us back our bicycles," which at first I did not understand, and then was told it was reference to the Nazi's confiscating Bicycles from the Dutch people to prevent freedom of movement and were being literally re-cycled to contribute to the severe metal shortage in Germany for the building of their new Panther and Tiger tanks.

As I went across to him to put an end to his insulting behaviour towards our German guests, he was so belligerent in his reply without further ado I head butted him off his stool. The resulting mass brawl, was a point of national shame and worst still nearly got me and Paul barred from the pub. We decided that the next time our German friends visited we would take them on a tour of the UK, far away from the small-minded nationalistic locals.

Despite my lack of experience, knowledge, and business acumen, I had a real go at being a commercial property negotiator and secured my first purchase of a property investment for a client for £110'000 which consisted of three shops and three offices at 110 Orpington High Street, followed by the successful sale of a shop and office at 55 Stafford Road Croydon for £50'000. This provided with a windfall commission to the tune of £330, enough to fund my package holiday to Spain to watch the 1982 World Cup. England had not qualified since I was responsible for them being knocked out in 1970 by falling asleep attributed to underage drinking and obvious parental neglect.

My plan to go with others started to evaporate as enthusiasm waned when the costs became clear and with Paul unsure if he was going with his family, I booked through Sportsworld the official and expensive travel agent. I chose to go it alone; I would surely make friends in Spain and my mates would have to watch me on TV having the time of my life. Eight years later Paul very generously paid for me and my partner of the time to go to Italia 90 which more than made up for his absence.

This was going to be the first time I travelled and stayed away all on my own, and although I was a little nervous of having no support at hand, my excitement at the prospects of being away for ten days abroad was visible. I was well prepared, having shopped intently to make sure I looked the part throughout my stay, and sat contemplating the feast of football, drink and sun that was about to emerge as I sat patiently on the platform of Coulsdon South for the train to take me to Gatwick Airport.

Arriving at Gatwick the feeling of loneliness eased as the terminal was awash with red, white, and blue and I was now part of an Army defined by my new uniform. The one overriding fear was that England supporters were certainly not welcome in Spain, or anywhere in the world given the unruly well-earned reputation we were not expecting much justice from the Spanish Police and my plan was to avoid anyone intent on trouble, but in an idealistic manner hoped I would stand my ground should we come under any attack. That fear just added to the excitement.

Everyone on my plane was bound for San Sebastian Airport in Hondarribia and then onto a small remote hotel in Cestona, a spa resort in the foothills of the Pyrenees mountains. I made a couple of friends on the flight who were both from Manchester, and when we started to descend, I became concerned as I looked out my window as it looked like our Pilot was putting us down into the Bay of Biscay, and this was a plot by the Spanish and French Government to murder all England fans on route in a cruel method of preventative justice. I did not realise the runway stretched down a very narrow strip of land along the river Bidasoa right on the French border.

Having landed safely in Spain we noticed oddly coloured Union Jacks on display in the airport souvenir shops. I chose to buy one of these red, white, and green flags and encouraged others to do the same.

Our hotel was a disappointment, we were miles from any action and Cestona was a sleepy town with little to do. I had to share a room and ended up with a middle-aged man who snored and smelled. In the morning at communal breakfast, we took our first wonder around Cestona. Our hotel was the only one in town, and the locals were obviously nervous about our invasion and everything was boarded up. Our temporary occupation illustrated by the mass of Union Jacks, St George's Cross's, and the new Red White and Green Union Jacks draped from every balcony.

In buying theses local flags, we had inadvertently made a brilliant mistake and scored a public relations Coup. These were the nationalist flags of the Basque who hated Spanish rule and had previously fought and continued to fight for complete independence. I had heard of ETA, Euskadi Ta Askatasuna ("Basque Homeland and Liberty") but had not attributed this organisation, which was often described as a terrorist organisation by the British and undoubtedly Spanish media, to my trip to Spain. According to the locals we were not in Spain.

I realised this was a quite different Country we had landed in, and we were possible more welcome than we understood given the history of the many English volunteers who died fighting the fascist Spanish rulers in 1937. Upon my return to England, I would read Homage to Catalonia by George Orwell, describing his experiences in the Spanish Civil War for the Basques and Catalonian's. German fans would have got a quite different reception, given Guernica itself was not far from Cestona, the place immortalised by Picasso's painting of the peace time bombing atrocity by the Luftwaffe, to support General Franco's campaign of terror against the Basque people.

So, although an accident, in the sense that had their flag had a different design, things would have been undoubtedly different, England Supporters apparently supported the independence of the Basque region, which no one had a problem with as the Basque's didn't have a national football team to compete with England, and we were about to take over the San Mames Stadium the home of the Basque team Atletico Bilbao as our home ground.

My first evening stroll in Cestona uncovered a bar which only revealed itself when we heard the unmistakable noise of a cheer prompted by a goal watched on TV in a bar. There was a moment of hesitation as we walked in to the suspicious all male young occupants, but then a friendly voice said welcome English. Knowing only a few Spanish words, and the Viva la España chorus from the holiday song that recently charted and having read the word for Basque here was Euskadi, I said the first thing that came into my head. "Viva Euskadi."

I expected a positive response, but the reaction was overwhelming. If we were looking to break the ice with the locals, I had just smashed up a sea of icebergs and within minutes there was a chorus of their local revolutionary song which included something like Viva Euskadi. Spanish was their second language, but they spoke and sang in Euskara. We were hugged, we were embraced, we were even kissed by our new congregation, and then the drink flowed, and we were not allowed to pay a peseta.

I learned that these young men were out commiserating because they had been forcibly conscripted up to serve in the Spanish Army for National Service, to serve a Nation that they viewed as a force of occupation, and unfortunately many would be leaving the village shortly and not be returning until we were long gone back in England. It was akin to conscripting young catholic men from Northern Ireland to serve in the British Army.

The next day was the first game, and we all loaded onto our coach for the short journey into Bilbao. We had a young girl who was brave enough to be our tour guide whose English was far superior to my Spanish or Euskara, however a grammatical error cost her dear. “We will arrive at our Destiny at about….” She was never able to finish the sentence as 50 young Englishmen laughed without malice as she turned her lightly tanned face into a fusion of red, and you could visibly see her hard-fought confidence drain away through the coach floor. It was not long before she was nicknamed Destiny and had to endure endless chants based on the British airways advert “well take good care of you, Destiny-Destiny”. Occasionally more explicit songs materialised which I hoped she would not understand.

Arriving at the Stadium it was obvious to all that I was very much the worse for wear given my late night with our conscripted friends, and my show-off breakfast that included more beer. As I entered the stadium I struggled to work out where my allocated seat was, and then spotted a space at the end of a row. The occupants of the next three seats stood up to allow me to pass not realising I had found my seat and as I looked up to explain I nearly fell backwards and rolled all the way down onto the pitch. I was sat next to Paul Heaton’s brother Adrian, his girlfriend Lorraine and his parents Horace and Doris. “Fuck me” I spurted out before realising I had left my language filter was back at the hotel.

San Mames Stadium España 82.

Given the state I was in, it was unclear who was more embarrassed, as I was hardly able to speak having become so dehydrated in Bilbao's sun, I was sweating alcohol faster than I could replenish it. Although excited to bump into the Heaton's in such a bizarre coincidence, given the tickets were bought through dissimilar sources and England's allocation was around 20'000, I was confused why Paul had not made the trip, after we had expended months discussing it. He explained later that he was initially prevented by his work, and when he was freed himself up there was no longer room in the family car for the 855-mile drive.

Fortunately for me, and the rest of the Country, Bryan Robson the England captain supplied a perfect distraction to hide my embarrassment and scored the fastest world cup finals goal from kick off in just 27 seconds, and England went on to win 3-1. The Croatian, Hakan Sukur now holds the record after scoring in 10.8 seconds in 2002.

I had not expected the boredom that would ensue between matches, my new friend Manc thankfully hired a car, and we were able to drive to a beach, and travel to a few remote bars, as Cestona remained something of ghost town. I had even contemplated catching the nearly empty excursion to Valladolid to watch the other group games, as we had tickets included in our package. We filled our time with a kick about, a few drinks, a few lengths of the Pool and then a kick about again. One person in our group was so bored he arranged for his wife to fly out.

England won their next game against Czechoslovakia guaranteeing qualification for the next round making the last game against Kuwait meaningless. On our last night in Cestona I wondered into the village and surprisingly found that a bar was open and inside were a few young people including girls. It had taken them over a week to realise that England fans were not going to burn down the village but had become just polite young men who were just boisterous at worse.

I struck up a pidgin English conversation with this young girl called Yolanda, with the Y sounding as an I. At this moment I was reasonably sober, as getting drunk had become boring in this environment and I was winding down for my return to England in the morning.

She invited me for a stroll in the warm humid night air, and we ascended one of the great hills that surrounded the town, talking aimlessly with little comprehension of each other's languages, relying almost solely on sign language, and when the point was lost I learned a new phrase "no es importante," Looking down on the Town we viewed an England fan running naked through the town draped only in a Union Jack, I covered her eyes in jest.

She took away my hand and gestured she wanted to look laughing, and then she reached up and kissed me. I had kissed girls before, but never in this sensitive and overpowering manner and in such romantic isolation in the low hills of the Pyrenees.

When we returned to the village, I felt really wanted for the first time in my life and this was more intoxicating than getting mindlessly drunk. I went back to my hotel room and held my breath as my roommate absolutely stunk of body odour, diminishing my loved-up aura, and making it hard to go to sleep in the humidity, especially without the anaesthetic of alcohol I had become reliant on. I cursed my luck that I had not met her on an earlier night, as there was no pretence of staying connected with such obvious barriers of distance, language, and culture in place.

I had considered staying on to watch the next England games, but I simply could not fund this, and anyway the remaining matches would be in Spain, not in the Basque lands where Yolande resided, and I was correct in my assumption that England fans in Spain were going to have a rough time from the locals, other fans, and the Police. So, I headed home to Gatwick as planned and was pleased to return to familiar surroundings, and my new job.

I watched England draw their next two games on TV but still get eliminated from the tournament without losing a game. Thankfully the España 82 format has never been used since.

# CHAPTER IX COME ON EILEEN

An old School friend Trevor Bloomfield invited me to go to Ireland for a holiday later in the year, he was so keen for me to go he paid for my Train and Ferry fair and we headed down to Longford where we were to stay with his Uncle and Auntie.

I was financially broke after my World Cup adventure so went as a kind of favour. My Grandad on my mothers' side was an Irish national, and my only earlier trip to Ireland was as a babe in arms in 1963.

The Barry & Sheehan Family on a Ferry to Ireland 1963

Val Sheehan my grandad was a hero of mine, an extraordinary card player, and repairer of watches. He was raised in Cork, and after emigrating to England became well known in London as the Head Chef of the Trocadero Restaurant in Piccadilly which closed three years after my birth and became a hotel. It has since become an amusement arcade, and later the venue for a Beautiful South private party.

After retiring with my Geordie Nan, Nancy, they retired to a cottage near Launceston Cornwall, something that frustrated my mother as at the time it could take about six hours to drive there.

However, it did provide a base for an occasional family holiday as they had a static caravan next to the small cottage where we stayed several times, although the journey there and back was almost a deal breaker with the six of us stuffed into a five-seater car.

Before moving out of Carpenter's Park near Watford, they had a house in Sheerness on the Isle of Sheppey, which we visited frequently which had a fairground close by with a crumbling wooden roller coaster "The Mighty Mouse", but Cornwall had Bude, and we could all learn how not to surf on cheap wooden hired boards that sunk instantly your body weight was applied.

Me and mum on the Whip in Sheerness

However, I do remember being excited about the visit to Tintagel and the Castle. I had loved Castles; and remember trying to bully my parents to take me to the castle visible at the end of the beach at Llorete de Mar on the Costa Brava without success. Over 40 years later I returned to this now unrecognisable tourist metropolis with my south east London Super Veterans Football Team the Old Gitonians and found time to try and fulfil a boyhood dream, only to be disappointed that the castle was now a private residence, and I could go no further than the imposing front gates.

I did not know what to expect from Longford, but much as I enjoyed going out for a drink every night, it became increasing apparent that Trevor's Auntie was seriously psychotic and extremely ill indeed, and her husband had turned to drink so that any car journey was a trauma for his passengers. Once driving us back from the local pub we were pulled over by the Garda, a common occurrence in County Longford which was by repute bandit country with highly active Provisional IRA units. The officer asked him if he had been drinking, to which he confessed he had a couple and was heading home. Expecting his immediate arrest and a long walk home for us, he simply waved him on instructing him to take care. Ireland was even less strict than England where the rule of thumb was not to drink more than two pints. We had been in the pub all day and our driver had consumed closer to two barrels than two pints.

Weeks before I had driven back from the Railway Hotel with Andy Sex when it was pouring very heavily with rain, conscious that I may be over the legal limit when I noticed I was being obviously followed by a Police Car who flashed me to stop as I approached the cover of a Bridge. Thinking quickly, I realised they wanted to keep themselves dry, so I decided to pull up past the Bridge and then jump out of the car and approach them in the pouring rain looking at the back of my car as if they must have seen something wrong to ask me to stop. It worked, they were reluctant to get wet and I ensured my positioning at their Car so that the driving wind and rain obscured by breath. It was a close call and should have been a valuable lesson.

The Government had started to campaign against drink driving, but the culture took a long time to change. It was normal for my dad to have a few pints and then drive us all home from a club, and this was the world I grew up in.

We did not do much but trawl the many pubs in Longford, to see if they were better than our favourite one which had the very shy Eileen pulling pints for us all day. To wind her up we would select Dexy's Midnight Runners on her duke box and gesture to her, and mime *"Come on Eileen, in that pretty red dress, my thoughts I confess verge on dirty, oh come on Eileen."* From that day forth she never wore red, most certainly not in our presence to be sure.

Something happened in Ireland that still haunts me today. One evening Trevor's Uncle asked for help as his dog had given birth to small litter of puppies and he wanted rid. I naively assumed he would take them somewhere else to off load them, but this was rural Ireland and after driving to a river he said he was going to drown them in a sack. All three of us were drunk and the two English boys realised the plot was cruel and asked if he could consider another way. He's response was to fetch a double barrel shotgun and proceeded to load both barrels.

This was not what we meant, but both were afraid to argue with an armed drunk. He tied the sack up, but the noise of the puppies, who obviously sensed the danger they were in, tore through my soul, and in disbelief we watched on in horror as this drunken maniac with a loaded gun fired one barrel at the sack falling back from the kick, and then dropping the gun.

The puppies screamed some were still alive but torn apart and everyone froze except for me. I could not bear the noise and incredibly for a 20-year-old, picked up the gun and put them out of their misery with the remaining barrel. This was the first time and the last that I would ever discharge a firearm, but the sound and image of those innocent puppies screaming and bleeding by the riverbank has haunted and traumatised me for life.

We drove back in silence, and I wanted to get back to England as soon as I could.

Arriving back in Coulsdon, I realised that I had spent far too much on my Credit Card in Ireland and for the first time was slipping into serious debt. My situation was exacerbated after I attended an impromptu meeting with Alan Best, who asked for details of all my potential deals in hand. Despite my lack of experience, I had made a success of the job earning well for the Company, but unbeknownst to me the realisation that the new partnership was a combination of two sinking ships hoping the other was more seaworthy was not working. After a further couple of frantic meetings, it was clear their combined ships were taking on so much water, and they were sinking into liquidation. The decision was eventually made by the Partners that I would be made redundant as they would re-model the company discarding sales and acquisitions, to concentrate on surveying and surviving the recession.

Using the template letter from before I circulated to local agents and received an offer from Maggs Edwards & Sharp based in Epsom High Street, Surrey They were very much a

Residential Estate Agency, but Tony Maggs wanted them to get more into the commercial sector seduced by the planned fifty-three-unit Ashley Centre Shopping Centre development in the High Street. Being impressed by my West End credentials he thought I was the person who could link his local knowledge with my commercial sales experience of acquiring property for his clients.

Unfortunately, his idea was flawed, the developers had already earmarked the vast majority of the occupiers, however he was right in that pedestrian flow would increase at the development end of the High Street, where rents would subsequently increase accordingly, which would create a great deal of movement in and out of the High Street, excellent pickings for a local commercial estate agent.

This was a cutthroat business, and despite my antics in Ireland, I was no cutter of throats. I had instructions to let a shop at one end of the High Street which we all knew would suffer after the development was complete, but I managed to get a buyer for the lease and was happy for the commission. However, when the interested party arrived with the paperwork to secure the deal and make it binding subject to contract, a sense of deep guilt and regret came over me.

The new occupant had by his own account re-mortgaged his own home to secure enough to pay the Premium on the new lease, secure the necessary business loans and to buy up enough stock to start his own shoe shop. It was clear to me that this would have been an enormous gamble at the best of times as he was going to compete against the giant shoe venders of the day, but while they were vying for position or signing leases in the new Ashley Centre or close to the entrance in prime positions, this charming dreamer was taking out a very expensive lease at the other end of the High Street, which would become a very secondary position in the coming year. It was all about pedestrian flow and the high street was about to change.

Even with my limited experience in the sector, I knew Shoe shops had to be located in prime position to succeed and although I felt morally obliged to let him know, it would have been completely unprofessional as I was acting for the owner who was selling up. The deal went through just before my 21st Birthday, and with it went my dignity. I had admired Ray Cottington's ruthless business streak but had failed to grasp that he was a shark operating in shark infested waters where everyone was a shark, but out here in the outskirts of London, in leafy Epsom there was an element of naivety, and I didn't feel like I wanted to be a predator, even though that was what I was hired for.

The brash overconfident negotiator who had discarded his shyness for playing the part of a "player" now had self-doubt, and it started to show. I fell out with Mr Maggs as he wanted me to focus on local business, and I was just chasing the commission and did not care where I could facilitate an exchange of contracts, while he was painfully aware about keeping a local reputation. I was not really interested in small local family businesses, I wanted to wheel and deal with the big boys, even though I was still very much just a mature child myself.

It was inevitable that we would be parting company and I was actively looking elsewhere, but then something that was also inevitable also happened to force my hand.

We had great Party's in Redhill and Reigate including one at my house while my Parents were away for a couple of weeks. I awoke that morning to find strewn bodies scattered around the house, and when I looked around for breakfast it became obvious that someone had removed all the labels from the tins and packaging. Eating for the next few days was something of a lottery as I was living out of tins.

As explained, I had had a narrow escape being pulled over by the Police when close to or just over the legal alcohol limit and had created strict new rules for myself which I had followed vigorously ever since, which often meant catching a Train to pick my car up in the morning, staying overnight, or simply not drinking alcohol when out.

The plan was to stay at Mathew Wyatt's home after his all day and night party in Redhill over the weekend. However, fuelled with intoxication and impaired judgement, rather than carry crates of replenishments back from the off licence, I chose to drive to the off-licence in a decision I decadently described later in the summation that I was too drunk to walk.

There was no rain, no bridge, just blue flashing lights spinning out in a visual type of morse code, this life is over! Hardly able to converse I was arrested and taken to Reigate Police Station and duly charged. I was fully cooperative and explained my stupid reasoning and how I needed my Licence for my job, and I was terrified of needles as I awaited the blood test. This created an element of sympathy which would not be around in today's culture.

It seems incredible now that I was released on bail that evening, still had my driving licence and my car keys, and the Police drove me back to the party on the grounds that I promised not to drive my car again until I was sober. I returned to the Party still in full swing and tried to drown my sorrows.

Someone gave me a lift home, and I remember waking late in the morning with an atrocious headache and decided to roll over and try to get some more sleep, but as I did, I noticed my blood sample from the Police Station sitting accusingly on the dressing table, for which I was free to get tested at my expense to confirm how much alcohol I had in me last night. I did not need a test. It all came flooding back, what was I going to do now?

I still had a few months grace as the Court case was not imminent, and I was legally allowed to drive until banned so I continued my job but decided to stop drinking any alcohol as I had started to realise that I obviously had a problem.

I went out on a jolly in the West End and remained completely sober throughout but was horrified when my drunken compatriots chose to gain access to the Nurses accommodation at a London Hospital where Joanne Goff lived, my companion in Germany. Visitors were banned at night, and this was only a clever idea if you were drunk but for me it was traumatic, and I did not want trespass or aggravated burglary added to my charge sheet.

I have never been able to lose the memory of a near naked Mathew Wyatt parading down the accommodation corridor in a cowboy hat, underpants, and long pink socks.

However, it was a lesson on how alcohol impacts on reasonable decision making. As we did not get caught and managed to escape the next morning unnoticed it was something of an adventure, but I was pleased that I had managed the complete day and night without a drink.

Paul had managed to pull together a very decent band who he unaptly called the Stomping Pond Frogs. It was made up of Chris Lang, Quinton Cook, and John Laurenson.

Paul and I had attended Tadworth Jazz Club a few times, and on one occasion accompanied by Andy Sex, we came close to killing ourselves. Missing the last train, we had no taxi fare between us. We made the ludicrous drunken decision to walk back home via the railway tracks. It was just two stops back to Chipstead, but firstly we had not considered if the line was live, or if there was any commercial or maintenance trains scheduled.

It was also well below freezing and we were constantly slipping on the icy sleepers as we pigeon stepped our way back down the line in near sheer darkness. When you travel by train it is amazing how you do not notice noteworthy features of the journey, and none of us recalled the Chipstead Viaduct which lay between us and our warm beds. We were lucky to notice it in the dark, but the drop of seventy-five feet somewhat sobered us up, and concentrated our minds being battered by a freezing wind.

Either we walked all the way back to Kingswood, adding hours to our journey, or we perilously navigated each slippery sleeper in the hope that if we slipped, we might not slip between them. Arms outstretched we carefully stepped on each sleeper in turn as if we were walking across a minefield until we reached the other side. Had it not been so dark, we might have spotted a pathway made for engineers' safety.

The jazz influence shone through with this new, vibrant band. When they played a small gig in Redhill it occurred to me for the very first time that there was real talent here, they were exceptionally good with the merging of rock, pop, and jazz, and they could play their instruments. The tolerance of the punk era, where anyone could be appreciated just throwing a guitar against a wall with attitude were outdated.

After a series of busking events, the Pond Frogs played the Lakers music venue in Redhill. A small venue, but well known in the County. Their performance there was outstanding, and they had metamorphosised into a sharp, professional, and very entertaining foursome.

They were supported again by an East London musician called Steve, a solo artist with a folk outlook but with a rock bite. He had biting left wing lyrics, so I became an enthusiastic fan. I remember spending time at the Lakers bar with him discussing politics, football, and music. He later changed his stage name to our mutual middle name, William and over a lengthy period has had a very successful music career as Billy Bragg.

For the first time Paul started to contemplate that he could make it in the pop industry and there was a real sense of anticipation about where this band could end up. Unfortunately, an element of common sense, and perhaps parental pressure led to Quinton choosing education over performing, and he made his way to Brighton Polytechnic, and the Pond Frogs croaked their last stomp. Fortunately for Quenton, whilst living on the south coast he developed his talents returning to perform with Paul in the Housemartins, and later becoming a disc jockey performing as DJ Quentox, developing his production abilities with Beats International and performing as Fat Boy Slim. Chris Land went to RADA and became a professional actor before moving on to a remarkably successful TV production career.

The combination of my impending driving ban and subsequent loss of job, and the break-up of the band led to a great deal of soul searching. Paul was from Sheffield and still did not feel at home in the beautiful south of England, and I think aspired to start a band in the North and knowing I was shortly to be at a loose end suggested we move north. Our fanzine in Reigate had been well received but to be fair circulation was in the 10's and only catered for a very few likeminded people. The big idea was to set up a proper fanzine, or alternative newspaper, and Paul I am sure had not given up hope of being successful in the music business as a performer.

The big question was where? I felt Sheffield was Paul's home town and thought it beneficial for all of us to be somewhere new. Perhaps a city we knew little about. I remember we tried throwing a dart in Paul's Garden towards a map of England to decide but it landed in the North Sea close to the Humber Estuary. I remembered being bored on a Saturday afternoon and betting with Trevor Bloomfield who would win the 1982 Rugby League Cup Final which ended in a draw. The team I chose randomly, Hull FC won the replay.

From the dart in the North Sea, and from this totally irrelevant logic suggested Hull as the place to set up our fanzine and perhaps Pauls new band, as one of my stipulations was that I wanted to live by the sea, not realising Hull over looked over the dirty brown Humber estuary, rather than the idyllic blue sea I imagined and had seen on maps.

No one could think of a band that came from Hull, so the idea generated some interest. To most people Hull was the forgotten city in Britain, famous only for its history of fishing, but the fishing industry had by now re-located to Grimsby. We agreed to stop and have a look at some stage in our journey.

Was Hull lucky for me? Would it be lucky for us? We guessed accommodation would be cheap but Hull had until this point had no significant successful musical history should Paul decide to pursue his musical hobbies. However, maybe that could be an advantage in the long run.

Both of us felt stifled under our parents' roofs, and the adventure was enticing so I contemplated the idea but was still undecided to take such a risk with my life. It was around this time our German friends said they were coming to visit again, so we planned to give my Austen 1100 a good send of and do a tour of the United Kingdom with our good German friends before my forthcoming ban. What an opportunity to take a brief look at Hull, and perhaps even find accommodation that suited.

## CHAPTER X

## WHEREVER I LAY MY HAT THAT'S MY HOME

With my old Basque flag attached to a roof rack we loaded up my car outside Paul's house in Chipstead where our German friends Alfred, Sabine, Berndt and Mario had stayed overnight. Paul's girlfriend Silly made up the group of seven in two cars. We had two weeks to go wherever we wanted and set of one August morning to pack in as much sightseeing adventures as we could and perhaps locate new accommodation for the move North.

We had no plan except I had a desire to reach the four most extreme point of the mainland having already been to Lizard Point and Ness Point Lowestoft, I had ambitions on the most westerly and northerly points of the UK mainland to achieve the full set.

We set of for the Peak District National Park and paraded up the M1, with the German Volkswagen always in my mirror as there were no mobile phones then, and so accidental separating could easily become permanent. We pitched tents on our first night, we had an old two berth, twos, company three's a crowd crawl in if you can, the Germans had a stand-up mansion masquerading as a tent, with all the mod cons.

After a difficult night we set off to explore the peak district, which Paul knew well from his early childhood in nearby Sheffield.

To save washing my hair I wore an old brown bobble hat throughout the trip, while Paul Young was dominating my car radio with "*Wherever I Lay My Hat, That's My Home*" a, which summed up our approach to our holiday with no itinerary.

We spent a few days camping in the Lake District, or at least the Germans did. Returning to our two tents one evening we were only able to count the one still intact after intense winds. The one with the greatest mass and therefore the greatest sail effect was still standing, but our small impoverished one was decorating a nearby tree, and it was not even Christmas.

Realising the cost of B&B was about £5 each per night, we quickly assessed that the English would be sleeping in the cars for the duration, or we would have to be teetotal. We chose the cars.

We continued our expedition up the west coast staying in various camp sites in the Scottish Lowlands. Understanding that Ard na Murchan, Gaelic for the hill of the great sea, was the most westerly point for the mainland, so we decided to take what we thought was a short drive there, but hours later, with nothing to view but flatlands and sheep we arrived only to realise there was nothing to see except a Lighthouse and a long drive back. My suggested diversion was a complete waste of time as I learned a short while later that Corrachadh Mòr  half a mile away the point we reached was a little further west, so we did not even reach our goal.

One night we made the mistake of staying in the pub too late and bedded down in the open next to a stream oblivious to the true menace of Scotland's wildlife. The most ferocious creature alive that would plague us throughout our Scottish adventure.

Inside my woollen hat, my face started to itch, I managed to pull it down over my face. The itching became very intensive to the point I jumped out of my sleeping bag in despair, and almost simultaneously so did Paul who seemed in the moonlight to be wearing a glass looking space helmet. Only this one was moving, and it was not glass. It was a swarm of Scottish midges chomping away at his face. Paul screamed "Trotsky" to me but not because of his predicament, but because he was viewing something identical around my head. As Paul started to run his helmet of midges followed and so did mine.

The same assault was taking place with our German friends. We were all being eaten alive and ran back to our cars where we bedded down seriously traumatised by this horror scene from a Wes Craven movie. We were very cramped, but no one wanted to be outside as we mercilessly killed every Midge that had managed to follow us into our car.

These insects bit so hard they drew blood and Paul's face reacted by swelling up in the morning. At the next shop we bought midge repellent, but this proved about as useful as a wet sock in a storm, except you could dry out a wet sock. The repellent did exactly the opposite as it said on the bottle, it attracted Midges who seemed to have adapted to the intended poison and it was now a food source, which they used as an appetiser before their main courses of English and German blood.

We were incredibly careful not to camp near water again, but these midges plagued us until we returned to the tame gnats of England. As a souvenir Paul and Susan bought me a large rubber fly which resembled a midge, McFly hung from my wing mirror which stayed a constant reminder of the imminent threat.

There was obvious football rivalry between England and Germany, because at this time we could brag about 1966 and the they about the great comeback of the Germans in Mexico in 1970 for which I remained entirely responsible for. We were yet to be humiliated on penalties as Italia 90 and Euro 96 were yet to be played out. A football challenge was laid down and the two international teams set forth onto the flat wet sandy beach in the neutral territory of Scotland, only the Germans would only have three players and England two. The goal posts made of a sandcastle each were set a foot apart to avoid the need for Goalkeepers given Sabine and Silly were not interested in being called up for this vital international. Alfred was a particularly skilful player, but I would say that Paul is the best player I have ever played with or against. However, Mario and Berndt were tactically clueless, and it was not long before England ran up a cricket score to Alfred's consternation. I had finally made good and redressed my faux pa in the Summer of 1970. My range of the German language improved during the game as Alfred shouted expletives at his fellow inexperienced players.

Most evenings we sat around illuminated only by a couple of camp lights playing Pontoon for loose change, or as the Germans called it twenty-one. The Germans of course were very well organised with their sophisticated stand-up tent, lights, cooking equipment, table, and chairs. Without their equipment we would have headed back south after a few days. None the less, we reached Inverness but did not see the worth in going further north so we headed back south.

On route we discussed Scottish cuisine, and Alfred overheard us talk about haggis but gave no credence to our comical explanation of a super large rabbit like creature with sharp pointy ears and a long curly tail. Despite persistence we were not believed, and the subject had been largely forgotten by the time we sat down for a pub meal. On the menu however was haggis, and the amazed Alfred apologised profusely for doubting our information and explained it to Berndt whose English was not as good as Mario's and Sabine's. We were lucky it did not occur to him to ask the local staff. I carried a hurt expression that he had not believed me. I then covered our tracks by conscripting our Scottish hosts in the game.

Haggis Hunting & Searching for the Loch Ness Monster

Every now and then on route Paul would lean out of my car window pointing across the Scottish tundra, "look haggis!" which they fell for every time. They were determined to spot a wild haggis before the holiday was complete, and we were desperate to keep them looking. Eventually a Scotsman ruined our English fun and we were never quite forgiven, a subject that would be raised on every joyful re-encounter with our German friends for many years to come.

As we headed back towards England down a long straight road Paul and Susan were dozing, and I completely sober, misjudge a second bend and managed to wrap my Austen 1100 around a wire fence, denting the near side.

I got out and noticed the Germans were uncontrollably belly laughing as they had seen the whole thing unwind, as my car wound up in the ditch. This was my first accident which was even partly my fault, and my last to date. In hindsight I may have fallen asleep at the wheel after a gruelling week or so on the road, sleeping on the ground or in a car must have taken its toll.

I suppose this knocked a small amount off the value after I was forced to sell it to coincide with my impending driving ban, but other than that nobody was hurt, and the Germans, although in no way responsible had their revenge for the haggis humiliation they suffered.

Our last stop before Hull, was to the Holy Island of Lindisfarne, which had two of my favourite things, a castle, and a brewery. The Island is only accessible at times due to the tide covering the causeway, and it was somewhat unnerving to drive along it as the tide was coming in and towards the end of the short journey you could be easily imagine we were on a boat, and there were several signs explaining emergency procedures.

Whatever our plans were now, they could not involve leaving the Island until the morning tide went out.

Lindisfarne is a fascinating place steeped in history, with a 1300-year-old Priory set up by St. Aiden who had travelled from the Scottish Isle of Iona at the bequest of King Ida to set it up. I could have remembered this from Sunday School back at St. Aiden's in Coulsdon, but this trivia could well have been delivered on my many truant days. Paul and I would one day visit Iona which was every bit as magical as Lindisfarne.

The castle built more like a fort, overlooked the rest of the Island, including the ruins of the Priory and after securing the obligatory bottle of Mead, we headed for the only pub.

The ten days of sleeping on the ground or in the car had taken their toil and I was restless through the night. The ruined Priory looked like the set from a Hammer Horror film and had bats flying around. I decided to test my nerve and took my sleeping bag into the priory ruins and camped down. I loved horror films but didn't care much for the Christopher Lee renditions of Dracula, much preferring the very creepy 1930's black and white repeats with Bela Lugosi which had terrified me as a child.

I managed to get some sleep. With just a hint of sunrise on the horizon I was awaken with the wind swirled around the ruins creating the music of the night, and within that sound on this very much deserted island I thought for a moment I could hear a voice blowing in on the wind. Not a normal voice, but a very sinister deep mantra, sounding a little like a huddle of male witches as I noticed more voices joining in. I lay silent wondering if my position could be seen by these spirits of the night.

It was now unmistakeable; I could hear human voices chanting in a ceremony of sacrifice and I could be that sacrifice. The howling wind, the noise of the bats, and now the witches lynch mob approaching I grabbed my sleeping bag and run as fast as I could back to the safety of the car.

As I turned the final corner at full pace, I frightened a group of Fishermen who were walking towards their boat, and all chatting in their Northumberland dialect which I was not accustomed to, but I ran past them not wanting to stop and explain how my terror had developed, as with deep embarrassment at my lack of courage, I realised I had been spooked by the wind carrying chatter of folk just going about their business before dawn.

The Germans were amazed by the North Yorkshire Moors landscape and we camped at the Lion Inn on the Blakey Road, surrounded in each direction by a sea of heather and not a tree in sight. A little over a decade later that pub became base camp for the film crew when I made my second appearance in a

Beautiful South video staged inside a London Black cab driving over the Moors, in One Last Love Song.

We arrived in Hull and bought a copy of the Hull Daily Mail. We searched the To-Let columns and found an abundance of cheap accommodation. We drew up a brief list and headed for a telephone box with a handful of coins. We were at first confused and then amused by the white telephone boxes, not understanding they were independent of the Post Office who ran the telephone system across the rest of the Country using a distinctive red.

We were looking for accommodation, and some room to set up our printing office for our fanzine/newspaper. Paul had asked Mathew Vincent a friend from his work at the Blind School to join us in Hull, so we needed at least three bedrooms.

We agreed to meet a property owner on Grafton Street which was close to the City Centre and had a pub which was built with no imagination, or concept of attracting passing trade. It was called the Grafton Hotel, but no one stayed overnight. However, across the road from our prospective house was a kind of off licence, but this place sold real ale from the pump. Who needed a pub when there was a bar across the road?

Sitting outside the Grafton Hotel Pub

None of us had ever lived away from home, and the excitement of this new adventure fitted rose tinted glasses to all the English viewers, but shock and amazement from our fellow travellers who could not believe we would contemplate living in such squalor.

We agreed to rent it on individual licences for £70 per month each, and after we returned to Surrey, and after we had made plans for the big move north, we said “auf wiedersein“ to our German friends. I attended Court and received an 18-month driving ban and a whopping £150 fine.

When I said goodbye to my mum, she seemed genuinely surprised I was moving to Hull, although I told her weeks before it did not register with her that I was moving out for good. I had felt a little upset that both my Parents did not seem particularly bothered I was moving out, now I realised I had been misunderstood.

The transitions in life are difficult for everyone, from childhood to adulthood, from being single to becoming a couple, becoming a parent, and then being a parent without direct responsibility for your offspring must be one of the most difficult.

The last of her flock were leaving the nest, and she was obviously a little upset. Des, and Viv were living locally, but Denise was living in Australia with her partner Liz Adams. She did not understand why I wanted to move so far away, especially without the security of work or at least an offer of a job. This was 1983 and Unemployment was at an all-time high. She was right to be concerned especially as Hull had one of the worst unemployment rates in the United Kingdom, with the Fishing Industry collapse a decade before and nothing had replaced it.

# CHAPTER XI ONE IN TEN

With a packed-up van sitting outside Paul's family home in Chipstead, which if I recall correctly was full to the roof and 90% of the belongings were Silly's, who also brought her cat Florence to boot. I first met Mathew Vincent for the first time. an intelligent shabby unkept young man who spoke in a drone but had no discernible bad traits that could prove irritating in our new shared accommodation, which was lucky as I had already paid a deposit and signed on the dotted line.

We arrived in Grafton Street and unpacked the van in a frenzy of excitement, tarnished by the discovery of large ball of furry mould which had grown inside the unused cooker since the property was vacated by Students before a sweltering summer holiday.

We were very hungry and went to the local store on Newland Avenue to buy dinner, a pack of rice and a tin of mixed vegetables. Sue and Paul were vegetarian so I decided it would be easier if joined them, and the household became a no meat zone.

There was one thing we had not really considered. We all assumed each other could cook but none of us could. It was on this first night that I ate the worst meal in my life. Starchy over cooked soggy rice, topped with tinned vegetable in a salted brine source, with ketchup for flavour. From this point on I was determined to learn how to cook, or I was going to starve to death. However, for the time being, we did have an array of takeaways at close hand, unfortunately it would be beyond our means to live on take aways.

Consequently, I did breach our vegetarian code once when I bought an egg burger from a takeaway but was challenged back at the house who saw the beef burger inside the roll. I explained that I thought it would only have an egg, but on biting into the burger it was just too tasty to discard. No one believed me, not even myself.

We had to learn a whole new language in take-aways, we did not know our Butties from our Chip sandwiches, or what a

Pattie was, which we learned was a deep-fried, battered sphere of mashed potato with sage, and it became a staple of our new vegetarian diet.

We celebrated our first working day by heading down to the Unemployment Office to sign on and complete our Housing Benefit forms to cover the rent which was due again in four weeks. Ironically UB40 were racing up the charts with "*Red Red Wine*" and to acknowledge their success I had gained my very own Unemployment Benefit Form 40 which sat proudly by my bed side table. I never imagined I would become one of their "*one in ten*", released only a couple of years before. I usually chose to walk to the Benefit office down the Beverley Road and noted with humour the Turner Furniture Store with the sexist tag "Everything but the girl," the inspiration for Hull University Students Tracey Thorn and Ben Watts band name who were yet to break through.

My benefit was suspended for giving up my job at Maggs Edwards and Sharp before I lost my Licence. It also became clear that they had done the dirty on me and were not intending to pay me commissions for deals I had put together which had now gone through on the grounds I had to be employed by them on completion. Threatening legal action, they paid the £330 outstanding which kept my head above water a little longer.

I also won my case at a tribunal and had my Unemployment Benefit re-instated.

I had become very political and saw my claim for Unemployment as a slap in the face for Mrs Thatcher, who had just won a landslide victory in a General Election after the popularity bounce of encouraging Argentina to invade their Malvinas, so that we could flex our empire mugging spoon and rout the tin pot army of conscripts with a very professional British Army.

I was introduced to everyone as Trotsky, which endeared me to some neighbours who regularly held Socialist Workers Party meeting in their home. They were horrified to discover under the influence of Alfred Wirth, I had joined the Ecology Party which then was very much in its infancy with a national membership of around four to five hundred, probably the same level of membership of the Labour Party in just the local Beverley Ward where we were living, which was only one of thirty-two wards in one City.

Next to the Unemployment Office in Alfred Gelder Street was an Unemployment drop-in centre called the Warren on account of its maze of corridors and hidden rooms. It was newly formed and included of a non-profit making snack bar, an art room, dark room for developing your own photos, a DJ room which pumped music around the building, and a counselling and advice section, and it was all free except the sandwiches and tea, which were sold almost at cost value. One of the volunteer workers there was a brume called Roland Gift who was playing in a local Ska band called Akrylykz but he would soon be on the move to better things as the lead singer of the Fine Young Cannibals and even starred in the 1987 feature film Sammie and Rosie Get Laid.

We were looking for support to design and print our local fanzine/newspaper, and we discussed the possibilities with Centre staff who were very encouraging. The self-appointed editor in chief dispatched his novice reporter, AKA Trotsky, to interview the radical left leaning Councillor Keith Russell about his campaign against the Benefit office so called Rabbit squads. These were Unemployed people being paid to snitch on other people who may be secretly working. Keith Russell was a giant of a man being well over my six feet, his left leaning views within the Labour party had made him a little isolated but he was very generous in helping with our first publication, and later he was encouraged to give up politics by being a shoe in for the Centre Coordinator position at the Warren which he diligently accepted.

I was also dispatched to undertake a football report on the Hull City versus Burnley match at Boothferry Park. I was frustrated that despite loving football I found it hard to write about it. That was my first and last attempt at sports journalism.

The first time I went back to London was for a CND rally. To save money, which was becoming scarce, I hitched for my first time, which was far easier than I expected. I only needed three pickups on the way until I reached the affordable London Transport network. Unfortunately, I had to walk a couple of miles to get to the M1 from my first ride in a Luton Van which picked me up on the Anlaby Road in Hull. As I walked briskly along, with a small rucksack on my back for company, I became aware that some ferocious guard dogs were running towards me, but I was protected by a large wire fence. Realising they posed no actual danger I felt brave enough to goad them a little for my amusement which had the desired effect. This great idea begun to unravel when they suddenly ran away in the direction I had already walked, but being suspicious of their sudden departure, which did not appear to be a retreat, I noted that a few hundred yards away, they had obviously recalled a broken part of the fence and were obviously trying to get free, so that they could have a late breakfast.

It is funny how you can run so fast when you need to, and I did not look around to see how close they were when I flung myself over a lower fence into a foray of brambles and stinging nettles.

Laying in agony and fear I kept incredibly quiet in the undergrowth hoping its smell may keep them of my scent. It took me a while to be brave enough to check if the coast was clear, but a valuable lesson had been learnt. After the rally I caught the coach back to Hull.

It was in the art room of the Warren that we produced some posters asking for musicians to start a new band, which were displayed in various locations. Whilst in the Warren we were asked if we wanted to go gliding, and it was completely free. We set of in a minibus and arrived at a Glider Centre in Pocklington and awaited our turn. It was here that I first became aware of Paul's fear of flying, but he hid it well from everyone else, and to be honest it is unsettling not to hear the comforting noise of an engine on an aeroplane, and when you land your bottom is only a matter of a few inches off the floor. I wondered if that was the reason, he had missed out of España 82.

Later we were asked if we wanted to go away on holiday with the centre to the North Yorkshire Moors. We jumped at the chance and headed off with about a large group of the unemployed and volunteer workers to stay rent free in a Quaker 24 bed Mansion in Hutton-Le -Hole. Barmoor House was extremely remote and surrounded my miles of moorland.

Being the only southerners, we were the subject of much attention. However, after being poked with sticks to check if we were human by the local youths, we were begrudgingly accepted with traditional Yorkshire hospitality.

We enjoyed horse riding, Orienteering, and Treasure Hunting which we were close to winning, and an array of other mostly outdoor activities.

Upon our return we all agreed to become volunteers, but when Monday morning arrived, I was the only one to attend and take up a role as a Volunteer at the Warren

Paul ramped up his advertising campaign for band members, placing one of the posters in our front window.

Meanwhile, we listened to the news on our shared house radio as US Nuclear missiles were being deployed at Greenham Common, in an escalation of the Cold War, where the concept of a short-range nuclear war was gaining a foothold under the guise of deterrence.

While Paul was out a student and would be musician called Ian knocked on the front door of 70 Grafton Street asking for Paul. Silly and I invited him in and found him funny and engaging, he was genuinely very funny and could easily have gigged as a stand-up comic. He made a good impression on the two of us, and it made me reminisce about my first meeting with Paul back in 1978. He was from Bristol and was studying Maths at

Hull University but had a similar sense of humour to Paul. I was confident they would get along.

The next few weeks I hardly saw Paul as I was volunteering full time at the Warren and Paul confined himself to collaborating with Ian and developing a few songs with the idea that they could try them out in the City Centre and earn money from the busking.

They had bought two blue yachting hats for props, and the three of us headed into Hull City Centre, my role simply to protect the money, look out for the Police, and pretend to be a fan to encourage others to stop by placing money in the hat, listen and contribute. I had perfected this art with the busking Stomping' Pond Frogs. Money was so short I would have to recycle my contribution often, but sometimes fell afoul of Paul suspicions that I was taking out more than I was putting in.

We headed for the busy pedestrianised Whitefriargate. As they strummed the first chords, I was unaware of the significance of what was in effect the very first public performance of the Housemartins. They were good and drew a crowd, but Hull being a poor City there were not the rich spoils the "Stomping' Pond Frogs" achieved through busking in various Surrey shopping centres, however at least now the money would be divided in two rather than four.

I started to get into a routine at the Warren and started to make some good friends. Chris Fleming the Centre-Coordinator was an expert psychologist, and a truly loveable person who would become a close friend and mentor. Mike Macklin aka Alfie was a biker hippie who I came to adore and there was an array of talented, sensitive, eccentric, and fun to be with volunteer workers. There was another local who we all referred to as Big Wally, and the apple of his eye, though not reciprocated, was the scouse Anne-Marie Tickle. Being ever so slight, even with her flaming red mane of a hairstyle to compensate, if she became Wally's doll it was odds on, he would break her before sunset or laying her gently on the roof the Empire State Building before getting shot.

The very educated Andy West was the counsellor who listened intently to every problem brought to him and was an expert in claiming benefits for others and this generous kind man was a local hero to every unemployed person who used the Warren, but the scourge of the Unemployment Benefit Office Staff next door. The woman's worker was Jenny Wildblood, who was a soft gently spoken, amateur actor, professional feminist, and an avid Guardian reader.

There were some broad rules at the Warren, which were underpinned by the Warren philosophy. This was a democracy facilitated by the three paid staff and the rules were written by the "customers" or service users. There were rival gangs in Hull, but this place was regarded as neutral safe territory, and Rocker, Punk, Trendy and Mod intermingled as if their uniforms were invisible, and occasionally reminisce about the fight they had between them over the weekend. The warren was a respected sanctuary much like a Church in the Middle Ages.

Next door was the Burlington Tavern, who's main trade was from those signing on, then local office staff for their wet lunch and then most evenings the staff and volunteers of the Warren. It became our unofficial office over the years.

A divide was developing between Paul and I, he was concentrating on the Housemartins, and I was throwing myself into youth work, and obvious tensions arose. When Mathew Vincent left, we needed a new housemate, and Jane Armitage arrived, a short round mod who had been part of a youth scooter gang and had in her words bettered herself to become a volunteer at the Warren. This ironically exacerbated my feelings of isolation in our home, Paul and Silly's relationship was becoming forever fragile which upset the equilibrium, and the introduction of Jane, who had the unintended ability to be a conduit of misinformed gossip created a palpable tension in the House to the extent that Paul and Silly started to discuss moving to Sheffield. I played my own part in those tensions and started to feel abandoned which exacerbated frictions in the house.

I was learning to shoot video and edit down footage using VHS crash editing and I became extremely interested in film making. However, at the end of the day staff meeting I left all the equipment out and switched on to work on after the meeting. We heard smashing glass, and two young people were found trying to drag the connected-up equipment out of the broken window from the alleyway between the buildings. When I was joined by big Wally, and the notorious Ronnie Howard the two would be thieves froze with fear, and we apprehended them until the Police arrived. This was Hull, everything had to be tied down and I was suitably admonished for my carelessness. Hull was a poor City and creating temptation was sometimes considered as bad as committing the crime.

In February, a friend at the Warren, a keen runner convinced me to sign up to run a half marathon to raise money for the Warren in about 8 weeks' time. However, after I was entered and started training for a week, Shaun England then explained it was in three weeks and it was a full Humber Marathon from Hull to Grimsby. He wanted someone to pace him, and he did not mind if I dropped out at the halfway mark. This deception I thought was selfish and somewhat arrogant, but in keeping with Shaun's attitude to life.

I could not afford proper trainers or kit, so I set off with Shaun wearing old plimsoles, and my winter vest, and a pair of old football shorts. I was exhausted by the time we reached the Humber Bridge, as the supportive send-off crowd had now dwindled as we had left the built up are of outer Hull, but I had managed to get into a rhythm with Shaun and our position at the rear of the large field of runners was improving steadily in that we were now overtaking rather than being overtaken, so we had probably judged our early pace well.

After descending the other side of the two-mile Bridge, I decided to run to the next water station and then decide whether to continue, but each time we got to one I found it hard to quit, and my pride enforced a resilience in me to wait until Shaun wanted to give up, even though I was aware he had been training for months and had taken everything very seriously.

We passed the halfway mark, and I was pleased that I had at least run half a marathon, but by now the distance between runners was such that we started to feel very lonely down the long winding country lanes, and occasionally we were completely alone becoming anxious we had somehow gone the wrong way. Without any warning Shaun just stopped, but my two hours of jogging was hard to stop and as I turned to Shaun, he waved me on.

Eventually I found some people to run with and made my way steadily through the Lincolnshire country plains, which were still part of the unpopularly named County of Humberside despised by the north and south of the Estuary in equal measure.

Occasionally we went through a village which supplied a boost as my small group of stragglers were cheered like heroes. It occurred to me that with seven miles that the pain was getting far too much to bear, my plimsoles had not provided any cushion and my legs and ankles hurt as much as my arms which had not done anything but be swung to and throw to maintain balance. So, I lowered them and then felt I might fall on my face, as I had no balance. There was nothing else to do but give up and so with just under seven miles left my brain instructed my body to stop.

There was a malfunction, my legs kept on running and were no longer under my control. The remaining hour is something of a blur, but as the mile markers started their countdown, I entered the outskirts of Grimsby and there were hundreds of people cheering clapping and shouting words of encouragement that I became tearful with emotion and a deep sense of pride. There was no giving up now, and as the crowds grew thicker, and the support intensified, I managed to scrape together enough resolve to keep going until miraculously I could see the finish line with its automated clock and the throngs of spectators and successful Athletes displaying their golden medals, all gleaming in the sunshine with their silver foil coats.

I was alone on the home straight and had the full attention of the large crowd, and I was lifted over the tarmac on a cloud of emanating good will to the finish line, unfortunately needing aid to stop as my prized medal was placed over my head in the Grimsby sunlight. I had done it. Shaun had not. I had a medal. Shaun did not. It had taken me four hours and forty minutes to complete without enough training and equipment. I was enormously proud of myself, but this did not sufficiently anesthetise my pained body. Shaun had actually got to Grimsby Leisure Centre before me, courtesy of the organisers mini bus which was sweeping up willing stragglers, and Shaun was very humble and truly impressed that I had made it and laughed when I told him I decided to quit but couldn't. I felt guilty that I had enjoyed his demise, and then felt very sad that he had worked so hard and had not been able to overcome the marathon wall as they call it.

Unfortunately, upon returning to Grafton Street I remained in bed for a couple of days hardly able to walk. I had not thought to try warm down and had sat on buses for an hour or so returning home.  When I received my photo of crossing the finish line, I noticed the time. Four hours, forty minutes, and thirty-nine seconds. I should have delayed my arrival by a second to round it up.

Our Proprietors decided to decorate Grafton Street and sent two young lads to disrupt our lives. After a couple of weeks their polite and courteous manner, turned into impolite and discourteous, and I for one started to feel very resentful about their presence. They had slowed work right down, were helping themselves to our meagre rations, and worst of all one of them was overtly flirting with Silly, who was reciprocating and enjoying the attention.

Emotionally I was still immature, I had left my family hundreds of miles away, and my group of friends were ceasing to be an alternative. The writing was on the wall underneath the fresh wallpaper.

It was no longer about what I would do if Paul and Silly split up, it was what am I going to do when they split up. I was torn between genuine affection for both, and selfishly upset for my self-preservation, like a child whose parents separate.

# CHAPTER XII HELLO

On Monday 9th April 1984 I organised my own Birthday Party. Paul was down south on band business but Silly preferred to stay. With new friends from the Warren and local neighbours, using the Good Beer Shop across the road as our bar, I drowned my sorrows. My consumption of alcohol had significantly declined in Hull due to our frugal new lifestyle, even though beer in the Grafton and across the road was significantly cheaper than Surrey, however the high in gravity real ale from across the road soon started to affect, exacerbating my melancholy mood.

I had noticed my Warren colleague Shaun England and Silly flirting with each other which I was not too concerned about as Silly was a flirt most of the time and had indeed driven off on a rival's scooter in Surrey once leaving Paul distraught before they got back together a short while late.

Sitting on the sofa Sue Tucker came and sat next to me. She was a Warren Customer and had presumably gate-crashed.

Through my drunken daze she spoke to me for a couple of minutes and miming to Lionel Ritchie's *"Hello"* which was playing, without any confirmation from me it appeared we were going out with each other, and we entered a long-drawn-out snogging session that killed the Party. She had taken out the host who had lost interest in his guests, and people started leaving.

Sue invited herself upstairs to my bedroom where we spent the night. In the morning Sue's pretty face was stained with last night's make up, her hair dishevelled, but she still looked beautiful to me, even with my hungover eyes.

However, it became apparent that while Paul was away in the South, Shaun England had poached his girlfriend, as I caught him discreetly trying to leave in the morning.

Silly had become a close friend and I was now torn, do I tell, or do I keep quiet? Either course of action would be explosive, and I genuinely wanted our Hull experiment to continue as I felt settled at the Warren and was expanding my social circle to even include girls.

On Paul's return it was noticeable to him that Silly's mind and heart was somewhere else, and I was sure he felt I had betrayed him, and he put himself in isolation and appeared to have something of a breakdown. A loyal friend steps up in these situations but I felt like I was part of the problem, and one evening it became obvious that I produced the straw that would break the camel's back. Bouncing down Grafton Street with two large plastic bags full of scrunched up clothes, underwear, and make up came Sue Tucker explaining she had been thrown out of her home and she needed to stay with me.

I did not feel like I had a choice, or the chance to consult my house mates, but her inclusion worsened an already fraught situation.

There was another problem I was due to go away for a couple of weeks.

The Warren had received sponsorship from Blue Circle Cement to send young unemployed people on a two-week cruise sail training with the Sail Train Association, but we were expected to do our own fundraising event. So, in full fancy dress, I dressed as angry of Mayfair created by Kenny Everett, we toured the old town pubs with buckets trying not to drink more than we raised. After advertising the fantastic opportunity to our Warren Customers, we only just scrapped together four people willing to go, and after the briefing meeting three dropped out. Faced with the possibility of losing further funding, Alfie and I were volunteered to go with the remaining customer Nigel, not really grasping what we had been set up to endure.

Angry of Mayfair fancy dress.

Leaving a difficult situation behind in Grafton Street, and after a long Coach ride up to Newcastle docks, we found the 135-foot, three mast Bermuda Schooner Malcolm Miller anchored majestically and glistening in the warm summer sky. Looking up at the yard arms it dawned on me that this was going to be no pleasure cruise, particularly given my fear of heights. The yard arms looked higher than the length of the entire ship.

Having been allocated lockers and bunks we set off for a local pub to get to know our new shipmates, under strict instructions to return to the boat at 10pm. This was not a recommendation, as it was barked at us in a way that made you understand you were under naval military command. What had we got ourselves into?

In the morning we were provided with practical lessons around the ship, how to tie a bowline knot, how to keep your heading while steering, basic navigation, and how to pull in unison with the rhythmic command of two, six, heave; two six, heave. We were then to pose for a photograph while all aloft on the rigging and yard arms of the ship.

To do this we then had to march to the sound of a slow drum beat up the ratlines to the Crow's Nest and then we were supposed to waddle out along the arms after hooking our safety harness on.

The STA Malcolm Miller

Stepping from the final ratline which was made of metal you then had to step onto and balance on the footrope which sunk under your weight and the weight of others, providing no sureness of foot, which presented my nervous system with the opportunity to operate its auto shaking mode and made it difficult to unhook my harness to get it attached to the yard arm. Because I had no safety mechanism in place, I lost it completely, and now people were climbing over me to go out on the arms.

I seriously contemplated that when I fell, as it was only a matter of time before I did, could I make it into the water and avoid hitting the deck, as in this way I might survive.

Sometimes you find the resolve you need to survive, and I managed to unhook the harness and get it attached and then cuddled the arm of the ship with both arms and started to feel a little safer. When everyone was finally in position the order went out and we were now supposed to stand up straight balancing on the rope, knees tight to the Arms with arms raised out sideways. I did my best, but it wasn't pretty, and at least I was some distance from any officers.

Our first destination was meant to be on the Eastern Danish Coast in the Baltic Sea, however lack of wind meant we eventually headed for sin city number one, Hamburg. Operating on a three eight-hour watches per day, I have fond memories of life on the Ship and experienced every weather conditional imaginable. Strangely one morning the most eerie and frightening weather phenomena appeared.

The sea was silent, and the ship felt static as if we had berthed in port and as I raised my head out onto the deck we were surrounded by fog and the sea appeared as flat as glass with no perceivable motion. The Beaufort wind force scale indicated zero. The captain was determined never to use our on-board motors unless it was an emergency, so we sat in the middle of the North Sea motionless awaiting a giant sea monster to engulf us and drag us down to Davie Jones's Locker.

On one-night shift in the early hours when most were asleep. I was starboard lookout and my good friend Alfie was at the wheel. Alfie was a long sufferer of migraines and tonight was no exception and he was not free to collect his medication for some time to come. All I had to do was keep my eyes peeled across a hundred and eighty degrees of circular horizon lit up only by the moon. All Alfie had to do was stare at the compass needle to make sure we kept course, easing the ships rudder left and right with a gentle swing of the wheel to correct any variance. This required a great deal of concentration, but I was aware from our gentle chatter he was suffering tonight.

In the early hours we were startled by the captain appearing in his dressing gown as he shouted angrily through the heavy wind "How's your head Macklin?" to which Alfie calmly responded, "it's not too bad sir, but thanks for asking." As I looked around, I thought the captain was going to self-ignite in rage as he hurled expletives at all three of us that the ship was miles of course. He had of course been referring to the heading of the ship and yes, Alfie had fallen asleep at the wheel. I wondered if I was culpable in this situation and then looking back on the ships trail of white water in the moonlight noticed that we may been drawing a circle in the North Sea for some time.

Thankfully for the entire crew there was a warning system in the Captain's Cabin, and they had satellite navigation at their disposal otherwise who knows where we might have ended up. When we approached Hamburg, I declined to volunteer to undertake the customary parade up the rigging.

As it happens, we ended up drinking on the Reeperbahn, former home from home for the Beatles, and a place where if you had the cash, you could probably buy anything or anyone you desired. I now understood more about why they changed their name to Beat Brothers while performing here, sounding like Penises might have drawn an unintended fan base. However, there were plenty of English "dicks" on shore leave that night.

The endless parade of sex shops, sex shows, strip joints, casinos and open-air brothels was a shock to the system, and it felt sinister and dangerous. I had been taken on a tour of Soho by Ray Cottington a few years before but that was like a corner shop compared to this American sized super store that was Hamburg. My new friend Taffy wanted to play the game, getting attention from prostitutes but then never going through with any deal as he had as little money as I did, but I sensed this was an increasingly dangerous game. I did not have the front to do this, and accordingly became aware that my Welsh friend was starting to attract attention from the many minders discretely watching over their merchandise. I gave him a wider berth just in case.

The next morning, we were still free to leave the ship until we set sail later in the day and I spotted two young girls admiring our Ship. I called Alfie over, and then tried to impersonate the swashbuckling film star Errol Flynn by gliding down the long mooring rope. They were suitably impressed and agreed to go for a drink with me and Alfie, but we had met them twenty fours too late and we set sail for Sin City two later that afternoon.

I can only imagine the captain had a thing for Sin Cities as he referred to them as our next port was to be Amsterdam. The only thing between us was a sever gale blowing fifty mile per hour winds, so that it was not safe to keep the sails up.

Given how pathetic I had performed while the Ship was moored in pleasant weather in Newcastle, and that I had managed to stay off the high rigging so far, I was now faced with a real-life threatening emergency brought abruptly to my attention by the obvious hint of panic in the regular crew's orders. I was not aware at this time that a similar Sail Training Ship heading for Nova Scotia in June 1984, was abandoned during a storm and 19 young people sail trainees like me consequently drowned in the North Atlantic. Having said that the danger all around us was very palpable, as the ship was being tossed around the raging sea with twenty-foot waves hitting us in every direction that the decks which I had so far seen as a safe place were now seemingly more dangerous that being on the rigging.

Transcending the wet ratlines in haste I was fortunate not to have to climb out onto the yard arms as the ocean swung the heavy mast about like a toothpick in a washing machine, and I bravely helped pull the clewlines and buntlines tight and stow the sails and tie down the gaskets from the least perilous position above the confines of the living quarters. Strangely being aloft while sitting in the docks in calm weather was more frightening than being in a storm at sea, as when you are in real and obvious danger, your fight and flight mechanism kicks in, and I was able to function when it really mattered.

My bunk was the second to last in the bow and I spent most of the night being lifted and dropped on to my harsh matrass until sun rise, but I didn't mind as I was at least still alive to suffer the lack of comfort.

As we approached Amsterdam, I volunteered to join the show, and parade up the ratlines to our positions on the arms, the overwhelming fear that had struck me down in Newcastle had been conquered, and I stood proudly, arms outstretched, balancing on the arms of the ship as we cruised proudly into sin city two. I can't remember a prouder moment in my life up until that point.

I found Amsterdam to be vastly different to Hamburg, with the red-light district far more relaxed and less threatening, but no one had much money left with the Purser and there were no overdrafts or credit at this floating bank. Consequently, we did the tourist thing of window shopping and then returned to the Ship earlier than expected.

We arrived in Hartlepool a good ten days after we had set sail from Newcastle not far up the Coast, but this had been an adventure of a lifetime and had boosted my confidence no end, and I had a formal qualification as a competent crew member for a sailing vessel.

We had taken a Warren customer Nigel, with us and noted upon our return that we had hardly spoken to him, which was fair as we were on different watches throughout. He was a young man who lacked confidence in even speaking to people in the Warren but had blossomed into a greatly confident leader of men during this voyage.

On the Coach back to Hull, I mentioned how he had changed and Alfie said he might have inadvertently been responsible for this through unintentional methods. During the voyage someone had warned me to avoid Nigel as he was dangerous, and I dismissed the comment out of hand knowing Nigel was a very shy boy whose presentation as a Biker with long hair camouflaged his very soft personality.

I was unaware that Alfie, being Alfie, had spread a false rumour around the ship that Nigel was on release from Hedon Road Prison for fire-arms offences during a Hell's Angel turf war. It was little wonder he commanded such respect on board, which had obviously boosted his self-esteem.

I returned to Grafton a changed man, and the experience was such that I had almost forgotten the problem I left behind, but I hoped it may have resolved itself. On the contrary Sue Tucker was still resident and had made herself extremely unpopular with everyone. It transpired that her story about being homeless had been exaggerated, and she had become a nightmare to my friends who demanded I showed her the door. The moment I mentioned it might be better for her to move out, she exploded into a foul mouth tirade, then broke down in tears before launching herself into another vicious tirade. Then without further ado she packed up her two plastic bags and moved out as quickly as she arrived.

Even though she left, things came to a head a short while later. We started to have very intense arguments about anything and everything, but probably not about the real issues that sat like lovelorn elephants in the room, and pressure was applied for me to follow Sue Tucker.

Shaun England irreparably broke up the household by snatching Susan Lillywhite's heart, and breaking Pauls. The brief introduction of Sue Tucker torpedoed what was left.

One evening I made a comment about how attractive I found my work colleague Anne-Marie Tickle, which clearly seemed to upset Paul. Despite working with her and living in the same house as Paul, I had no idea he was seeing her. This was a sign of how far apart we had grown in the same household that I didn't even know who his girlfriend was anymore.

It was not long before I moved out and took up residents in another shared house in a ten foot off Ella Street ten minutes down the road while 70 Grafton Street became the hub of the Housemartins now including Ted Key and our old friend Chris Lang from our Reigate days. Silly went to live with Shaun England.

I saw some of the early Housemartin local gigs in working men's clubs and a few years later at the New Adelphi Club which opened in 1984 for live music owned and was managed by Paul Jackson. The Housemartins as a foursome signed their first record deal here with new label Go Discs but the first release in 1985 Flag Day did not chart. I was given a free copy of the single, but Paul and I were no longer in each other social circles. I had found a "family" at the Warren and he was working flat out to launch his musical career.

The Adelphi car park had been carved out from the terrace of housing in De Grey Street by the Luftwaffe during the Hull blitz. Hull was obliterated during the war something historians omitted from the history books due to the British Propaganda policy of hiding the true extent of German success. Hull was bombed every bit as much as London and Coventry.

I watched a lot of bands here including the Gargoyles, with enigmatic Eddie Smith as a fearless front lead singer backed up by Ted Key and Hugh Whittaker. I also watched The Red Guitars who were Hull's most well-known band at the time, and the lead singer Jerry Kidd's partner Jeanette Eddisford was now my boss at the Warren. I was a regular attendee at the Adelphi but missed out on the early pre-charting performances of the Stone Roses, Pulp, Radiohead, and Oasis.

However, at the height Liam Gallagher's fame some ten years later, I was invited by Paul Weller's Personal Assistant to the Oasis Christmas Party in London, and ended up boozing with him in his Hotel room all night, or at least he did, apparently, I collapsed on his bed in the early hours and left the next morning in disgrace.

# CHAPTER XIIITWO TRIBES

Living on the Limes, in Ella Street I continued attending local Ecology Party meetings in the Bluebell pub which was around the corner from the Warren. The June 1984 European Elections were approaching and I wanted a local candidate.

I had learned so much about Green Politics from my German friends, and I wanted to deliver this radical approach to politics in my own community however it was explained that the sum total of funds was nowhere near enough to fund the required deposit, and I then learned that the Ecology Party had not ever put up a candidate in the City Council Elections even though there was no deposit and all you needed was ten signatures.

I self-funded a leaflet in April 1984 for the Avenues area where I lived and distributed it by myself to all four thousand households explaining that constituents were being denied the right to vote Ecology during the Euro Elections because the UK Government was holding them in a first past the post system of voting when the EU had adopted proportionate representation allowing for green representation.

That summer Frankie Goes to Hollywood dominated the charts for two months with *"Two Tribes."* I had first become aware of this exceptional track in the Silhouette night club before it charted.

On Wednesday 30th January 1985 I took a quick train excursion to Hillsborough as my beloved Chelsea had drawn Sheffield Wednesday in the Quarter Final of the League Cup. It was an amazing game and is still talked about to this day. Lame Chelsea were losing 3-0 at half time and so brought on the speedy winger Paul Canoville for the second half, who scored in matter of seconds from the restart. By the time he scored again with just five minutes remaining Chelsea were leading 4-3.

There were not that many Chelsea fans on the terrace of the Lepping Lane end most were in the seats above, but we had all gone berserk, and believing the game was done and dusted many, including myself thought we would try and get back to the Station to avoid the rush and started leaving the Stadium still listening intently for the final whistle. In the last minute of injury time Sheffield Wednesday were awarded a penalty.

Every Chelsea fan ran back into the stadium, through the central narrow tunnel onto the terracing, and before the penalty was taken, I felt I was being crushed against the barrier and was unable to breath. This lasted for about ten seconds which was exceptionally frightening. The pressure subsided but I was deeply concerned that if the crowd had been far larger this could have been a profoundly serious incident indeed. The penalty was scored, and the tie went to a replay, but at least I was alive to watch it on TV.

I was squashed in the very spot where Ninety-Six Liverpool fans would be crushed to their deaths just four years later, but on this night, no one was interested in crowd safety, and the South Yorkshire Police viewed everyone as a criminal so our safety was never a consideration.

I wrote to Sheffield Wednesday Football Club to explain my concerns but received no reply.

The Warren was challenged to a game of Cricket by the adjacent Post office sorting office, but we realised we didn't have enough staff to put up a team, but at the meeting we realised we had not considered the female staff. It was explained to the Post Office that we would play mixed gender cricket if they fielded a minimum of five female staff. Our female staff were keen to play but none had ever played before and had to be shown how to hold a cricket bat and bowl with a straight arm.

Building on this we decided to make it a fundraising event and secured free alcohol from the local Brewery which we could sell to players and supporters alike, we arranged for a barbeque to sell food, we managed to secure equipment from the Yorkshire Cricket Club, who also allowed us free use of their A list infrequently used professional ground at the Circle on Anlaby Road. This ground was the first temporary home of Hull City Football Club in 1905, before building Boothferry

Park. They would move back to the circle in 2002 in the newly built KC Stadium.

We managed to increase the match into a mini tournament by adding two other teams from social and probation services. With safety in mind, I devised more written rules, including that you could only bowl underarm to the batswomen, an innings would be limited to twenty overs with each player except the wicket keeper bowling at least two overs, and we brought the boundary in much closer.

On the day with the barbeque sizzling, the cold beers stacked into large tents, the sun out with no rain forecast, everything had gone to plan until the Post office team arrived. They had brought eleven young men intent on winning not really understanding the spirit of the day, we negotiated new rules. They would have to choose five players who were only allowed to bowl underarm and would also have to bat using their weaker side, which they reluctantly agreed to do.

As they argued intently about who was going to be a girl, comparing looks and chest sizes, we were busy planning our strategy and guessed they would follow traditional Cricket logic of putting in their best batsman first and lead off with their best bowlers. So, we reversed their strategy for our innings to chase down their score of 85. As it happens our female bowlers were amazingly effective bowling under arm, as the batsman found it impossible to anticipate where the ball might end up.

First people in the crease were our ladies who had instructions to play safe for an over. block or just let the ball past and run any byes that may come your way, and then take more risks and make sure you are out at the end of the second or third depending on circumstance.

Our strategy came to fruition just over halfway through our innings, where Guy O'Connell and I found ourselves partnered and facing only the remaining underarm bowling from our trans gender postal worker. They had used up all their good bowlers and now as each underarm ball was slowly presented to us on a light soft bounce, it was dispatched for four runs almost every ball and it was not long before we secured victory with two very good batsman in reserve.

We played fair for the final and lost, but we did raise a fair bit of money, and made many reliable professional links between staff.

It was clear that the Hull Ecology Party was very much a debating society managed by Helen Dixie and her well-meaning sister from East Hull, who understood the issues around the Environment but were not political beings and had no desire to be in a position of power and were content with the monthly social meeting at the Blue Bell. I followed up this leaflet by trying to stand in the local election but my limited understanding of the strict process of nomination fell afoul of the Returning Officer as one of my signatures were not on the electoral register and did not count, and it was too late to do the paperwork. I was however able to stand next year as there was an election schedule every year in Hull.

Paul Heaton had previously managed to navigate the bureaucracy when he stood with three others in the made up Put Hull Back into Yorkshire Party.

A vacancy developed on the Ecology Party National Council, its governing body lead by the charismatic Jonathon Porritt, who later became chief advisor to the HRH Prince of Wales. I was to represent the Yorkshire and Humberside region having been volunteered by Helen to distract me from my local mission of campaigning in our city. I therefore put forward and elected unopposed onto the Council and after a brief handover from my predecessor, I headed off to London for two days on a National Express Coach and stayed at one of the Co-chairs houses in North London Professor Paul Ekins.

The meeting lasting two full days, was all about internal squabbles, and there was a clear divide between pragmatists, and idealists. I felt out of my depth and remained silent until the matter of the ongoing Miners' Strike was raised and what should be the position of the Ecology Party. Jonathan Porritt turned to me and asked what the representative from Yorkshire and Humberside thought on the matter.

For the best part of year, the Miners' Strike had dominated the political agenda, and although I supported the Miners in principle, I had not done anything to get involved to which I now feel somewhat ashamed. Paul on the other hand had worked tirelessly helping to fundraise with the local community and had stood on picket lines as the Government tried to starve the National Union of Miners back to work, by snatching their funds.

Before the dispute, a large storage of Coal was deliberately stockpiled to counter strike action designed to avoid a repeat of the power cuts of the 1970's that had provided the Trade Union with a convincing victory over the Ted Heath Conservative Government and facilitated my early candlelit chess lessons.

However, Jonathan's question had thrown me, as the last two speakers had just supplied powerful and compelling arguments for closing the coal mines on ecological grounds, as using coal fired energy was unsustainable. The Manifesto for a Sustainable Society written well before the dispute confirmed this as policy.

I was not sufficiently eloquent to respond as I would have liked, having been put on the spot, I felt unease at my political direction into Green Politics, for when it was introduced to me by my German friends from Dietkirchen, they explained a radical departure from mainstream politics whilst remaining very much on the left of the political spectrum. My gut feeling was that the Ecology Party in England was very much in the middle and would not be supporting a Trade Union dispute when it involved a struggle to further pollute the environment, and risk global warming.

I sat on the fence, explaining that communities needed jobs, but we needed to radically overhaul our energy policy, re-deploying miners into sustainable energy. However, the Miners' strike was a marmite issue, you were with them or you were with the Government. It was a real dilemma for me. I was a socialist and trade unionist, but also understood the issues around the real-life threatening dangers of global warming.

Returning to Hull, I realised that the Ecology Party position, on the Miner's Strike, or lack of it was going to be a problem in the Socialist Republic of Hull.

The Blue Bell was also the meeting place of an informal alliance of various animal rights groups, and Silly got me involved with this group who were very different in their approach to activism than the local Ecology Party. I had also become a member of CND and had attended a camp outside a local American Military Base that supposedly housed medium range Nuclear Cruise Missiles.

Susan Lillywhite (left) and I at an anti-circus demonstration.

I attended the Ecology Party conference held in Malvern that year, and we agreed to change our name to the Green Party and were confident that we were set for a breakthrough, but we were deluding ourselves, although there was some growth, the electoral system was never going to provide our small support a voice in Westminster.

I was involved in a few public protests, when the Circus came to town with their array of tamed and caged wild animals, we managed to get our protest pictures in the Hull Daily Mail, and we also got similar coverage when we staged a protest outside

Hull's Reckitt & Coleman who amongst many things made pharmaceuticals which we assumed required animal testing.

We engaged in some activities which were described as direct action, which was our way to describe minor law-breaking to make a political point. Paul did not get involved in in this activity, although he supported the overall cause as much as Silly and I, he felt that my involvement was more to do with the excitement of planning, executing, and getting away with these operations, and to be fair on reflection he was right.

My one venture with the Hunt Saboteurs ended with the armed Huntsmen imprisoning us in our hired minibus, an action completely against the law carrying a heavy sentence but was deliberately overlooked by the Police who were obviously very cosy with the organisers of the Fox Hunt. Their actions apparently justified by a few Saboteurs who in the past had broken the non-violent code and offered violence to the red devils on horseback, rather than sticking to laying false trails to confuse the hounds.

In Hull the group operated as the Hull Animal Rights Group and was a mesh of smaller groups with specialist interests, and collectively we hired a bus to attend a national demonstration to get a fur farm closed in the Midlands. Accompanied by fifty-five activists including Silly, this demonstration was at the time of the Miner's strike and the Police were organised in military style. The scene resembled a war game from the Napoleonic era, with small square brigades of Police lines in full riot gear their shields and helmets glistening in the morning sun and behind them the cavalry lined up in reserve. This pattern was repeated around the farm as protesters encircled the battlements. Had we brought enough vegetarian sandwiches we could have starved them out.

I had watched a lot of violence on TV as the last national Miners' strike unfolded, and even though I was aware that the BBC were editing material to favour the Police and paint the striking Miners as the initiators and perpetrators of violence, I knew what was coming from the Police here and I became very scarred. To be fair the protesters were very organised as requests were made through several loud hailers and when we started to encroach towards the Police lines, I became aware of the sound of barking Police Dogs still hopefully tethered. It was ironic and unhelpful to the Animal Rights Brigade that they were about to be attacked by animals.

The battle lasted for hours, there was no chance the protesters would break police lines and there was no way the Police could disperse the thousands of protesters who only slightly outnumbered the Police. So ensued a game of cat and mouse, the police lines opened several times, and the cavalry charged knocking protesters to the ground with the horse's torso or from batons swung at any head they could reach.

They were not interested in arrests, the Police wanted blood that day and it would take many more years before my respect for the so-called upholders of the law was restored.

Once the injured were ferried to hospital in makeshift ambulances, and the coaches headed back to the four corners of the Isles. The animals destined to be skinned awaited their cruel fate as if nothing had happened.

However, the farm was closed shortly afterwards, probably due to the economic cost on Policing further protests, and sixteen years later all fur farms were closed as this cruel practice was finally abolished.

This was brutal, this was Britain in 1984. Eric Blair's vision of the future was developing before us, and this was before the introduction of the world wide web.

I had become suspicious that I was being followed sometimes but put this down to my fantasy thinking and overrated sense of self-importance. It was just that when I drove down to London sometimes, or to Party meetings in Yorkshire, there always seemed to be a car just about visible in my mirror maintaining my speed, regardless of if I speeded up or slowed down. My paranoia was worsened when I started to hear clicks on my telephone line as if there were a third-party present.

My involvement in Animal Rights dwindled after an Irish fellow activist, inventively called Paddy, was arrested, and placed in a wagon that bore his name. He painted the local fur shop with MURDER and ALF (Animal Liberation Front) for the umpteenth time that month, only this time the Police were waiting for him, and the look outs were clearly not doing their job, however I did manage to avoid arrest by hiding in a darkened shop doorway for some time. I had to scurry back home in the early hours with Silly along a discreet route to avoid any patrol cars as I was carrying spare paint.

Some of the activists were also perhaps a little too passionate and seem to care for animals above human beings, and I had a vested interest in not adopting these extremist speciesism beliefs. Apart from being human myself, holding that view in modern society must have been a daily torture and many of these activists were traumatised by the conflict between their lives and their beliefs and were deeply unhappy.

I decided to concentrate more on Green Politics with the Hull Green Party who's manifesto for a sustainable society had some very progressive polices on animal rights. This was a labour dominated City where locals joked if you put up a sheep with a red rosette it would be elected, and sometimes they did.

My leaflets had generated some interest in the Avenues, and few additional members joined, notably John Wonacott who was a local teacher living on Ella Street.

We had a surplus of teachers within the tiny membership, and they were unable to stand in an election, so it was difficult to find volunteers who were fine with declaring their radical politics and understood they had no chance of getting elected. However, for the forthcoming 1985 elections I managed to persuade four people to stand in their wards, with the other twenty-eight wards having no representation. However, this meant we were entitled to some media coverage and we were each given a short piece in the Hull Daily Mail. With no national coverage, and the local electorate having not even heard of the Ecology Party our vote share was obviously derisory; however, I had the best result in the Avenues gaining exactly 150 votes.

During the count in the City Hall, I was a little taken back that only the winning candidates would address the small crowd of activists dawning their mostly red rosettes with an occasional blue or yellow one, and a rare green one, especially as it was being broadcast live on both local radio channels. I was remarkably disappointed and indeed frustrated that the Sunflower seeds I had brought to the Count were now redundant unless I took matters into my own hands.

My result in the Avenues was one of the first to be declared and as the newly elected labour Councillor left the stage, I grabbed the microphone before anyone could react and started my speech explaining that I was giving a packet of Sunflower Seeds to each winning candidate, to sow their seeds of doubt and our seeds of hope that Hull would become an ecological and sustainable society one day.

The Civil Servants in charge were both horrified and slightly amused at this breach of protocol, and I was quickly ushered off the stage. It worked, it went out on the radio, and then BBC Radio Humberside had some time to fill so I managed to get a full interview and providing the platform we craved.

The Government were planning on raising the Parliamentary deposit from £150 to £1000 per seat, which would make standing very unaffordable for many local Green parties. I was recruited into a secretive team to organise and implement newsworthy peaceful demonstrations against the rise as the Party of 500 was facing electoral oblivion as the national cost of £650'000 of standing was a long way beyond our reach. Each national member would have to contribute £1300 each, before any costs of campaigning could be considered. The Government, backed by big unrestrained business were looking to silence the growing green voices. We had always campaigned against any deposit, preferring an extension of the number of nominees to deter time wasters.

Meeting in Hull, we devised our plan, and started to procure the equipment we needed, and to undertake a reconnaissance of our intended target, the House of Commons. The plan was to abseil onto the floor of the house from the viewing gallery with flags and banners. The equipment, to be made of rigid plastic to avoid detection, was to be obscured around our bodies on entry covered in foam. We were serious, but our plan was never implemented as the Government agreed to lower the deposit to £500, and we were instructed to stand down.

In principle I do not agree that a financial deposit is fair in a democratic society, as it discriminates those with less means. Although I did appreciate the explanation given that the intended target of the Government was the far-right National Front and the British Nationalist Party who had grown faster than the Green Party in the late 70's.

However, it would not surprise me if the same civil servants used a similar explanation to the far-right parties, that their intended target was those loonies in the green movement who wanted to abandon our nuclear defences during a cold war.

One of my recruits to the Green Party cause was John Wonacott who was a great strategist and identified that there was a lot of enthusiasm in the Avenues area of Hull, but they were not turned on to activists if they had to go to a City Centre pub to meet, and suggested we hold local meetings. The constitution of the Green party was to act locally think globally, and anyone could set up a local party.

We also had a mole in the TGWU, who was feeding us information about the Labour Party strategy towards us.

So, we set up the North Hull Green Party, meeting locally boosted attendance significantly and informed the Region not expecting any controversy. At the next Regional Meeting there was a motion from our friends in East Hull to disband and re-join the Hull Green Party. Given there were now about thirty odd members in the Avenues Ward of the North Hull Constituency, and only a handful east of the river, we understood that they felt abandoned, but the motion was ridiculous.

They put their case, they had not been consulted, we had been undemocratic, we had unilaterally broken up the agreed structure, and they felt betrayed. In response I launched into a considered but impassioned speech in response. This took me by surprise, because I had never considered myself a good speaker up until this point but my passion was aroused, and the room remained silent and attentive throughout.

I started out by saying, nothing has changed for our members in the east, the Hull Green Party had just grown too big and needs to localise and decentralise its activities in a City of a quarter of a million. We have not replaced any structure; we have just built firm foundations under it. I went on, North Hull is part of the Hull Green Party, not set up to compete with, but to nourish, support, and encourage our friends in the East, and indeed we are currently working to help the development of a West Hull Green Party, all under the umbrella of the Hull Green Party. My master stroke was then to nominate Helen Dixie to become coordinator of the Hull Green Party to oversee the three new Party's when West Hull launched in the next few weeks.

In hindsight our discussion was ludicrous, we only had a hundred members in Humberside, with a third living in a square mile in Hull, but strategically we had shaken off the shackles of the debating society that was, and we now had an active decentralised party to get our message across.

Money was short with the North Hull Green Party and the Hull Animal Rights Group funded our campaigns with an occasional jumble sale, something picked up in the lyrics of the Housemartins first single Flag Day, *"So you thought you'd like to change the world, Decided to stage a jumble sale, For the poor, for the poor. It's a waste of time if you know what they mean, Try shaking a box in front of the Queen."*

One of John Wonacott's masterstrokes ideas to organise a community green educational trip to the Centre for Alternative

Technology based in Llwyngwern Quarry, Pantperthog, Machynlleth, in central Wales. The centres mission was to educate by physically illustrating sustainable ways of producing and saving energy to offset mankind's dangerous route towards climate change, which at the time was referred to as global warming. We managed to fill a coach of residents and their children, charging extraordinarily little in this allegedly non-profit excursion, as we accommodated everyone in a local youth hostel.

As the coach journey was long, we supplied soft drinks and home-made sandwiches which we sold very cheaply to our captive audience. The centre was excellent and very educational but above all it was inspiring. We recruited new members, and by accidents made a profit of a few hundred pounds just from the soft drinks being sold at 5p a cup with two four-hour journeys either way.

I was still single and seemed to attract the attention of one of the Dixie sisters, recently divorced sister-in-law who seemed to follow me around a lot. She told me she was thinking about learning to drive, so I agreed to provide some free lessons to smooth things over with our East Hull comrades. However, despite our significant age gap of about twenty years she flirted during our lessons and we ended up an item for a short while which clearly did not go down well in the Dixie households.

Just for the record, many of the things I campaigned against, have been realised. The fur trade has gone, commercial vivisection has gone, Fox Hunting has gone, the hole in the Ozone layer has gone, Short Range Nuclear Cruise Missiles have gone, and the world has finally woken up to the perils of unsustainable growth and climate change.

We were determined to do better the next year and were better organised for the 1986 campaign and were now benefitting from the change of name to Green Party. My first political lesson in life was that regardless of how well you prepare, how clear, concise your message is, anything can happen to destroy completely, or boost your success like outside events completely out of your control.

Press button phones were still relatively new in 1985, but when I called home to my parents in Coulsdon someone from the TGWU (Transport and General Workers Union) in Hull answered. Confused as the numbers were not similar, I tried again and this time someone from Hull Greenpeace answered. I just started pressing any buttons to see if the device was broken, when an operator intervened and asked what number I was trying to call. I told them the number and they connected me. I thanked her and she replied that she was pleased to help, only she mentioned my name. I asked her how she knew my name, there was a silence and she eventually responded your registered to this phone number. I said no I'm not, this is a friend's phone.

I was now convinced the phone I was using had become a listening device for Millbank, as described by Peter Wright in his once banned book Spy Catcher, and that I was indeed followed as I drove around the Country. Obviously, the spooks had a technical issue that day, with the chances of accidently being connected to two overtly political numbers were millions to one, there was no doubt I was a person of interest to the Security Services.

Later in the year the Guardian Newspaper reported a leak at MI5. Cathy Massiter alleged that there was widespread surveillance of all organisations that were anti-nuclear, including wiretapping, physical surveillance, and infiltration. These disclosures have never been denied. I am convinced that I was the subject of ongoing intrusive illegal state surveillance for several years.

Although it was a cause of celebration to have our collective paranoia exposed as being justified, it paradoxically created mistrust amongst all the groups I had become associated with, and I indeed felt suspected of being a traitor, being the outsider from the south. This corrosion of trust was perhaps something the state had deliberately organised. Perhaps the leak from MI5 was not a leak, but an effort to put a cat amongst the pigeons and disrupt the organisations that they perceived as political subversive.

# CHAPTER XIV CHAIN REACTION

The Housemartins had two John Peel sessions under their belt and were becoming well known and were building on their success. Donna Summer released "*Chain Reaction*" in the spring of 1986, without any foresight of the irony of events that would unfold before the world.

On Saturday 26$^{th}$ April 1986, I was busy distributing leaflets for the May 8th Hull City Elections, which among other things warned against the dangers of Nuclear Power. At the same time Ukrainian engineers in Pripyat were busy with their contribution to my election campaign. Commencing a safety test on reactor four of the Nuclear Power Station in Chernobyl, they accidently caused a nuclear chain reaction, causing a complete meltdown and a subsequent fatal explosion killing thirty-one Ukrainian Engineers, and over time indirectly ending the lives of between four thousand to two hundred thousand prematurely depending on who you believe. This is still the worst nuclear disaster in history and it took nine days to contain the massive outage of radiation that spread right across Europe including my home in Hull.

The terrible news dominated the last week of the election campaign and suddenly the Green Party were newsworthy. I was invited to BBC Radio Humberside and the local private Viking Radio to give interviews, trying not to sound too "we told you so" and hopefully explaining the gravity of the situation given the lifespan of radiation and its health risks, and the death toll would be rising significantly over many years to come, and that Britain must review its energy policy as Nuclear Power was not safe.

We obviously did a lot better that year, my result was close to five hundred votes but was still only about 15% of the vote, and not enough to break through.

The next election we reached our peak and managed to field a full slate of candidates across all thirty-two seats and managed a far better result than the national average for the Green party.

In September 1985 I had started a low paid part time job with the Charity Hull Architecture Workshop Ltd., based in the old High Street, as part of the Governmental Community Programme. Our role was to facilitate community design and bring a wider appreciation of the architecture of the old part of the city. I learned that the local church foundation bricks were the very first bricks ever used in construction within Britain, after the crusaders returned from the middle east with new ideas from their spoils, and the introduction of a key stone in constructing an arch.

We arranged a light festival with fireworks for the City Council to celebrate the new space age Tidal Surge Barrier placed overlooking the Humber Estuary to protect the River Hull from flooding the City at high tide, but our most sustainable project for which I am intently proud was the award-winning design of the Fountain Road Community Garden.

There was a history of children getting into difficulty, or indeed on one occasion dying in one of the drains that ran through the city to offset flooding, but as it was not possible to build along their banks, nature had grown to obscure the risks of a steep bank into deep water, often filled with unwanted bed frames and bicycles. Our vision was to turn one of these strips into a safe community garden.

Coordinated by my colleague and eccentric friend Tony Mercer, we toured schools and community centres with a moveable model. The local people young and old designed the garden to meet their needs, a play area, a quite sitting area, and a beautiful garden of wildflowers and shrubs that would need little maintenance. We then managed to get many volunteers to put the project into practice but used professionals to restore the broken section of the road facing bridge wall.

I managed to fundraise from local business and entered the project in the BP Environmental Community Awards to which we were announced the annual winners. The garden is still a community asset some thirty years later.

Geoff Haslam who was the manager, had a pet project in designing and restoring a dilapidated fishing boat called the William McCann, into a community resource to take people on short boating trips down the Humber Estuary and beyond. I occasionally helped with this work, mostly applying marine paint, which I found far more difficult and energy sapping than any domestic painting I had ever undertaken, but as the project neared completion we held a party on board.

I was at the time friendly with a girl called Patricia Dennison, we hung out together but were not what anyone would describe as in a relationship. As the party ended, we were invited to stay the night on board, and a crew member assuming we would agree had made up a bed for us to share. I would have been happy to crash out together but Pat wanted to go so we left in the early hours in a taxi to our respective homes.

The next morning the weather was very stormy when I awoke, and downstairs my house mates were watching live TV coverage of a sea rescue on the Humber, as a small ship had got stranded in the moving sands which the Estuary was renowned for. It was said that if you knew how the tides worked at specific times and places you could walk across the Estuary, though I never considered trying it. As I snuck into my morning cereal, I could not help noticing the resemblance of the woman, who had clearly lost her dignity, wrapped within the legs of an RAF rescuer as she was being winched up to a helicopter hovering above the small, stranded ship. She looked a lot like Carmine, a fragile lady who I worked with at the Hull Architecture Workshop and had been at the Party the night before.

As I watched the drama unfold the next person on the winch was unmistakably the one and only Tony Mercer with his wild hair and long grey beard. I found out a short while later that the party had continued into the early hours, and the crew and guests had got so drunk that they thought it would be fun idea to take the ship out onto the Humber at first light.

I felt a sense of relief as the situation looked perilous, then paradoxically jealousy that the party was still evidently going on and I had missed out on the adventure. Nobody was physically hurt, and the ship could be re-floated at high tide, but reputations were sunk, and I had missed out on a helicopter ride.

The Housemartins had released an album London 0 Hull 4 and had released another single but had not managed to get into the top 40 of the UK singles charts, but they had attracted a local following, and some national attention.

When the Germans wanted to go back to Scotland in 1986, Paul dropped out of the trip as he was concentrating on his new career, and there was a deep sense of frustration from my German friends and I, that our magical holiday could never be re-created. I went, but with the addition Alfred's son Fabian Wirth still too young to appreciate the Scottish wilderness, and we were very restricted on what we could do with a toddler, and the holiday was somewhat flat. I decided when I returned to Hull, that I needed to put things right with Paul, his dream of pop stardom had yet to materialise, and we had gone through far too much to give up on our friendship.

Up in Scotland, one morning I awoke a little early and decided to go for a stroll when I heard the strangest of noises. In the undergrowth I could see something moving and it appeared to have a plastic white pointy head and was making a shrill sound that was unnerving. I noticed the undergrowth obscured what appeared to be a concrete trench, perhaps a remnant from the last war, and what I now understood to be a yogurt pot was trudging through the undergrowth in this trench shrieking at the top of its tiny voice. I managed to get into a better viewing position, and realised it was a hedgehog which had appeared to have forced its head through the carton and was wearing it like a dog's cone fitted by vet to stop them from licking their wounds.

I was highly amused by the mess this little guy had got himself into, then realised that he may be starving to death which would account for his shrieking. I didn't even know hedgehogs made sounds, but I jumped down, chased the hedgehog into a corner and managed to pull the yogurt carton off, which came away with a pop. The hedgehog stunned appeared to make a sound like "thank you" but not speaking hedgehog I cannot be sure what the noise made meant, except it was not the traumatic shrill I had been listening to.

I could not wait to tell my fellow campers about my adventure, however there was a problem. I could not get out of this trench as the sides were high and the undergrowth too fragile to take my weight. The ground softened by weeds was hard to launch from. It occurred to me that I was not in ear shot of anyone, out of sight, and trapped. It seemed that I had sacrificed my life for a hedgehog who now had ample things to eat, my only meal would have been the hedgehog I just saved but I had lifted to freedom.

Fortunately, in a life and death situation ideas can emerge to save you, and after a few attempts to climb out I came up with the idea of binding greenery together which then became strong enough to take my weight and I was able to get my fingertips onto the top of the concrete wall and clamber up.

I was only trapped for about ten minutes, but it was very scary due to the isolation, and when I returned to camp as a hedgehog saving superhero, I was brought down to earth by the Germans remembering the infamous Haggis gag just assumed it was another Trotsky story.

It was my own fault as I had in the past been found out, exaggerating or embellishing things to improve a story, but mostly for entertainment purposes. Suitably punished I was more thoughtful on how I told stories from this point forward.

I was lucky that my next Scottish adventure had witnesses as I was tucking into some fresh fish and chips, I was attached by a Scottish Gull in such an aggressive manner, despite my hunger and recourse to more cash, I surrendered my dinner to save myself from further divebombing from the Scottish equivalent of the Luftwaffe.

On route back down to Hull we stopped in a pub somewhere in Northumberland, and I spotted the Housemartins on a duke box. After investing 10p to hear what it sounded like, intrigued as to how it had managed to get onto a duke box, especially so far from Hull. I listened to the opening chords of Happy Hour for the first time and at once thought this is good. This is incredibly good.

The bartender, obviously a fan started to jig gently behind the bar, and I enquired if he knew the song. He told me in a gruff Northumberland accent that it was number 3 in the charts. Had this been the time of mobile phones and the internet, I would have sent congratulations, but I was far away with no means of communication other than a telephone box, but 70 Grafton Street had never been fitted with a telephone. I understood this was a game changer, and his life would never be the same again. My German friends could not believe it, but I felt an ebb of sadness that any attempt to put things right with Paul now could be perceived as trying to jump on his new gravy train.

It would be a couple of years later that I reached out to Paul after the Housemartins split up in 1988, and in the meantime, I had a life to lead of my own. However, he did call me to warn me that journalists from the Sun Newspaper were tracking down his friends and acquaintances looking to find any dirt, and I gladly promised not to talk to them.

The Housemartins brand was northern working-class lads. Inevitably the Sun exposed their partial middle-class background, with images of their large, detached family homes in Chipstead and Reigate. What had really upset the establishment was his support for the Miners and his Socialist and Republican views. When being interviewed by a reporter they suggested the Royal Family bring in a lot of income for the nation, Paul flippantly suggested then why not chop them up and sell them off. They had already dug out his lyrics to Flag Day about try shaking a box in front of the Queen and the video to Happy Hour mocking male office stereotypes at lunchtime could easily have been associated with the sexist misogynistic male Sun employees of the time.

The story was a substantially unfair, they had excluded Paul's Sheffield roots, or the poverty Paul had I had endured in the early days of Grafton Street, which had no heating system, and we rationed the two-bar electric fire when it turned below zero outside. The Suns' cowardly intervention did nothing to dent the chart success of their third single, but locally some people in the community took offence, believing their working-class neighbour was a fraud.

The Warren was considering taking young people potholing as an offer was made by some experienced cavers to take some of our young unemployed with them. Unsure about the suitability of this type of activity, it was decided to send a handful of volunteer staff on a taster day. I volunteered along with Shaun England and his new girlfriend Sue Lillywhite, and so a handful of us set of to the peak district to Transend a Grade 2 pothole "*Easy cave with minor difficulties*" with two seasoned Cavers.

Wearing all the proper kit, red boiler suit, helmet with attached miners' lamp, and thick waterproof boots we each stepped inside the darkness in turn as we walked easily down steep inclines. I trailed Shaun and Silly and it became increasingly difficult to navigate as the rock was very uneven, and visibility was restricted to the range and direction of your own lamp. The constant sound of running water was a reminder that these caves can flood very quickly, and perhaps my last choice of methodology of death would be to drown in cold water in pitch darkness miles underground.

I started to be unnerved by the occasional scream ahead as my colleagues tried to overcome certain obstacles on our descent into the depths of hell. Not being able to see what problem they met exacerbated the danger in my mind out of all proportion. I was however reassured by the seasoned professional Steve bringing up the rear right behind me. I could at least turn to him for re-assurance.

Although we had climbing ladders, thin metal rolls of thick entwined wire with metal struts that could be rolled out and fixed to the rock, as this was a grade II experience I did not expect to do much climbing, but after about half an hour in, I was confronted with a short fifteen foot drop, and although I had difficult turning my back on the drop and trying to find a foot hold in the narrow ladder which had no room to spare with my size eleven boot, I managed to climb down the ladder to a safe plateau below where everyone was waiting. Of course, I had a safety rope attached and Steve aided my decent before coming down himself unaided.

The next obstacle was a so-called cheese press, where the rock narrows above and below and you must squeeze your way through. It didn't help that Shaun England, having already squeezed through said imagine if there was an earthquake now as I was compressed like a piece of stilton, with my confidence being squeezed out of me like excess fermenting milk.

As we moved on down into the dark abys, I became aware that an obstacle ahead was causing some consternation. Nigel, who had been on the Malcolm Miller with me, had delayed going around this pillar shaped rock and allowed my friends to overtake him. He was being encouraged from the other side to grip his fingers and toes hard into the rock and move quickly to avoid falling into the large shallow looking pond which was preventing a straightforward journey. Without warning, he disappeared into the water slipping like a sea lion into the dark water without a splash or sound. All I could see of him was his lit lamp under the black water, and then a panicked face and dog paddle arms as he frantically swam to the surface and was pulled to safety.

I was next. I thought about quitting but understood this was no longer straight forward given how deep we were and I would need someone to get me out of here. So, I nervously gripped for dear life and managed to successfully get myself around the smooth slippery rock onto the other side.

Thanking Steve for his encouragement and advice, I asked him about the type of hazards you would expect in a more difficult grade of cave. He only mentioned grade five severity in his reply, and it was then that it dawned on me, this was a grade four cave, and considered difficult even for seasoned cavers.

My nerves were already shattered when we arrived at what appeared to be a hole in the wall, which others had already descended through. When I looked down it was pitch black which was due to an overhang which had also made the ladder difficult to access. Steve had me tied and supported but turning my back on the darkness and a drop of unlimited depths, and with the difficulty of finding my first ladder rung, I started to panic, just like I had on the Malcolm Miller.

Calming myself and only being able to hold on to the top of the ladder with fingertips, as it was hard against the overhanging rock, I managed to take small steps down the ladder, but it started to sway. As I took each step down into the darkness the rocking continued. Gently at first, then I was swinging like a pendulum inside a grandfather clock and fearing Steve would not be able to hold me if I fell off the ladder, I started shaking to the extent that my miners lamp came free of my helmet but still attached to the battery, it was now shining in my face completely blinding me in the darkness.

I was going to die in the next few seconds I told myself, if I didn't calm my body and stop swinging, I would shortly fall to my death possibly taking Steve with me.

Calm, calm, calm was my mantra as I managed to stop the severe swinging. Then a familiar voice said "Trotsky, are you getting off or what?" I was only about 2 foot off the ground with my antics being observed by everyone in disbelief.

I was done. My nerves were completely shattered and it was agreed that I would not make the final descent into the large cavern below and await everyone's return. However, as Steve descended the next ladder, I was alone, deep underground by myself, at risk of drowning in a flash flood, being crushed if in an earth tremor or earthquake, or worst still my battery could run out.

Ascending was much easier, and I was truly grateful to get back to the surface, but the Warren never commissioned these well-meaning guys again, as the guinea pigs all agreed that this was a little too dangerous for the clientele of the Warren.

I vowed not to undertake any more dangerous sports and immersed myself during the summers in taking young people on adventure trips to the Yorkshire Moors and Dalby Forest. I really enjoyed organising the Orienteering, treasure hunts, and what we referred to as search and rescue to test the newfound skills of our intrepid young people.

On one occasion my role was simply to drive the mini bus to collect everyone off the moor after they had undertaken a mock search and rescue, and I would be the mock ambulance to collect the casualty and all I needed was a radio message and coordinates, so I slept in the van overlooking miles of desolate terrain. I received a message saying they had lost sight of our young people and could I drive to a viewing point over the valley to see if I could spot them with my binoculars. To get there I would have to descend and up the other side of a steep valley.

Halfway down I got the message they were found and I should return to my position, but rather than drive up the other side to a turning point, I decided to try and turn around on this single-track road. As there was a break in the stone walling for an entrance which ran downhill to the farmhouse a mile or so away. I swung the large 15-seater minibus around and as I turned the steering wheel to re-ascend the steep hill, my efforts to drive off were impaired by the thick mud my rear wheels had met and I started to descend a few feet backwards.

The harder I tried to ascend, the faster I descended now being at least 100 meters away from the safe tarmac of the lane above, I decided to radio for help but found the signal was now lost.

I panicked a little more and sunk a lot more. The track was thick wet mud and I had sunk unable to move up or indeed down anymore. Having a large group of vulnerable adults at risk of the harsh moorland weather, I went into basil faulty overdrive, if I had a branch available, I would have given the minibus a John Cleese style damned good thrashing. However, the nearest tree was probably miles away so I worked out the only option was to hope that there was someone at the farm who could help and I waded through the mud down to the farmhouse.

Fortunately, they were in, had a tractor, were willing to drag me out for £5, and were not too condescending and mocking of my predicament, and as they hauled me onto the reassuring safety of the tarmacked lane, I anxiously awaited the first communication of the Radio hoping it wasn't about the disappearance and search and rescue of an ambulance.

I got away with it, no one had noticed my absence in the hour it had taken to get free and re-connected to the radio.

I enjoyed these outdoor pursuits so much that Chris Fleming suggested I undertake a formal qualification in Hill Walking and so I set off to a training centre where I learned about mapping, weather forecasting, health and safety, bivouacking, and all things outdoors. I felt I was excelling and was looking forward to the last day which was described as classical abseiling.

I had never been abseiling due to my fear of heights, but after potholing I felt I could bounce down the side of a hill with some confidence, with all the safety equipment and ropes attached. Unfortunately, I misunderstood the term classical as meaning "traditional, standard, conventional, orthodox or usual," but no, in the world of Hill Walking classical had a whole new meaning. It referred to having no equipment except a single rope, although we were allowed a helmet.

The exercise was to illustrate how we would get a group of people off a hillside if the weather posed a risk. The Moors can become an extremely dangerous place at truly short notice, there are sheer drops from crags and scarps, and if the mist and fog rolls, which is why mapping work was so important needing to know exactly where you were always. Of course, everyone could be attached to a rope and lowered down, but what about the last person? If you had to drop down in stages you could ill afford to leave a rope tied and it would have to come down with the last person. We were being trained to be the last person. This was Classical abseiling.

The drop was sufficient to realise that if you fell you might not die, but you would probably break most of the bones in your body. Obviously, I went last hoping to get some practical advice from my more competent trainee's. With my rope secure around a rock, through my legs and over my shoulder I had to turn my back on the steep sheer drop and allowed the rope to burn into my clothes as I held my weight trying to allow the rope to slide gently through my hands. It was not long before I was upside down, foot entangled grasping on for dear life, and having to be rescued myself. If I had fallen, being upside down, I may well have broken my neck. Here I was risking life and limb again. Even though I made a mess of this exercise I did complete and therefore became the proud owner of a competent hill walking certification.

I was now back at volunteering at the Warren and socialising with some of the staff. Chris Fleming often invited us around to play a board game called Diplomacy, a war game set before the first world war, where you had to negotiate trust and peace deals or suffer or inflict betrayal.

I had seen a few students come and go from my shared student house, from Peru to Germany, but the arrival of three English rugby players hastened my departure.

I moved out of The Limes into "Faulty Turret's" on Spring Bank West where Alfie and his girlfriend and another friend called Brian lived in what can only be described as a hippy commune. The property stood out along the terraced house as it had a castle like turret as a feature. I have never smoked, and that includes joints, but the place smelt of cannabis, and when there appeared to be lack of supply in the city, we joked that we could harvest the wallpaper which was stained with years of reformed resin. There was a constant flow of customers to the house day and night, and it was tradition to let anyone in.

No one in the house was getting rich, as the official residents were not suppliers or dealers, but the house had a reputation and to a stranger it would have been difficult to understand who the official residents were as so many people stayed overnight without invitation. In hindsight it is a wonder we were never raided.

This happy place was more of a slum than Grafton Street, hence it's nick name Faulty Turrets, but my ground floor bedroom was spacious and had the fantastic feature of my large double bed sunk into the base of the turret that expanded the room in one corner. It had four narrow full-length windows semi-circling around the headboard. I became very fond of a regular visitor called Emma Lutley, but she only had eyes for Brian.

Across the road from us was the Western Cemetery, which was rich in history and overgrown in the greatest tradition of a Hammer Horror film. We sometimes spent summer evenings sat amongst the gravestones, or if we were flush, we would wonder down to the Polar Bear my new local pub.

Alfie and I became members at the local Casino. I was overly cautious not to get addicted and made effective plans to ensure I didn't and introduced very specific rules about frequency of attendance, length of stay and maximum spend. I would take a single cheque for £20 to be cashed for chips, would always leave before midnight, and never take my wallet. If I spent all my £20, I would have to walk nearly two miles home for lack of a taxi fare.

There were some evenings I did very well, receiving my cheque back to destroy and pocketing over a £100, but most nights I lost my £15 very slowly with cautious bets.

Apart from being extremely exciting there was free snacks and drinks, and the entertainment of other people winning or losing big time. On one memorable occasion a young man the worst for wear, was politely asked to place his last bet before leaving, being a little drunk, and upset at the decision he slammed down £5 in chips on eight black, which came in to the embarrassment of the concierge, and £160 worth of chips was being passed his way which he had difficulty in collecting.

The anxious concierge obviously impatient reminded him he still had chips on the table which were still resting on eight black. Before he had the chance to collect the Croupier had spun the ball announcing "Plus d'enjeux" in their usual awful Hull French accent, so etiquette would not allow him to pick up his chips until it had landed, which it did, on eight black.

His eviction from the Casino had engineered for him a return of £360 pound in a couple of minutes. Obviously, they swept his money off the table as quickly as you can say "putain," and escorted him to the cash desk to cash in his small mountain of chips. They had done him a favour as they had denied themselves the opportunity to get their money back.

# CHAPTER XV THE LADY IN RED

After six months I was eligible for another Community programme and jumped at the chance to work for the local Health Authority part time, producing videos to promote their work in the mental health department. I was assigned to a portacabin in the grounds of Tilworth Grange in East Hull. I started with Mike Verdun who was to produce computer programmes to facilitate learning, and we were expected to collaborate. Our Manager John Lutkin was a narcissistic womanising power-hungry civil servant who had dreamed up this media department to flatter his own ego and income. He took joy in pointing out he paid more income tax than I received in gross salary. We had no real purpose or direction, but we were free to play as we saw fit and get a modest salary.

Most of the Residents had severe obvious disabilities, except some of the women who all lived in the main building who posed a real threat to Mike and me, who despite their old age seemed to be very fruity and could have been the inspiration for the BBC Fast Show characters "young man" who chased young men around.

For an entire year we were given no guidance, no projects, and produced virtually nothing for the health authority of any value. However, I did spend my time developing my skills in production. The highlight was filming Mr Lutkin singing to Residents on a guitar, who seemed to believe that by being filmed he was in some way on Top of the Pops, and his cheesy performance and comments between each corny classic was a point of hilarity for which I had to work ridiculously hard to avoid severe belly chuckling camera shake.

The only production for Hull Health Authority of any note was my edited version of a water disco which imposed images and special effects of staff bouncing Residents in the swimming pool to Billy Joel's Uptown Girl.

However, when my sister Vivien announced her wedding to Geoff Barrett in the summer of 1986, I had the perfect idea for a wedding gift. VHS cameras were becoming mainstream, and several Wedding Video companies were setting up, but I borrowed the equipment I needed and set off for Coulsdon. Knowing St. Aiden's, I could plan the shots in advance, and would not need lighting as the building had huge stained-glass windows which produced a perfect white natural light.

I like to think I captured the joyful day and managed to edit down the footage to the background music of Sue Pollard's *Staying Together*, from the TV Documentary Series *Marriage* which was airing at the time. Their Marriage produced three beautiful new grandchildren for my proud parents, Nicole, Danielle, and Lisa. Unfortunately, the theme I chose didn't do enough to keep them together and my video masterpiece is no longer on my sister's viewing list.

I was not sad to have completed a year at Tilworth Grange, but the mystery of the strange woman in the main block was finally resolved when I heard news that the main building was going to be closed and the strange women released into the community. I was told that they had all been here since their teenage years when they were committed for falling pregnant out of wedlock before the war. Some fifty years later, with their lives stolen by the state, and so institutionalised it was going to be equally traumatic for them to leave as it was to arrive, they were being evicted to be provided with "Care in the Community." This new Government policy was to effectively close asylums and institutions. If anyone ever points their finger at other Countries cruelty to their own people, I make a point of telling them about the forgotten women of Tilworth Grange.

Annoyed that our familiar social, after work, was going to be delayed by a political meet at the Warren I attended the steering group committee for the Hull Young Person's Housing Campaign set up by Andy West who was dealing with ever increasing levels of young people becoming homeless in his counselling and advice section of the Warren. Andy was compiling statistics and drafting a report to submit to Hull City Council under the title *"No Fixed Abode"* pushing for a change of policy to consider young people as suitably vulnerable to be re-housed which currently was not the case hence the increasing case load.

The Committee was chaired by my political rival Keith Russell, who was at once suspicious of my attendance explaining this was not a Party-Political issue. He was obviously more concerned about his platform in a city where Labour had no chance of losing overall control for the foreseeable future, rather than allowing the Ecology Party to be a green wedge on the issue which may have achieved faster results.

However, I agreed not to use the issue in forthcoming elections and tried to contribute as best I could. After the publication of the NFA (No Fixed Abode) report the City Council wanted to silence the rebel Keith Russell so they made the committee an offer of money to set up its own hostel for homeless young people. So, in conjunction with the Church of England, Doorstep of Hull became a charity and we set about identifying suitable property, and planned its development into a suitable core hostel, which would be the fulcrum in which floating support workers would be based to support young people in the community and move on from the hostel into their own accommodation.

At the Warren and the Hull Health Authority I had learned a great deal about film production with our VHS cameras and the ability to edit and mix sound, and I went about producing a documentary about homelessness using the theme tune of "Don't Give Up," performed by Peter Gabriel and Kate Bush. Interviewing various young people, Keith Russell, and Andy West on camera, and then splicing this together with still photos taken and printed by Barry Thompson. Tommo as we all referred to him was a fellow southerner with a rich cockney accent, very tall and lanky, but with a great sense of dry humour and we became good friends.

The Video was used for fundraising purposes and distributed accordingly and it was something I was proud of; my first film screening was well received.

There had always been an element of sexual politics at the Warren, but after returning from my recent Hill Walking Course I became aware of the new woman's worker who referred to herself as Lissa, although her real name was Wendy. She had moved to Hull from Stourbridge in the forlorn hope of making it as a singer, song writing, guitar playing, actress. I think she was also a big Paul Heaton fan, and moved into a flat in Grafton Street, which was obviously not a coincidence, being just a few doors from Paul.

It wasn't her fault but she was very attractive, and she knew it. I could see the distraction this was going to have and it wasn't long before most of the male volunteer staff had asked her out. I didn't like her, she was brash, argumentative, and worst of all she had a brummie accent.

Chris De Burgh had had a song out called the *Lady in Red* that summer and it played in my mind frequently as Lissa had this habit when she was heading home from work of lingering by the exit fiddling with her bright red umbrella, even if it was not raining. She often wore red for attention, and she could not be more obvious.

It was unclear who she was interested in at the Warren but I knew Tommo was interested, and to avoid any suggestion of dating Tommo, Lissa, her friend Anne Marie Taylor, and I went out for a few after hours drinks, in what I hoped would assist Tommo with his desire to date the girl he was becoming a little besotted by. I was his wing man, and Anne Marie was Lissa's chaperone.

This became a regular occurrence, and the foursome soon turned to a threesome as Anne Marie found alternatives as she noted along with me that Tommo's near obsession was not reciprocated and things were becoming tense and boring. When I discovered that Lissa lived on Grafton Street just six doors from Paul Heaton, and when I explained how we knew each other she asked me repeatedly for an introduction. I was aware that Paul was now living with a girlfriend called Karen, who might on reputation rip Lissa's head from her shoulders if I introduced them. So, I thought the best way was to knock

Paul up one evening with Lissa and see if he fancied a pint in the Grafton Pub. In truth I didn't want to introduce them, but I did want to catch up with Paul.

Perhaps I had an unconscious desire to be with Lissa, but my loyalty to Tommo would not allow me to consciously consider this, but after Lissa became aware that Paul was not interested in her, and was very devoted to Karen, we ended up at her flat later that night with just the two of us.

Something was developing between us and the next few threesome evenings with Tommo became more tense as it was obvious that something had changed and each time, we went out there was a standoff about who was leaving first. It came to a head one night when I explained the situation with Tommo who flew into a rage.

A week later he attacked me in the street without warning while I was with Lissa, which didn't end well for him, but painted me in a very unfavourable light as everyone knew about his obsession, that we hung out together, and that I had in his words nicked his bird as if she was a possession controlled by the  man who saw her first regardless of her needs and desires.

Beating him up emotionally and now physically was regretful, but circumstances played out as they did because although fun to be with, he was not a very desirable person to get involved with and had no obvious prospects other than a life on the dole. I on the other hand did.

I was due to leave Hull shortly to attend Bradford and Ilkley Community College, as I had successfully received an annual £3200 grant from Humberside County Council and been accepted onto their two-year full-time Youth and Community Course. It was not practical to commute everyday so Lissa and I agreed our fling was not sustainable and I set of from Paragon Station on the Train to Ilkley.

I remember it was raining heavily as if orchestrated to match my feelings and shed some tears when the train eased out of the station, on the first leg of my journey to Bradford & Ilkley Community College. At first, I considered it absurd to be so smitten after such a brief relationship, but then realised it was much more than that. I had given up Hull as well, my home for the last four years. At the time it felt like a greater transition than the one when our gang of four first travelled up the M1 to start a new life.

Rick Astley had invaded the airwaves with "*Never Gonna Give You Up*" contradicting my resolution.

My home was now next to the Ilkley Moor *bah tat*, and I did not know anyone except for Jane Armitage who had also managed to get on the Course.

Jane had wanted me to share a private house in Ilkley, but my experience of sharing a house with her convinced me to stay in the Halls of Residence. My first room was in the listed Wells House which was the main building. It was a very lonely existence, and this was the first time in my life that I was older than the people around me, I was a mature student at twenty-five.

The lectures, classmates, and the feel of the course were all very encouraging, but the evenings were mind numbingly boring, so I succumbed to travel back to Hull at weekends and stayed with Lissa. Her small bedsit in Grafton Street was extremely basic with a small bedroom, with a kitchen area. Mr Chapman the elderly Proprietor made a business out of buying up cheap property, converting them into bedsits, and then letting them exclusively to young girls. He collected his rent early on a Sunday morning and let himself into each bed sit with the keys he kept without warning, no doubt hoping to catch his tenants in a state of undress or other compromising positions. Lissa always had her rent ready, but if she didn't, I am sure Mr Creep Chapman would have preferred to be paid in kind.

I was convinced by my new student friends to transfer out of Wells House into the adjacent annex where it was far more social able. I became particularly good friends with Steve Suckling my neighbour and the mad bright red headed Sally who would brighten anyone's day. Had I started Student life in the annexe I would probably have not returned to Hull, especially as Sally had a friend who took an instant like to me. She also had a boyfriend who she had left behind and was suffering similar angst and loneliness.

I decided to reduce my weekend trips to Hull and concentrate on my work and new social life, joining the mixed gender hockey team and a couple of political societies. I regretted my trips back to Hull as they were motivated by selfish need, but now by cutting off Lissa I was also being selfish and was torn apart with having two feet eighty miles apart. If both actions were selfish then I should choose the one that best suited me and I decided that I had a new life to lead.

Some weeks later, sitting in the student bar on a stool propping up the bar, my hands were covered by female hands, but as I turned to greet one of many suspects, I noticed in the mirror Anne Marie Taylor, and was shocked to find Lissa had just turned up speculatively with her old chaperone.

My new student friends, who I had yet got to know very well, or trust, or for them to trust me, were brilliantly discreet and Lissa was mercifully not introduced to her many rivals.

I felt compelled to try and keep two worlds running simultaneously and spent the next two years commuting via Leeds station every weekend and holiday period. Without discussion, Lissa rented a second-floor attic flat on Westbourne Avenue, and this became my new Hull base.

I really enjoyed the Course and had to undertake working placements by arrangement and had a short spell at Horsham Youth Club which I hated and then in the second year with Barnardo's in Hull with their youth offending team which I loved and where I had to produce a Crown Court Social Enquiry Reports, and spent two weeks working in a care home for teenagers. I also had to support staff in delivering the caution plus programme for new offenders to examine their thought processes when they committed their crimes.

Having interviewed a teenager who was a prolific thief and burglar, I set out my report and took advice from the various staff about content and language and was fairly pleased with the result. I was then to attend Crown Court all day to get a feel of how the system worked, and to watch the case I had reported on. I was assured that it would be very unlikely that I would have to go in the witness box, but it was therefore important that I left no nuance in the report that could provoke such a thing.

I sat in Hull Crown Court intently waiting for my case, chatting to Social Workers and Solicitors, and felt very relaxed in this environment. The case before mine changed all that. After lunch there was a new judge who seemed to be impatient on the speed of proceedings, and I was told they wanted to get off to the Golf Course to get a round in before darkness fell. However, he was in no rush in the preceding case as after reading all the reports he asked that the author of the Social Enquiry Report take the witness stand.

A small panicked stricken female Probation Officer scuttled into the witness stand, trying to arrange their paperwork in order but obviously failing by the nerves generated by the shock of being called. The Judge proceeded to take the report apart verbally, piece by piece leaving the probation officer close to tears. It might have been better for him to have ripped it up and thrown it at her, as this wouldn't have taken very long, but his forensic dissection of her analysis and recommendations lay like confetti slowly falling over her during her public and professional humiliation that lasted a good ten minutes.

I was next, and I considered running out of the Court, or refusing to acknowledge who I was, or claiming I had left the building. Before I had time to assess what I could do, I was pleased that after reading my report he thankfully did not comment at all.

I enjoyed the eight weeks at Barnardo's, there was a great banter and one of the administrators kept a book of odds for custody or non-custody which we could all bet on after reading each case.

Part of my placement was to undertake some shifts at a Children's Care Home called Sutton Place. Arriving at this secure Care Home I was introduced to the staff including the manager, who would go on to become a County Counsellor. This was a real change of gear, there was a sinister atmosphere in this large building which I assumed was normal for such a place, and it was not long before the deeply disturbed children sounded me out, with one youth who I will call Ian, asked if I was going to visit him during the night. At the time I assumed this was a ploy to get under my skin, and to test my resolve. Later he was extremely aggressive with me without any provocation or reason but I managed to bring him around and develop a decent understanding. These children were all disturbed but I had an intuition that there was something else wrong here.

I was only to do three-night shifts over two weeks, all together to keep my hypothalamus in check. I chose to have these at the end of this two-week placement within a placement. On my last night the fire alarms went off late in the evening, which were wired directly to the local Fire Brigade. It was a deliberate false alarm but we were unable to stop the Fire Brigade arriving and checking things through. About an hour later it happened again, this time the children evacuated properly, but once again it was a false alarm. The disgruntled fire brigade was less polite this time and suggested we get the alarms checked out. Both alarms had shown up as coming from the girl's dormitory but there was no obvious fault.

Just as we thought the night was slipping into a natural slumber, the alarms went off again, and I strolled up the stairs to oversee another tiresome full evacuation again. The boys needed no prompting, but this time they were shouting "Fire", "Fire" and as if I was reading the script from a Faulty Towers episode I stated, "there's no fire," but as they screamed back in unmistakable terror, I realised they were not making it up. I noticed the hallway was filling up with thick black toxic smelling smoke from under the girl's dormitory door with an accompanying flickering light.

I froze, I was stuck between opening the dormitory door, understanding that this could be extremely dangerous and spread the fire, and the very real danger the girls were in. Experienced staff took the decision for me and tried to open the bedroom door, but it became obvious that it had been obstructed on the inside, and probably on purpose.

All four of us shouldered the door and managed to slide the barricade made up of furniture over to supply enough room to squeeze in. We agreed to go in with nose to the floor and form a chain to which I was at the rear. This was never going to work unless the girls reconsidered about committing the most atrocious and horrific method of suicide imaginable, and fortunately one did, followed by another. As the barricades were pushed further adrift and I could see through the thick smoke that they had lit a bonfire of so-called flame-retardant furniture which was burning ferociously and the flames were now running across the ceiling in a backdraft. My head was burning, my eyes streaming, and I was relieved to see one of my brave colleagues unceremoniously grab up the last girl and drag her out to the hallway.

Soon after, the Fire Brigade arrived and spent the good part of an hour hosing down the dormitory, while we sat shell shocked overseeing the eight children in our care and pondering how close we came to someone dying.

The boys were returned to their dormitory and the girls were placed in the lounge under constant watch until first light, when the first of the vehicles would re-locate them. It was an awfully long night, and it was only at sunrise that I remembered that this morning I was supposed to prepare for the visit of my tutor from the College to assess my placement performance and learning. I had learned a lot.

After the Girls had been re-located, my tutor arrived horrified by the tale of the night before, but still had the good sense of humour to open my tutorial with "So Ray, how do you think things have gone?" Brushing away the fire grime from my face, smelling profusely of stale smoke, and looking like a badly put together Guy on the morning of 6th November, I replied "I've had better nights."

I learned a great deal at Ilkley, but perhaps the most overriding life enhancing thing I took away from there was a real insight into my own attitudes to race and discrimination. Our class spent many hours debating issues around discrimination, particularly around racism, with the insight of a diverse group of students and a safe but challenging environment I managed to at least loosen the shackles of white privilege and become a member of the whole human race.

I qualified as a youth and community worker and was proud that my mum and dad attended the award ceremony in Bradford, I now had a level four qualification and the ability to earn a decent salary for the first time since leaving Maggs, Edwards & Sharp six years before.

On 15th April 1989, I sat down to watch on TV the FA Cup Semi Final between Liverpool and Nottingham Forest being played at neutral Hillsborough. I was initially impressed how many fans they seemed to have managed to pack into the stadium, and then flashed back to my recent experience of being seriously squashed in the Lepping lane end. Even from the TV gantry view it looked very uncomfortable. The game was abandoned and then it gradually became obvious that fans had been crushed and many appeared to have died.

My thoughts turned to my very frightening experience there just a few years ago and could easily imagine how awful this situation was becoming. Much has been written about the Hillsborough genocide, and anyone who has followed the narrative will understand that this was and remains a significant stain on our coronary justice system, with essentially a state sponsored cover up of some of the facts to protect the culpable which remain still to this day. Think Hillsborough, think injustice.

Returning to Hull I was quickly able to secure some job interviews and after interviews I had a choice of two offers but chose to start work with the Hull Liberty Trust, financed by Stonham Housing Association who had a twin ex-offender hostel on Westbourne Avenue just a few minutes' walk away from my new home.

My association with the Warren was now over, Chris Fleming had started his own management training company and Keith Russell had become the new Centre Coordinator having given up his seat on Hull City Council. The Warren had also moved premises out of Alfred Gelder Street into Queens Dock Avenue nearby where it still operates as a youth project much valued by the local community. I no longer felt welcome with most of my friends having moved on.

The Warren had given me so much, and I in return had given it years of free service, but I cherish the memories, the things I learned, and the people who made it such a brilliant place to work.

Paul Heaton had formed a new band the Beautiful South and released their first album *Welcome to The Beautiful South* in October 1989 which was very successful with two top ten hits, *You Keep it all* In and *Song for Whoever*.

One Sunday he rushed back to Hull to play Football, and still without a driving licence Paul invited me to drive him to Bristol to re-join the bands national tour. This was my first experience of touring and I was in for a shock. Unlimited alcohol and anything else to get you high was available. I found the experience profound, such adulation bestowed on my old friend was exhilarating, but I was also ashamedly a little jealous of all the attention he received. It was an extraordinary night, and an insight into a different world.

I had already started a new job at Liberty Trust, on the same day as Sandra Broughton in two new identical rolls as Project Workers, under the watchful eyes of Dick and Elaine Pooley.

The two hostels owned by Stonham Housing Association, were divided by a drive. Together they had room for just over twenty ex-offenders, with two large industrial shared kitchens, two long gardens. The two lounges were luxurious, extraordinarily equipped with the most expensive furnishing imaginable and giant-sized cable linked colour TV's. There was also a sleep-in room for night shifts, and a small flat at the back which housed the Pooley Family with their two sons Timothy and Simon.

Elaine Pooley was a strong, large, well-mannered woman who had an authority and purpose that was at first unnerving, but it didn't take long for her sensitive side to materialise. Dick I initially found frightening. Although short in stature, and mature in age, he had looked as if he could rip your head off with his bare hands if you so much as looked at him the wrong way. This is what years of Prison can do to a man, as he had spent most of his life incarcerated at her majesties pleasure. He met his wife to be on visits, and he attributes her love and support for turning his life around. Upon leaving HMP Dartmoor he set up home in Hull with Elaine and started to allow former inmate friends to stay with them upon release to help them get themselves on their feet.

A point was reached when things become too much, and at some stage, a Housing Association offered to buy some property, and the Probation Service agreed to fund the running of a small ex-offender temporary home in Westbourne, run by Dick and Elaine. It had now grown to include the neighbouring house, and it was now that they felt the need to employ staff.

Once you had earned Dick and Elaine's trust, which was not readily given, they were very warm and generous people. Dick was like a dynamo, despite being a pensioner, he was making up for lost time, and nothing could be done fast enough.

He also ran the Hull Liberty Trust Furniture Project, which collected unwanted goods that were in reasonable condition, and delivered these to people in need around the City. The ex-offending residents could volunteer to drive and collect and deliver and were rewarded by having the pick of furniture when they moved out into their own place. Due to the recession, Associated British Ports kindly donated an unused warehouse on the docks rent free which was an Aladdin's cave of junk and second-hand sofas, beds, wardrobes, chests of drawers, standing lamps, TV's, washing machines, cookers and just about anything you could or could not imagine people might give away.

New health and safety legislation killed off the project as it became illegal to provide second hand electricals, but over the many years of operation over a quarter of a million items must have been distributed to families in the City, which statistically means that everyone living in Hull received at least one item from the Liberty Trust over its years of operation, and as far as I am aware none of the furniture donated or distributed ever caused an accident.

The one down-side of the establishment was that if residents were not on the van that day there was not much else to occupy their time, but we supplied an invaluable service to the Probation and Courts services. One of my roles was to assess suitability of applicants currently in Prison, and so I undertook many professional visits in various establishments throughout Yorkshire and Humberside.

This was a very unorthodox but innovative project that ran two oxymoron reputations, we were either viewed as saviours of the poor, or a cover for unspeakable crimes.

There was no doubt in anyone's mind that a lot of expensive items did not reach their intended destination, and the practice of elderly people hiding their savings taped to the bottom of their furniture was common, but of course when they passed, this ended up back at the warehouse and no doubt it was often re-cycled in the local pubs that night.

However, the obvious risks of using former prisoners, many convicted for theft and burglary, was obvious to all, but some in Authority believed that Dick was Fagin rather than Robin Hood.

The one area I was certainly uncomfortable with was on advice I never looked up resident's offences until I had got to know them, and I became aware quickly that one of the houses had several what were referred to in those days as Schedule 1 offenders, or people who had committed sexual crimes of rape, assault, and paedophilia.

This was a very well-guarded secret from the local community, and we were the only move-on route for people who had committed these types of crimes, which in effect distorted the proportion of high-risk re-offending we were taking. In hindsight we should have spotted that by unwittingly concentrating likeminded sexual predators, we could worsen their behaviour.

Early one morning a Resident told me the Police were here. This was not unusual as we cooperated all the time with them and they often just popped in for local intelligence. This time however it was a large group of CID and Stonham Regional Staff. Dick, Elaine and their sons Timothy and Simon had just gone on holiday and effectively left me charge with Sandra.

I was told that they were investigation sexual abuse in the project and that staff, including me were suspects. I was then interviewed by Stonham Staff who explained they would be managing the project, and I was to follow their instructions, and await my interview with the Police. I gathered from the line of questioning that the overall allegation was that the Pooley children, and others were being abused by Residents, and that we were not safeguarded children at the project.

I went home devastated, frightened, and sick to the stomach. Had I in some way not seen the signs. Looking back now I would never have countenanced the idea of children living on the same site as paedophiles, be it in different buildings, but I felt very naïve that I had been drawn into this working environment without consideration which I had begun to consider as normal. It wasn't.

The investigation cloud hung over the building for a few days and concluded without explanation or outcome except the

Pooley Family all moved out to their permanent home in a local village, and we converted their flat into offices and existing offices in each building back into bedroom increasing our service capacity. Strict limits on housing sex offenders we self-imposed and agreed by the authorities, but no one apologised.

To clarify, no sexual offences were uncovered, no children had been visiting sex offenders at night and the Pooley children had not been exposed to any unwanted behaviour. However, it came to pass through the Probation Service who leaked information pinpointing the source of the allegation that a prolific sexual offender, who believed paedophilia was a form of sexual orientation and should be a protected characteristic had been fantasising about the Pooley children. He then recalled them to others in a perverse game of arousal, and at some stage the difference between fantasy and reality were merged that some people believed the fantasy as real, and reported this to their respective probation officers, who then went about starting their own discreet investigation before alerting the Police to the allegations of systematic abuse behind closed doors in leafy Westbourne Avenue.

Behind the scenes this had sent a shock wave through Stonham Housing Association who were by far the largest provider of ex-offender units in the Country, and the days of Liberty Trust, run by an ex-convict were numbered despite the changes that had been made.

Amid all this turmoil, I was enjoying a great social life between the Grafton and Mainbrace pubs and occasionally the Silhouette Nightclub.

Paul was now living with a new girlfriend Gillian Mead, a seemingly frail but sensitive woman who to me resembled a very young Doris Heaton. The four of us were frequent visitors to the Jewel of Asia on Beverley Road, which became something of a bad habit for me having already had a meal at tea time, and then ploughing through a three-course meal in the early hours after a session in the Mainbrace.

Paul was aware of the stress I had been under at work and had the idea and to just go on a short holiday to Scotland in the morning. The four of us set off for Oban, then took the ferry to Tobermory and then onto the remote religious island of Iona. We stayed in Bed and Breakfasts throughout. Perhaps this was my most relaxing holiday ever, and something I needed to release all the grief I had endured at Liberty Trust.

When the Beautiful Souths second album Choke was released, they achieved their first UK number 1 single "A Little Time" penned by Paul and Dave Rotheray but sung by Briana Corrigan and Dave Hemmingway.

A bands second album is always difficult, but this was real cause for celebration and Dave ordered champagne all night at the Grafton Hotel to mark the occasion.

I made a little time myself to visit them on tour promoting the album and enjoying the riotous after parties. I was particularly partial to Belfast and Dublin nights out and would always ensure I was free from any obligations elsewhere when the dates were announced.

**PLACES WORKED**

Dudley Samuel & Harrison 11 Bruton Street Mayfair London.

Best Gibson Holdsworth St. Georges Walk Croydon.

Maggs Edwards & Sharp High Street Epsom Surrey.

The Warren Alfred Gelder Street Hull.
The Architecture Workshop entrance High St Hull.
Tilworth Grange Salthouse Road Hull.
Liberty Trust Westbourne Avenue Hull.

# OTHER PLACES

The William McCann in dry dock Hull.

Cane Hill Hospital Coulsdon and its Water Tower

The Railway Hotel Reigate, Dietkirchen Germany

# CHAPTER XVII WONDERWALL

In early 1990 Paul assembled several of his friends and their girlfriends to attend an all-day promotional filming session at a local pub called the Haworth Arms Beverley Road which at the time had a private room upstairs. He explained it was going to be a wedding reception so dress for the part but no one was getting married. Apart from the bride who was a professional actor the film crew wanted as natural event as possible to capture the mood of a real wedding, so we were plied with drinks from early in the morning until close to early the next morning.

Each of us were given small scenes to perform, mine being in a toilet washing cold water over my face to sober up, and building playing card towers. Poor Lissa was also confined to a toilet but she had to sit on hers. I was unaware that my tiny cameo in *"Let Love Speak Up Itself,"* would open things up for me in years to come. Apparently, I was told I was a natural performer and had an interesting face.

Paul Heaton had travelled to Italy many times as he had a new passion for Italian Football and had been a guest on Channel 4's Italian football magazine programme. Due to his newfound wealth, he was able to pay for me and Lissa to attend the World Cup in Italy for a week with him and his girlfriend, staying in luxury hotels and travelling by train between Turin, Verona, and Milan. We watched Brazil play Costa Rica, Belgium play Uruguay, and West Germany play Colombia.

It was a fantastic experience for which we were incredibly grateful, but I did feel uncomfortable feeling very naturally subservient to Paul due to the economic contrast, something that was missing in Scotland in the economy bed and

Breakfasts. It brought back uncomfortable memories of my days in Hill House. There was something else that was troubling me. Lissa became very cold and argumentative when we were alone and I could not believe that staying in such luxurious Italian hotels, with some single rooms larger than our flat back home, there was no romance in her. She was prickly and distant but also seemed overawed by the experience. Her head seemed turned, but it was away from me.

Back in England with an obvious friction, our German friends turned up in Hull, who were always welcome, but this time their timing was unfortunate. They sensed the issues between Lissa and me, and Germany had to Play England in the semi-final and it was not safe for our friends to watch it on a public TV so they crammed into our tiny flat as the penalty drama unfolded both parties trying to be polite while tearing our respective hair out of our heads. It was agony.

A short while after the world cup was done and dusted, Lissa felt compelled to come clean with her guilty secret and confessed that she had slept with one of my friends before we went to Italy. This was devastating and from the heights of Italia 90 I was now in an awfully bad place and sunk into a deep depression.

I moved out and used the spare sleep over room at work until I got myself sorted out.

It was not long after that we were subjected to a stringent unnotified financial audit, with Dick and Elaine's role under scrutiny, but once again despite a few book-keeping mistakes, there was nothing to show any irregularly, and we had to adhere to a few minor recommendations. They did insist however they I should not be using the sleep over room but seemed understanding that this was very temporary in the circumstances.

I got a message at work from Lissa, who said she wanted me to collect the rest of my stuff, however the truth was that she wanted to see if there was any way we could get back together and explained her part in her recent recklessness, and it appeared to be a one-off drunken moment of indiscretion much regretted by both. I had to find somewhere to live or give it another try so I did.

My salary was now enough for me to get a mortgage to buy a small house, and we moved into a two-bedroom house in Granville Avenue which sat between the Avenues area and Newland Avenue. Unfortunately, we were persuaded to take out an endowment mortgage, which was later exposed as being mis-sold. We received compensation and our mortgage was turned into a repayment one, but this unfortunately raised our cost of living. I had no plans to be a father, but it seems I was settling down. Sean Barry was born on 27th April 1994 at Hedon Road Maternity Hospital Hull. That day something changed in me, being a proud dad, I was not sure I could tolerate working with child sex offenders anymore.

Chelsea reached the Cup Final that year but were humiliated by Manchester United at Wembley. I was spending a lot of time at the Mainbrace Pub run by Martyn Goulding, who became a great friend, enhanced by our joint passion for Chelsea. I was playing Sunday league football for the Grafton Hotel Pub Team, who I also managed. I had also become good friends with Dave Rotheray who lived either in the Grafton or his adjacent house. Most weekends a large party of us would end up in Hull's nightclubs, our preferred destination being the Silhouette Club which had been set up by the gay and lesbian community.

We sometimes also attended the gothic styled Spiders nightclub which many say was the inspiration for Hull born Mick Ronson's band the Spiders, who was the very much underrated guitarist who helped David Bowie's rise to superstardom in the early seventies. Other clubs had a male predatory feel to them, but this club was also a haven for straight women who did not want to be harassed by testosterone and alcohol fuelled attention.

Dave invited me to play Squash with him, and I eventually joined the Hull & East Riding Squash Club on Chanterlands Avenue North. We were quite different players tactically but well matched and decided to play a tournament of first player to win ten matches, the looser paying for an entire night out. Interest in the Grafton intensified as things remained very equal, with many side bets being waged adding to the pressure. The night before the final game, with the score nine each, I couldn't sleep which is why I may have succumbed to lose the final match.

People were gravitating to this new exciting social scene, and one person would in time become the spark that could ignite any igneous situation that arose or created by them. Steve Clark from Sheffield arrived on the scene, a short man with a shorter fuse. If you needed a definition of small man syndrome, then Steve Clark would be the example I would offer up. Just over five feet tall, he was introduced to me as Sparky and in early days was good fun, but his mood could turn in an instant, reminiscent of the famous Joe Pesci scene in Goodfella's, only Sparky would only say he was joking if he felt he needed to back down.

He was invited, or he invited himself, onto Beautiful South tours, and from the outset seemed happy to intimidate anyone who he felt had rubbed him up the wrong way, or publicly insulted him. His attitude to women was one of possession, conquest or bellicosity, and his attitude to Briana Corrigan was undermining at best and aggressively hostile as worst. Although Briana never to my knowledge said she left the band due to Sparky, I certainly know he was not an advertisement for staying around.

I had concerns when he started to see one of Lissa's new friends Helen Kirk, a blonde bright girl who was full of fun and was enjoying life to the full. It became clear that after a while Helen wanted out but was afraid to break free, feeling that she would be the one isolated from her group of friends as everyone feared Sparky.

Things were brought to a head when Lissa and a friend called Alison were with Helen offering support, when Sparky tried to fight his way into Helen's home in a very violent and intimidating way, and in doing so assaulted Lissa.. It became obvious that this should have been a police matter, but Helen did not want to involve them.

The next time I bumped into Sparky he blanked me at first, and then tried to dig me out, saying I had been saying things behind his back which I would not to his face. All the time he was swinging a small weapon about with intent. It was now or never, so I told him straight, whatever your problems are with Helen is your business, but you do not touch my girlfriends or any of her friends again. He was not used to confrontation but his reaction was to launch an attack, which found him on the floor screaming while I held him down, he spat, *"I only need one chance to get you, and I will."*

Holding him down, I said something like same mistake will end in the same outcome, only each time you come for me the consequences will be worse for you. If you are wise, you will go home, pack and catch the next train back to Sheffield.

His humiliation was public, and his aura of fear was broken, and it was not long before he left our social scene and then moved out of Hull. Whatever reason Briana Corrigan left the band, Sparky's departure had come too late.

I had toured with the Beautiful South across England, Scotland, and Ireland whenever I could, usually at my own expense but being able to crash in various hotel rooms that were often vacant due to overbooking, and crew members returning to their families occasionally when reasonably local. This became a very hedonistic lifestyle in stark contrast of the conformity of my work supporting the criminal justice system.

Back in the summer of 1991 I had driven Paul back from Sherdley Park in St Helens where the band had played the day before. We had attended a Party after the gig, and Paul talked endlessly about a girl singer he had listened to while I was very much incapacitated through over indulgence, unconscious and out of ear shot, I had missed her impromptu shy performance. Although an amateur, Paul was excited about her voice but was unaware of who she was. After Brianna left the band, Paul managed to track her down with the aid of a local friend in St. Helens to a mini mart. She was then invited down to Westside Studios, and Jacqui Abbott replaced Brianna as the female vocalist.

The Beautiful South's popularity and longevity were in decline towards the end of 1994. In the Autumn of 1995 Paul asked me to do another video with him on the Yorkshire Moors, where we had enjoyed one of our first outings as unemployed youths with the Warren. They were going to release a best of album, usually the death toll of a band in decline. I caught the crew bus out of Hull in the early hours and headed for the Lion Inn on Blakey Road. This Inn was a stopover place in our tour of England and Scotland with our German friends. It was also made famous by a double-glazing advert. The isolated pub is surrounded by mile upon mile of windswept moorlands. To my mock surprise the bar was open for us at 8am.

I was unaware at this stage that the storyboard was essentially just Paul and I in a taxi and when the crew were ready, we took our places having sunk a few pints with the blessing of the Crew, because we were supposed to be returning from a great night out. I had become a little self-conscious as a few weeks ago, I had woken up with a stinging hangover, only to find on soothing my head that all my hair was gone, or at least shaved down to a few millimetres. It took me a while to remember the day and night before when our friend big Kevin Warcup decided he was getting a crew cut during our drinking session and for a laugh we went to watch the carnage, only due to intoxication and a sense of bravado all took the chair, and four of us were simultaneously cropped. When I returned to work on the Monday, Dick Pooley's response was "you look like a fucking convict."

No acting was required, I was just playing me, and as we were towed around every part of the Yorkshire Moors, I did not expect this additional *"One Last Love Song,"* to get any significant airtime, but I really enjoyed the day. My only instruction was not to look in the camera, which was difficult given its remarkably proximity, with the camera protruding from the replaced driver seat. We filmed passed sundown, with different people taking turns in the towed Taxi, while Paul and I topped up our liquid refreshments, when the video appeared on a Saturday morning programme for a celebrity review, the accomplished BBC journalist Michael Burk commented that the fellow next to Paul looked legless. He had obviously not lost his journalistic observational skills.

Against everyone's expectations the Best of album went to number one in the charts, and our video was playing everywhere you looked, and I was starting to get recognised. However, as I parked up my rusting car close to my home on Reynoldson Street, a woman scoffed at me with distain saying, "with all your money you'd think you would buy a better car."

It had not occurred to me that people would now think I was rich, and not that I had given my time voluntarily. Paul had treated me so often this was not a subject for discussion, and to be honest the video production company were paid to make the video and paying for performances was up to them.

The success of the Album pushed the band up a level, and the future looked bright for everyone associated with the business. I received a VHS version from the production company with a note from a West End Casting Director suggesting I give her a call as she believed I could find a lot of work in the industry because I had an interesting face and was obviously at ease in front of a camera.

In contrast, I was offered and accepted a short secondment in Scunthorpe to manage a small home called Foxton House for people with drug dependencies. In hindsight I believe this was the regional mangers idea to try and isolate and expose Dick and Elaine as senior management had seen too much smoke and assumed that their reputation could get burned. Had Dick not had a criminal record, which was now very historic and no longer pertinent, and had been a middle class academic then things would have been undoubtedly ended up differently, as Dick was a victim of the severe prejudices afforded ex-offenders by the very organisation that were publicly decrying such discrimination.

My reputation was also suffering in Scunthorpe. A resident asked me if I had a petrol can in my car as he had run out of petrol in the town centre. My first suspicious thought was what did he really want with petrol, as I had an inkling that he had previous offences for recreational arson, so thinking quickly, or not as the case turned out, I went with him to check out his story. After putting a litre of petrol into my can at the local garage we approached his car and it was then that I noticed that he did not use a key to open the petrol flap, and the car had been left unlocked.

Without warning the police sprung their trap, I was under arrest on suspicion of car theft and was explaining myself down at the Police Station who released me having been in custody for over an hour.

Foxton House was managed by a committee, on agency management terms with Stonham, just as the Liberty Trust was and there was a direction of travel with the Housing Association to standardise processes and this would involve changing the relationships of projects and bringing them in house under direct management control. When it became clear to me that Foxton House Committee members did not support the introduction of the required measures for Stonham Housing Association to comply with Housing Corporation's Key Lines of Enquiry standards, I reported this and my secondment was brought to an abrupt end.

Back at Liberty Trust we had had some changes of staff over the years, and a new brash Richard McKinnon became a Project Worker. Even though I never gave him my address, he turned up at my new house to lend me a hired copy of the Lion King so that my newly born son could watch it. He's father was a Director for another Housing Association. What I did not realise about Richard was that he was close Stonham's new Regional Manager Sandy Smith, something he never disclosed.

It was not long before Stonham made their move to centralise their activities, but with the Liberty Trust, which was unique in being set up from scratch by the Pooley's, they knew they would have a battle on their hands.

Dick was actively looking for ways to become completely independent but Stonham had the freehold of both properties so he grew increasingly frustrated.

It felt like we were just waiting for Stonham to pull the plug or take over the project. When it came in late 1995 it was swift, Dick and Elaine were suspended from duty, and a new manager was imposed over me. I put in a formal complaint that I as Deputy under my contract of employment I should be acting up in these circumstances but this obviously didn't fit their strategy of searching for anything, they could terminate the contracts of Dick and Elaine.

Similar things were happening around the region and having discussed this with my trade union we organised a joint meeting of project leaders in Scunthorpe to discuss what was going on. After a frank and honest dialogue, it was clear that Sandy Smith's role was to clean out all staff who were not in favour of transferring their contract and allegiance to Stonham from the respective agencies we all worked for.

At the time Oasis spell binding *Wonderwall* was being played everywhere, and some of the lyrics became my personal anthem. *Today is gonna be the day, that they're gonna throw it back to you, by now you should've somehow, realized what you gotta do.* The song is about an imaginary friend stepping in to save someone in difficulty, and it was very apt at this anxious time.

A couple of days after this meeting I was summoned to Leeds to face a disciplinary investigation meeting into harassment of Sandy Smith on the grounds of her gender and sexual orientation. Due to the absurdity this was later redrafted as simply harassment. Not understanding the bigger picture, and following what we agreed at the meeting, I denied any knowledge of it, only to be found out by the intervention of Richard McKinnon being a star witness for the prosecution. I had forgotten I told him I was on my way out to meet other project Leaders, and he had taken no time in ensuring Sandy Smith and senior management were aware, so I fell straight into their trap.

I do not recall anything at the Scunthorpe meeting that could be construed as harassment, but the denial of the meeting by the attendees, and the fact that Sandy Smith's role was not popular, and people feared coming under Stonham direct management, there was enough evidence to secure gross misconduct  charges for all that attended.

Losing this income meant paying my mortgage was obviously going to be exceedingly difficult, and we thought long and hard about what we could do. Sean was just two years old, but I was not comfortable for him attending the local primary school, as John Wonacott my Green Party friend, had painted a very bleak picture of the poor standards of education there, and we were considering a range of options. I decided to call the Casting Director and she gave me some contacts in the industry and I decided that given the circumstances I should take a chance on a new career back home in the beautiful south.

I decided to appeal my dismissal at Stonham, not because I felt I had a chance of re-instatement, but because they would pay my fares to London, I could see my parents and offload some large items for our move south and meet up with Paul who was performing on Top of the Pops at Elstree Studios. He arranged for my pass and we met in the canteen. While waiting the young actor Paul Reynolds introduced himself having recognised me from the video and then delighted in telling me all about his recent role with Christopher Eccleston in the 1991 film release *Let Him Have It* which I remembered well. He also told me about the children's TV programme Press gang for which they received a BAFTA which co-starred Dexter Fletcher and Julia Sawalha, who's sister Nadia I would later work with.

However, it was clear his career had apparently peaked, which concerned me as I was gambling my life on the impact of a short pop video, and this guy couldn't find much work after appearing in a major successful movie. This was also my first experience of entertainment one-upmanship where the not so successful try to make themselves feel successful by bragging about the roles they have done and have been promised in the future. This would become a mainstay of my life for the next six years.

Top of the Pops was a disappointment, the studio was tiny, and the crew did not seem genuinely nice to the teenagers who have queued expectantly outside for many hours and of course everyone was miming, but it was nice to meet some of the other stars. Along one of the corridors there were what looked like the remains of pornographic images stuck high up on walls. I was told that another band had stuck them up as they displayed photoshopped images of the Spice Girls who were performing in the studio. Snoop Dog the rapper managed to maintain his super coolness even in this environment, which is more than can be said for the obviously offended scary spice.

I was yet to know it that I would attend these studios many times over a few years as this was the home of the set of Albert Square for the BBC's EastEnders.

# CHAPTER XVII MISSING

Moving back into my parents' home in Nutfield Road Coulsdon, some thirteen years after leaving the roost was a difficult transition, but my mum had the chance to become a mum again with little Sean, and my retired dad was happy to have more people to talk to and help around the house. This was a temporary arrangement until we could find our own place, which needed to be close enough to my parents for any babysitting duties, and close to a station that could get you into London quickly.

I had hardly unpacked when an agent rang to offer me a driving job in the ITV production of The Knock. I was unaware at the time that my friend Chris Lang was formerly one of the writers for this production.

This was my first paid job as a jobbing actor, but I had failed to understand the nature of my role. I was ill prepared for this cutthroat industry where you were the commodity, and you could be treated like a star one day, and a peasant the next depending on your importance to the production at hand.

I spent the day driving around a deserted Woolwich multi story car park having set of from home incredibly early to arrive for my call time of 6am. I was almost late as I took a wrong turn as I approached Woolwich and became very anxious that I might be late, a sin that I was told could lose you a day's work.

We filmed into the night, and my driving colleagues rubbed their hands together as the overtime clock kicked in which significantly raised the pay. I was a good driver and this was quite easy money and I drove home in the late hours exhausted but knowing that my Self-Employed status had got off to a very quick start. However, from the long conversations I had with my fellow performers, it seemed that they were doing this work for a hobby, for extra pocket money.

When I explained I was with Lee's People they explained he has a huge book and is renowned for making a profit from your casting picture you pay for, then gives you one day's work, and then you can sit around for months on your backside, unless you are one of his favourites. The first doubt materialised that I may have misunderstood the note from the Casting Director.

As asked, I checked in with the Agent every week, but I was not offered anything, and each day that passed the advice to find different agents became increasingly the obvious thing to do.

Paul had sent me his new album "Blue is the Colour" which I at once warmed to given it had the same title of the cheesy Chelsea FC song.

*Rotterdam* had already charted well, and although I liked the music the Beautiful South had produced so far, this album made me a genuine fan which I still rate as Paul's finest work, giving due credit to his co-writing partner Dave Rotheray.

I received a phone call from Eddie Singleton, who had become a friend after he moved to Hull, a worldly Scouser from Kirby who had a sharp wit, was genuinely warm and had been genuine fun to be with. He was an ex-boxer, but not as successful as his older brother Joey, who won the British light-welterweight title in 1974 and after two successful defences, lost it to Dave Boy Green in 1976 at the Royal Albert Hall.

We had previously travelled together for a Liverpool Chelsea game at Anfield, and just for laughs, and a dare we swapped tickets, so Eddie watched the game amongst the Chelsea faithful, and I stood on the Kop.

Eddie had had an accident for which he was compensated which he invested in attending a private film school, but his career had floundered and was looking around for projects. The band agreed he could produce some work for a backdrop for the forthcoming Beautiful South Tour and they paid him handsomely in advance to cover his expenses.

Eddie was calling me to ask if I was free to do some acting in Leeds to help him out. Being a close friend, we did not discuss money and I set off for the location at Original Oak Pub in

Headingly which had been taken over by our good friend Martyn Goulding after leaving the Mainbrace Pub in Hull behind.

It didn't go well, Eddie was a crew of one, trying to set up, direct, and film was not ideal, and he had asked friends to perform who were less than professional, and only came for the free bar promised. I also noted for the first time that his habit of tucking one arm away was to hide his disability, having had a hand amputated. I noted our mutual friend's lyrics to a track off the Blue is the Colour album. *The Sound of North America* had these words "*You can fight with anybody with a glimmer of a chance, but god help the boxer with no hands.*"

Being the only professional in the room, be it that I was still very new to the industry, I helped where I could. I have always had an interest in film production, and this was an ideal time to learn. I considered that knowing more about what goes on behind the camera was important to understand what to do in front of one.

Eddie managed to shoot some scenes of us propping up the bar, but it took the best part of the day, and his cast were becoming increasingly the worst for wear, and with it so was Eddie's irritation. I had never experienced this in him before. We stayed the night, and in the morning, Eddie persuaded me to spend some time with him to help him shoot some more scenes.

I cleared it with Lissa, who was not happy being stuck with my parents without me, but I explained it was work and if an agent rang, I would ensure I could get back. As it happens no agent rang, and days of filming turned into weeks.

From the outset, Eddie never shared his plans, he had a rough idea in his head what he wanted to film but it was chaotic. I understood from being on professional sets how much work and how many people were involved in the logistics to produce just a few minutes of footage, Eddie had been commissioned to provided footage for only about twenty minutes and with all his technical know how he had almost zero artistic imagination, or organisational ability.

We hired a car, loaded the blonds and red heads, tripod, camera, lenses, film rolls, the jells, clapperboard, so that the back wheels sunk to the floor and we set of with a vague plan, no storyboard or even treatment. The only plan shared was me being filmed in various well-known locations around the UK which could excite a local following during the tour. The locations creating the interest not unknown me. After a week travelling around different sites with a short film of me running about wearing the same coat, we stopped in cheap Bed and Breakfasts, or with friends, and covered the mainland of the British Isles.

What Eddie was essentially trying to do was to produce four pop videos for *Rotterdam*, *Liars Bar*, *Have Fun* and their cover of Fred Neil's, *Everybody's Talkin'* which featured in the1969 film Midnight Cowboy. After a week, in my opinion we had about a minute of usable but boring material, and perhaps enough to be the spine of Liars Bar filmed at the Original Oak.

I did make what I thought were some helpful suggestions, but they were shrugged off, this was Eddie's project and he made it clear this was not a collaboration, I was just here to aid him. Towards the end of week two, things had not improved, and it was unclear if it was possible to produce anything of use for the Concerts which were getting ever closer, and post-production would also take up a lot of time especially given the chaotic nature of the filming.

In a panic Eddie drove us to his sisters' home in Kirby where we stayed a few nights and hired a small studio. He had the promising idea of using toys and models for some scenes for Rotterdam, and we shopped for our models Barbie, Ken, and a pink toy car accessory, and I helped him build some background scenery and we started to get somewhere, and he started begrudgingly listening to my suggestions.

For three days we worked night and day, and finally had something reasonable in the can, but we were still too far short of what was needed. Eddie was not pleasant to work for or with, he was quick to temper, and snappy. His humour and good nature only returning when we were no longer working and relaxing.

Everything but The Girl named themselves after the strapline of a Hull Furniture shop called Turners, and they had *Missing* on a regular air play on the radio, which was a constant reminder I had gone missing from my family. We agreed that I should go home to Surrey for a couple of days, which gave me time to unwind and apologise profusely to my Parents and Lissa for going astray for so long, but they understood I was working, and I argued it was better than waiting by the phone which had still not delivered any positive calls from agents.

The two days back home gave me time to reflect, and I used what little knowledge I had of storyboarding and came up with an idea for *Everybody's Talking*. Listening to the song and lyrics I mapped out the story of a young homeless man in Hull walking the streets feeling excluded, and mirroring scenes from Midnight Cowboy.

So, I went to work designing a series of shots mirroring the same scenes I watched repeatedly from the film and then choosing similar locations around the City of Hull which I knew so well. Furthermore, I had it planned in such a way, that it could all be shot in one day. When Eddie returned to pick me up, I showed him my work which he at first dismissed out of hand, but the pressure of time convinced him to try it as he still had not produced an effective plan of filming for the massive gaps that remained. I had also storyboarded *Have Fun* but I kept this back and time ran out to put this into action.

We found our young pretty man in Steve Hind, a regular at the Mainbrace Pub and convinced him of his future stardom. He even had a cowboy style jacket and boots and we bought him a cowboy hat to match and took him out on location. The first shot was for Steve to walk through Victoria square which was renowned for pigeons, the idea that he would stir them into flight, giving us a long-drawn-out slow-motion scene as they flew away from him paralleling his homeless existence of repellent isolation.

We were not recording any sound so we could speak as we shot, but rather than give a hand signal to Steve, he shouted across the square, which meant the pigeons were already off before he could start his walk. We tried it again but this time there were too few pigeons.

I could not have produced anything without Eddies encyclopaedic technical knowledge of filming, however in time Eddie passed the artistic reigns over to me, and I started to direct the shots, and we put together something passable that I was proud off. However, in hindsight had I been given some artistic control earlier instead of being used just as his assistant at his disposal, we may have produced something reasonably decent.

When the concerts came, I invited my parents to watch at the Royal Albert Hall. I had not been able to see the rushes, or the edited versions of our films in advance, but Eddie assured me they all looked good. Paul confirmed that Eddie had been paid for the production and enquired what Eddie had paid me. I explained we were still to work this out, but having spent over thirty days, or 300 hours working for with him, I felt I should be paid at least double the going rate just to have put up with him.

As the Concert unfolded, I cringed a little at *Rotterdam* and *Have Fun*, our videos were corny, but it also kept cutting out which I couldn't understand. We had also obviously shot on the wrong type of film for this size projection as it looked grainy, but I thought that might look deliberate so we might get away with it. However, every time it returned to the screen it was out of step with the lyrics. The film was either predicting or way behind the story.

When the band performed Liars Bar the images behind them got worse, it was so out of synchronisation it was almost funny, but again I hoped people wouldn't notice, but again it kept cutting out and reappearing. I went to where Eddie was sat by some controls and realised, he was struggling to keep it together. He explained we had timed all the shots to coincide with the recorded versions, but the live versions were performed at different speeds.

It was a disaster. I suggested cutting to a blank screen was worse, and just let it run out of time. He did have the ability to speed things up or slow them down, but he had got into such a flap he had become too anxious and conscious of failure he was falling apart at the seams.

I was fortunate that my baby, *Everybody's Talkin'* was performed at the same speed as the single and had no reliance on the lyrics and it looked alright in my view, even quite good from a biased position, enhanced by no intervening blank screens.

It seemed that the Royal Albert Hall was an unlucky venue for the Singleton family some twenty years apart, but my mum was full of praise, but my dad gave me a look. I could almost hear him thinking out loud "I have had to put up with a terrible two's toddler and your girlfriend for a month, for this?" I tried to pay for their taxi home, but they were always too proud to take anything off their own grown-up child.

As everyone was packing up Eddie approached me and gave me an envelope of cash, which I stuck in my pocket, and at a discreet moment I took a sneak peek. It contained ten £20 notes. I quickly worked out my worth, excluding being away from home every night. I worked around thirty ten-hour workdays, which meant I was valued at around 66p per hour.

In his defence, he had paid for my accommodation, and meals from his budget, which amounted to about a £1000 given we shared a room. I later asked Paul what Eddie had been paid and it was an astonishing £10'000. I could tell Paul was not happy with the work but he knew I had sacrificed a great deal to help Eddie, so he refrained from critiquing our work too much. When I got home, I worked out our rough costs. He had hired his film school's equipment at a nominal rate of a few hundred pounds, shared a room with me when we had no one free to stay with, and not paid anyone else except for a few drinks in Leeds. With the hire car and petrol, he had paid himself well over £7000 and chose to share less than four percent with me.

I was incredibly stressed out when I returned home to my parents' home and my eczema which had steadily got worse over the last week or so, became so bad that I went to the Doctors as the over-the-counter cream I bought seemed to be exacerbating it. In shock, I was diagnosed as having scabies and I was to trace everyone I had been in touch with and let them know given its high-level contagion level. I was disgusted I had brought this back to my elderly parents, my partner and child. We disinfected everything and the lotion we all had to apply was disgusting. The only place we had stayed other than hotels in the last week or so was Eddie's sisters in Kirby. So, I rang to find out and it was confirmed this was where I caught it.

I never spoke to Eddie Singleton again, and if I ever had to it would only to demand the £3'300 money owed to me and try and pass on an infection. This is the reason why I just love it when Chelsea beat Liverpool.

I had managed to rent out my House in Hull, so I started to get some income, and Lissa managed to get a job with the Probation Service, so we had an income to get a flat. This was the start of a new career for her having given up being a solo singer guitar player, or actor. We rented a top floor two-bedroom flat on the Brighton Road Purley with a London

Black Cab Driver as our landlord, who was very friendly, and allowed us use of all the garden for young Sean to play in.

# CHAPTER XVIII DON'T MARRY HER

In the late summer of 1996, I received a call from the production company who made the Video on the Yorkshire Moors, checking my availability and they also wanted Lissa, and we both jumped at the chance to perform.

I was now a Chelsea member and attending most home games. Fortunately, the two-day shoot did not overlap any matches.

Sean was packed of to my mothers, and a car was sent for us. We were chauffeured majestically through London in the early hours and arrived at a large, detached house in North London surrounded by the largest crew I had encountered so far. The song was Don't Marry Her Fuck/Have Me depending on the sensitivity of the media outlet

Although nervous for the first few shots I was given plenty of encouragement from the Director Liam. I was aware that they were under incredible pressure to get through the exceedingly long storyboard within a set time, and they were frantic in setting up each shot as quickly as they could, so for my part I wanted to ensure I became known as the one take kid.

For two days we worked from first light and into the dark evenings. Being the subject of the Video was exhausting, and the way it was shot meant that I hardly saw anyone else except Liam, Jacqui Abbott my fictional mistress, and the wardrobe and make up girls who shamelessly flirted with me until someone told them the other actress was my partner, which was a shame because I was enjoying the attention.

On the second day we were provided with stage school children to adopt, who came accompanied by their pushy

chaperone parents. I was not keen on having to play with them, and pretend they were my little cherubs, so I had to dig deep and act the part, which was after all what I was being paid for.

The money helped keep us going, and I believe the media coverage helped to get more work for me. I had a photographic shoot with Bella Magazine as a Mummies boy for an article, it was all over in a couple of hours and it paid well. If I could land this, then perhaps I could get a commercial where the real money was.

I approached two new agents, Galloways for walk on parts, and Mugshots for Character modelling, to see if I could use the momentum of the charting video to sustain a career. Galloways was everything that Lee's People were not. Gilly Moore interviewed me in depth and provided an in-depth assessment of what I could offer, and what the agency could provide.

This was far more impressive than Lee Towsey's interview, which was more of administration exercise, as he didn't care if you had talent, looked good, if you had your book fee, he was happy which is probably why he never got much work for his people, as Casting Directors needed to have superhuman powers even to pick up his casting book due to its weight and volume. I did upon his advice join the Film Artists' Association a branch of BECTU to cover walk on parts in independent television.

I was suitably impressed with Mugshots who in their offices had ample evidence of the success of their character models hung from the walls of their office in Soho. They quickly secured me some photographic commercial work for Cable and Wireless and the new TV Cable company Telewest. These shoots were full day and I had been unaware to that point how much work can go into a single frame.

In the new year things were going well, but I felt I needed a flexible back up plan to ensure we had enough income. We could survive on Lissa's income, but we both wanted much more than that. My landlord suggested I undertake the London

Knowledge as this was entirely flexible to the extent that you could pick up fares on the way back from any film set.

I undertook the necessary police checks and was interviewed at Penton Street but realising getting the full London Knowledge could take at least a couple of years, I chose to try and obtain a suburban badge first which would be much faster to achieve. To get income in, I took a job at a Private Hire company in Sutton Surrey quaintly called Kwik Kabs, signed up for the Sutton and Merton Yellow Badge.

I balanced my time between doing a little taxi work, learning the blue routes through Sutton and Merton, and doing what I loved, modelling and walk on work in the entertainment industry. My 35$^{th}$ birthday arrived, and it had become plain that my experiment was working out. I was dismayed in 1979 when Thatcherism arrived in Britain and for half my life to date the Conservatives had ruled Britain but as May 1997 arrived there was real hope on the horizon, Chelsea had reached the FA Cup Final and Labour appeared to be favourites to win the General Election. Not only that I secured tickets for my first Chelsea FA Cup final.

A week before the cup final, I travelled up to Liverpool and attended the Hillsborough Justice fundraising Concert at Anfield. As The Beautiful South were performing, we were provided with a box, and I enjoyed performances from some of my favourite bands including the Manic Street Preachers, Stereophonics, and the Lightening Seeds.

It felt like a joyful inspirational afternoon and evening, but after several speeches the horror of Hillsborough started to hit home again. When the large crowd spontaneously started chanting *"Justice Justice,"* it made me very emotional. Eight years had gone by, and those who were so obviously culpable had still not faced any justice beyond their own guilt.

I had attended the Tottenham Manchester City replay game back in 1981 when a fellow Chelsea Steward had rung me as the club had given him a bunch of their allocation away for free. Most City fans had spent everything they had on the

Saturday drawn final and simply did not havc thc funds to return. We obviously supported Manchester City standing on the terraces that night in a three-quarter filled Wembley won by the remarkable and iconic Ricky Villa winning goal.

By the time I took my nieces boyfriend Andy Watkins to Wembley, Labour had won a landslide victory and I was walking on air as the news rolled in about changes in Government direction and Chelsea's opponents were the very beatable Middlesbrough despite their international stars.

Walking up Wembley way to support your team is a rite of passage, not being able to remember the 1967 final, and been confined to watching the 1970 and 1994 finals on TV, my boyhood dream had been realised. After all the pomp and ceremony was over, the game seemed over in forty-two seconds as Roberto De Matteo opened the scoring for Chelsea, which was wrongly accredited as being the fastest Cup final goal in history, which should be acknowledged to Wednesday's Fred Spiksley in 1896, where some reports say he scored in twenty seconds against Wolves at the Crystal Palace in South London. Even Everton's Louis Saha's 2009 goal against Chelsea in twenty-five seconds could not beat that, and it didn't count for much as Chelsea beat them anyway. However, I was close to being present at the fastest goal in both World Cup and FA cup history.

Chelsea went on to win 2-0 on this magical warm May afternoon just under three weeks since John Major was evicted from 10 Downing Street.

I was developing a whole new group of friends, socialising more in London than in Coulsdon. My first attendance at Penton Street to be judged on my Knowledge was a truly frightening affair. It is run in a very militaristic and intimidating way, summoned to stand before an examiner who would not even bother to look up at you, and they would simply say something like *"take me from the Sutton Arms Public House to Thomas More Catholic School Purley."* You would then try and recall the journey road perfect, leave Sutton High Street on the left, left Carshalton Road, Forward Ruskin

Road, right Boundary Road, Left Stanley Park Road, forward Stafford Road, right Forrester Drive, right Plough Lane, left Russell Hill, left Russell Hill Road, set down on your left.

Of course, it never went that smoothly, under intense pressure you were bound to forget a road, especially when they simply changed names without you having to undertake any imaginary manoeuvre. You had to reply snappily without hesitation to pass, even getting it right was not enough, and you had five routes per test. The worst thing was that you didn't get any feedback except you had not passed, and the date of the next test which if you had done well would be shortened and if not lengthened.

As each test approached, I drove round frantically trying to cram in places of interest and on route my anxiety levels clouded my memory and cognition that I may have forgotten my own name. I felt like a sheep to the slaughter each time I went, but I did start to make progress after a few months and the tests were coming a little quicker and perhaps the yellow badge was within my clutches if I could just up my game.

The problem was that I was becoming too successful in the entertainment busy and my diary was filling up, and so my taxi work which aided my knowledge learning, was on the decline. My knowledge progress stalled, and then seemed to fall back.

Sitting in my Volvo 360glt which Martyn from Hull had sourced me for a very reasonable price I was waiting for my next fare in Sutton High Street, contemplating the best way forward. As I set of, I spotted a familiar face staring back at me from a Bus Stop advertising hoarding, then another, and then almost everywhere I drove I was confronted with images of myself smiling back at me advertising Telewest Cable Television. Perhaps this was the road sign I was looking for. This proved to be a lucrative contract, the model fee was good, but the image rights depended on usage and exposure, and I was one of four faces shown all over the metropolis. This was shortly followed by a poster campaign for Cable and Wireless.

On the Friday evening of 5th September 1997, I took a fare of four young women from their home in Sutton uptown to the Comedy Club on Oxenden Street London, and after dropping them off tried to arrange for a lucrative return pick up later in the night but without success.

There were no Satellite Navigation aids in 1997, although I did have a decent walking knowledge of Central London the one-way systems were still a curse, and I tried to navigate the local roads to head back south. I really didn't want to go down Pall Mall as this was pushing me up towards Piccadilly and I had become frustrated at my lack of competence. As I approached the junction of St James Road, I was stopped by a Policeman and I became aware that something was going on as there were TV cameras and the paparazzi all around. I could not believe my bad luck and decided when I got back to South London, I would stop for the day. Sitting there for some time at the front of a que of cars being held up some gates opened to my left and the flashing lights erupted into a frenzy.

To my astonishment a funeral parade emerged, and it quickly dawned on me this was St. James Palace, and the coffin was the recently deceased HRH The Princess of Wales, described by Prime Minister Blair as the People's Princess. Here I was live on international TV sitting in full view in my car moaning about the hold up. I felt an incredible sense of shame as I had been just as moved and angry at the nature of her divorce and death and had a black silk ribbon attached to my aerial as a mark of respect which most taxi drivers had done at the time.

Due to my earlier experiences with the security services, I had read a book before these events that chronicled alleged political assassinations by the Spooks who hide in the shadows of legality, whose gruesome trade was dressed up to be disguised as accidents or suicides. One of the methods used was to use a military flash gun weapon to blind a driver to force a hopefully fatal accident, usually in a tunnel or a wooded Country Lane. Even if Lady Diana were not pregnant with Dodi-Fayed's baby, the fact that this was a rumour, would certainly have panicked the authorities, that an heir to the throne could be of Islamic stock. For me there was a motive, and the means to carry out such a dastardly deed and perhaps one day the truth will out, as it often does.

The first assignment I had from Galloways was for a new 1997 BBC production called "*Bloomin Marvellous",* and I was to play a radio programme director. Making my way to the BBC centre at Wood Lane I really felt I had arrived giving my name in at the reception and being given a pass to the Studio.

I had not been given much information, but I was suitably wardrobed and having my makeup put on sat next to the star of the show Sarah Lancashire who was well known for being in Coronation Street for a long time but having left she was looking to expand her career and this situation comedy was the vehicle the BBC had chosen for her.

I was given a copy of the script, and after leafing through it realised, I had no lines, but had one simple prompted action, to give a thumbs up. That was it. I was disappointed. It didn't take very long to film my scene and I was finished by lunchtime. I checked in with the Assistant Director who confirmed I could go, but then said see you back here at 6pm. I looked quizzical. She explained that there was a live performance tonight in front of a studio audience.

My car was in South London, so I could not earn any money, and it would be pointless to spend money going home for a few hours which is all the time I would have so I spent hours in the BBC canteen noting the various faces of the BBC coming and going.

I had so far always been comfortable in front of a camera, but never performed in front of a live audience since my tiny part in the school play many years before. All I had to do was pretend to be directing a Radio programme, twiddling nobs, and waiting for my cue to give a big cheesy grin and a thumbs up to Sarah.

After eating and drinking my way around the vast array of BBC dishes, which would not have been out of place in the refectory of Redhill Technical College canteen, I returned to the studio nice and early and when in position I made the mistake of looking at myself in a monitor for the first time. These were usually never in a performer's eyesight but catching a glimpse of myself made me very self-conscious especially with the headphones I had to wear which made my silhouette resemble Micky Mouse.

I had not realised that my performance was not important live as they already had what they needed in the can, but as it happens everything went smoothly and I had secured my first BBC contract appearance, which was a steppingstone to getting the Holy Grail for actors, an Equity Membership Card.

I soon started clocking up my BBC air miles with a walk on part in Albert Square delivering drinks to Nadia Sawalha's Night Club. I would repeat this delivery role a couple of years later only this time to the Queen Vic'. I was very impressed with the permanent outdoor set at Elstree Studios, I had been unable to sneak a view when I attended Top of The Pops but having watched the programme when Leslie Grantham and Anita Dobson were the fulcrum of the story it felt very surreal to walk around the market.

The BBC did not waste their money, I also had to do background outside that evening. We all had a few changes of clothes so that we could pretend to be someone else or the same person on a different day. As the sun sunk behind the tall surrounding buildings on my first day of shooting, it became very cold and Queen Vic looked very inviting emanating a warm glow from the lights inside. Knowing I had a few minutes break I thought I would shelter from the chilly wind and went to go inside the Queen Vic for my first time. Only I didn't, as this was only the outer shell, the inside was half a mile away in an internal studio.

In February 1998 I had what felt like a dubious call to a church hall in Virginia Water Surrey, with no instruction on what to wear, but we were told it was for a rehearsal for Tonight at the London Palladium which had not been on TV for some time.

As we arrived there were no cameras, no lights, no trucks outside, and I became suspicious that something was not quit right here. Inside there were just a couple of young men, some kettle drums and an elderly gentleman wearing a tracksuit who greeted me very enthusiastically as if I was his friend?

Out of context it took me a few seconds to recognise it was Bruce Forsythe. I was overawed, he was a legend of Saturday night entertainment, and he was genuinely excited to see each of us as we arrived greeting each of us in turn with a clasped handshake and offering to make us all drinks.

The idea behind the day was for the four of us to test out audience participation games for the forthcoming live shows, which he was hosting to celebrate his 70th Birthday. He was thrilled to be doing it, as this was the show where it really started for him and he hadn't starred in it since 1964.

It was such a privilege to watch him, perform without effort, he had the innate ability to extract humour by embarrassing someone, without humbling them.

When it was my turn to try and bounce a tennis ball across two kettle drums and hit a cymbal placed just beyond, he accused me of cheating because I was in front of the line. Looking down I was clearly behind the line, and sensing an injustice he approached me, put his cheek to mine and compared nose sizes, joking your nose was over the line. You could not help but laugh at this self-depreciation, and his very good-natured constant mocking.

When the show was broadcast live the audience members were obviously more nervous and struggled to win, something Bruce had predicted in response to our feedback that the games were a little too easy.

My big ears also came to be of use when it was arranged for me to be an audience plant for BBC's "*They Think It's All Over*" sports quiz panel show. No one should have noticed the ploy as I was slipped into the audience que right at the front so I could get to my pre-destined seat. This was so Jonathon Ross could recognise me and then find me easily, after the audience were in place.

The game was that Gary Lineker would hide in the audience and Jonathon Ross was dispatched to find him and would deliberately venture to my seat and pick me up by my outstanding ears in error. I was not told in advance about this public humiliation so I could react accordingly. My audience neighbours felt sorry for me, but I kept the secret that I was being paid for my trouble.

Some comedies are so funny, it can be exceedingly difficult not to laugh and ruin the shot. I met Frank Kelly in the makeup room of Channel Four studios. This was a long daily endurance for him to transform into Father Jack. A young Graham Norton was also on set. I was to play, with a few colleagues a recovering alcoholic at an Alcoholics Anonymous Meeting on the Irish mainland which Father Jack was to attend in error due to his short-sightedness.

He only had five single word lines of "Drink," but the delivery was sufficiently funny to make it hard to suppress a grin at the very least, hence my hand covering my mouth in contemplation. I had not watched *Father Ted* up until that point, but I became an enthusiastic fan of the Craggy Island saga forthwith.

Tizer was rebranded with a new mascot, known "Ed the Head". Ed appeared as a red-coloured human head, the top of which was opened so that Tizer could be poured.

Throughout 1999, I was getting great exposure and income from a Tizer Ident for the Chart Show every weekend. Questioned by Ed the Head, I played a music contestant who couldn't get a simple question right and was then lambasted and advised to fill my head with Tizer.

I did a Lambton's Beer commercial in 1998 dancing an Irish heavy jigger with Neil Morrisey looking on in bewilderment, which I never saw, and the lack of repeat fee's reflected that. Fortunately, they only filmed my bottom half, so not revealing my incompetent dancing technique.

I returned to EastEnders many times doing background and walk-ons. Barbara Windsor was playing the part of the very stern Peggy Mitchell, and during a setup of an interior shot in the Queen Vic, something made her laugh, and she chuckled just like she used to in her dumb blond Carry-On days. I embarrassingly laughed out loud it was so infectious.

In 1999 arriving on the EastEnders's set one day, I discovered that Galloways had not mentioned that I had been chosen to take on an enhanced walk on role as a Brewery Delivery Driver with my colleague Xavier on a zero-hour contract, as the story line involved problems with deliveries to the Queen Vic'.

Apart from the main players, there was also a group of actors who played identifiable characters, usually as market stall holders, and we had joined their ranks. I had several simple scenes over the coming weeks with Craig Fairbrass and Mike Reid. As is customary in the industry we were never told it was our last day, and we were never called back. The reason became obvious when the storyline unfolded a month later.

Rumours were circulating that Mike Reid was demanding more money from the BBC who were not being responsive, and so he gave them an ultimatum which was rejected. Publicly he retired exhausted, but when he sadly passed on a few years later, it appeared he had debts close to a million pounds, which might explain his anxiety around income and subsequent ill-health. His demise signalled mine, as the script writers erased him, the story line, and my little role in one swift rewrite.

Every further call to the set over the next two years, which were very minimal was something of a humiliation, as they were aware that I had been seen before as an identifiable character, so I was usually limited to doing what many referred to as the walk of shame. Inside the studio walking past the Café window changing jacket and then walking back, while the crew filmed inside. Even when being a customer in the Queen Vic', an Assistant Director said I was too prominent and moved me far away into a corner. This was the first warning I had about having a little success, famous people sell things, as does the person next door, but if your face got known you could not be that person next door anymore, or famous enough to sell, and it was advertising where the money is. I was slipping through the cracks.

In 1998 I was very much aware of the issues around the murder of Stephen Lawrence five years earlier, his racist murderers were yet to be convicted. I was asked to attend an audition to be one of the perpetrators in a new docudrama, which I refused.

If I had been cast in such a role, after airing I believe it would not have been safe for me to walk the streets of South London again, although a month later I was happy to be booked in as one of a crowd of demonstrator protesting outside Hannibal House at the Elephant and Castle during a mock-up of the public enquiry.

It is somewhat healthy to vent your anger at injustice, but this was not real. It was, however, very realistic. There was no obvious barrier at times between the actors and people just going about their daily routine. It was also difficult not to hate the five poor young actors on the receiving end of a torrent of abuse, and missiles hurled towards them each time they walked up and down the ramped entrance. The actors were deliberately kept apart from us by the director to facilitate genuine anger. It is easier to bestow violence on someone you have never met.

Of course, the missiles were stage glass, or made of soft rubber, and they knew we were just playing our role. As the day progressed, I sensed that that our numbers had swelled a little, and it became clear that word had gone around that Stephen Lawrence's killers were at a fresh enquiry, and some people came down to watch or seriously have a go, and our acting colleagues only had Supporting Artists dressed as Policeman to protect them. Fortunately, if they mistook the actors for the real thing, they probably mistook the Police Uniform for the real thing.

I believe the real Police turned up in force to keep an eye on the situation, but they now ran the risk of being gently assaulted by Supporting Artists. The Directors hope of creating the tension of the real event was profoundly realised and the outcome was achieved with the recreation being difficult to distinguish from the actual news footage.

Docudramas were usually more fun, and I really enjoyed assassinating the Archbishop of Canterbury in his Cathedral, recreating my school play role almost two decades earlier. Another programme which recreated an aeroplane crash I found very harrowing. I am not a nervous flyer but sitting in an aeroplane with your seat belt on, as artificial wind and rain is sprayed past your small round window, it was hard to remember we were parked in an aeroplane museum, when they announced engine failure and to brace as we ditched into the sea.

TV Commercials pay very well, and I spent a lot of time undertaking many castings, for just about any product you can think of. Occasionally you got lucky and you face fitted, but success was more like a game of roulette with all your chips on one number, if it came in you were rewarded with four figure sums for sometimes a day's work, otherwise you just watched your chips be dragged off the table as you funded endless trips into the West End.

Acting as a bartender for a couple of days in a Greene King IPA commercial, I uncovered something of nostalgia. *Only Fools and Horses* had stopped their regular series some years ago, but they were still commissioned to do a Christmas special each year. Being a major fan, I would have loved to have participated, but was never called. Dropping a tea towel, I was using as a prop, I knelt behind the bar to pick it up and noticed in large letters, "BBC Nags Head OFAH."

My nickname of Trotsky had often been morphed into Trot, or Trotter. So, here was Ray Trotter Barry serving behind the bar of the Nags Head. Holding up the bar flap I chuckled to myself about the iconic moment David Jason fell through this gap in the Yuppy Love episode, before getting back to serving up another pint of soapy stained water for the umpteenth take.

I supplemented my income with a door-to-door delivery driver for Lynx, who had just won a contract to deliver prestigious Marks & Spencer home wear and goods. Dressed completely in a green uniform with my fellow seven green colleagues we entered the busy Lynx warehouse in Coulsdon to see how big our individual rounds were, covering all of Surrey. There were less than thirty of the distinctive green parcels in an ocean of thousands of others, and the embarrassed manager divided them up accordingly warning us not to return to the Depot before 4pm, some eight hours later. I only had three parcels which were all within a few minutes of each other, and unfortunately, we were fitted with revolutionary computer tracking equipment, the first of its kind so we had to spread delivery out to fool head office.

The next day I used Sean's old cot mattress to get some shut eye between deliveries, and one day forgot to close the side door spraying a Woking roundabout with rolling green parcels, but the job was overall very uneventful.

Although trade increased significantly it was not long before they reduced staff on the specialist contract, and I was forced to work on the usual HGV deliveries which I hated so I quit.

I got a call to Finsbury Circus to undertake what would be my last appearance in a Beautiful South promotional Video for Liars Bar. A far better version than the earlier Singleton version. I had to learn a dance routine the day before, which was not my forte. My fellow performers were all professional dancers and even though this was a supposedly easy routine I still struggled.

It didn't help that my Tramp's outfit hindered free movement, and I was tempted by Paul to have a liquid lunch, something which in my new line of work was a definite faux pa. I had convinced myself that I should be in character as a drunken street homeless loser, but the outcome was that towards the end of the shoot, I could tell the Director was not particularly happy with my performance, and that was the last time they called me, and the last time I drunk alcohol while working.

I did do a few other Pop Video's for other bands, from Genesis to Prefab Sprout, but never as a feature artist.

The Genesis pop video was flawed as they expected a group of background artists, to wear their own smart business clothes in the City of London, and repeatedly fall to a wet concrete floor as if they had been shot repeatedly all day long. Even with the introduction of knee pads it never looked remotely realistic, as this action was effectively a stunt risking significant injury, and no one was taking that chance for a couple of days background fee.

# CHAPTER XIX SEASONS IN THE SUN

Lissa wanted to buy a house, and with some manipulation of my self-employed accounts we were able to secure a mortgage for another home and keep Granville Avenue as an investment. We moved into a two-bedroom terrace house at 166 Chipstead Valley Road opposite St. Aiden's Catholic Church, about a mile from my parents and very close to Coulsdon town centre and its two railway stations. It was bright but very narrow, with a small rear garden banked up sharply for start of the valley upward slope. It was very convenient, but like Granville the front door opened into the living room which I hated.

We agreed that Lissa would pay the mortgage, which was about the same as the flat, out of her regular income from the Probation Service and my fluctuating income would support our flexible spending which included holidays abroad. The house had a great old-fashioned looking kitchen, but the rest was modern, and I felt we did well to secure if for £100'000 given this was Surrey. The mortgage in Hull had become almost insignificant through inflation, but the rental income and indeed the value of the asset steadily increased.

My income, although inconsistent averaged out rather well. I did a promotional advert for BBC's *Match of the Day* as a bored DIY shopper waiting for the football season to begin. No acting needed there. I played a robbery victim for the groundbreakingly good sketch show *Goodness Gracious Me,* and a 1960's Policeman in Sky Tv's *Good Ship Citizen.*

Sean was now attending my old Primary School, and my mum was always on hand to look after him if I was working which I was doing two or three times a week. At the time I felt guilty to impose and my mum never once complained, and in hindsight she managed to spend some really wonderful time with one of her growing number of grandchildren who she adored.

My relative success in the entertainment and advertising industry seemed to be viewed through Lissa's eyes with an element of disdain. It was ironic that early on in our relationship I was working in the criminal justice system supporting ex-offenders in the community while she was giving up her dream of becoming an actor and singer songwriter. It seemed every success I had was a tiny stab to her heart, as we had effectively switched roles, and I was doing the one she really wanted. This was somewhat muted when I secured an appearance on BBC's production of *Nicholas Nickleby* for Sean who was only three years old at the time which made us both very proud.

However, I sensed a change in her when we secured the house, she became more independent from me, and detached and the relationship started to struggle. There were no rows, or fights, but something had gone.

I tried to re-impress her, buying her a new designer suit for her Court Work, a holiday to Rhodes, but that was ruined by a heat wave. The fact I invited my sister Vivien who was now divorced, and her three young daughters on the holiday was a sign I was concerned about spending so much time together. It didn't help that to cover Viv's costs we opted for cheap accommodation which had no air conditioning and temperatures soared close to 50 degrees Celsius. The beaches burned your feet, the sea gave little chill relief, feeling more like a warm bath, and with no air conditioning, my niece Danielle become quite unwell.

I forgave the sun for ruining our holiday, but never the tabloid of the same name for their coverage of the Hillsborough disaster, and I was not told that a Commercial I had been signed up for was for the Sun Newspaper until we were part way into filming in the changing rooms at Brisbane Road, the home of Leyton Orient Football Club.

Westlife thankfully kept the awful Millennium Prayer by Cliff Richard off the number one spot for the forthcoming special New Year's Eve a cover of *Season's in the Sun,* the tune of which I was very familiar with as it was often the accompaniment to a Chelsea terrace chant relating to the cowardice and speed of retreat of other football fans. However, it took on a whole new meaning with the burial of my political principles.

The habit of going to Germany for New Year had dwindled over the years, but we realised there was no better place to see in the new millennium. Flying separately several of us met up in Dietkirchen where we celebrated a fantastic international New Millennium. I confused our hosts by setting of a Rocket at lunchtime to celebrate the new millennium in Kiribati in the pacific, and every hour through the afternoon and evening as the New Millennium in Germany and then the UK which had now caught up with the idea of fireworks for new year.

We all lost interest when New Year reached the USA due to excess alcohol, and indifference to a Country that was not particularly popular in these parts, partly due to the positioning of their nuclear weapons on German soil. It was amazing to celebrate this once in a life time new year in Dietkirchen

In the new year, an Irish girl called Elaine and I were successful in being chosen for a Courts Furniture Bank Holiday sale commercial which we understood would only be repeated for a few days, so we did not expect a big pay out. The shoot only took a few hours as we sat on beds and admired them in the usual cheesy style. What we didn't realise was until a few days before the Mayday bank holiday is that it was aired repeatedly on every commercial channel for most commercial breaks for about five days, and the money rolled in accordingly as it was shown thousands of times.

I followed this up with an inflight advert for Virgin Airlines playing a Mr Bean type character, and I assumed I was a lot cheaper than Rowan Atkinson. I also promoted the new *Elvis Presley 50 Greatest Hits* album, by miming to Suspicious Minds as I listened in on a private conversation as a BT Engineer.

*One Foot in the Grave* was one of my mum's favourite programs, and I took immense joy in telling her in 2000 I had a walk-in part pencilled in.

I was lucky to get the part as the agent for some reason thought I had a tattoo.

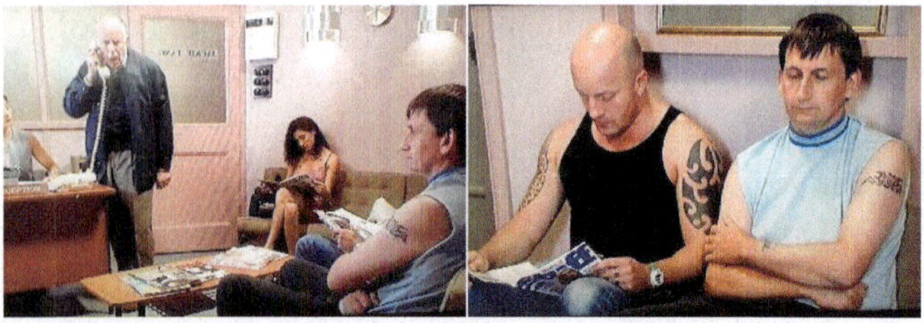

I was re-united with Xavier, who did have plenty of tattoos and an actor model who I had previously shared the Telewest adventure with. When the Assistant Director realised, I had no tattoo she said she would arrange one for this evening's filming. I have a terrible fear of needles hence my lack of tattoo's and when I started to turn white, she added don't worry it will wash off.

This again was filmed in front of a live audience, and it was easy just sitting in a Tattoo Artists waiting room flicking through magazines, while Richard Wilson went into character having a meltdown realising, he had sent Jean Warboys, played by Doreen Mantle, to get a tattoo of her teeth.

My mum also loved *As Times Goes By* but when I got the call for this it was very much forgettable background work. I did other live studio audience comedies such as BBC's "*Gimmie Gimmie Gimmie*," starring Kathy Burke, but mostly in a strictly background capacity.

Having briefly met Graham Norton in 1998 filming Father Ted, he was now an up-and-coming talent with his new TV show *So Graham Norton.* I was cast for an opening credit scene as a pall bearer who would drop our coffin to rush home to watch the Irish Comedians new chat show.

Having auditioned for an Ident for Guinness for the forthcoming televised Rugby World Cup to be held across the United Kingdom and France, I was excited to get the call and made my way to Twickenham for filming. The audition involved drinking Guinness and then being lifted from my seat by other surrounding spectators and catching a rugby ball.

When I arrived, I realised that this was a large call, with a lot of background booked to fill in the surrounding seats for a wide shot. I had developed a friendly rivalry with a colleague who had similar attributes to me, and we therefore competed for many modelling and TV contracts, so I thought I would rub it in that I was the feature artist today, so I asked him if he knew who the feature artist was, and he replied "me."

I laughed and said so you know it's me then. He looked genuinely surprised and said very earnestly no, it really is me. The agent had neglected to tell me I had been booked for background, and I had kept this date free prioritising it over other less lucrative work offered. It was funny, but my nose was firmly out of joint, and my expected four figure earnings shrunk with my ego down to a few hundred pounds.

Some days you would be treated like a VIP, and the next like a servant, or worse, depending on your status on set. Doing background for a Tesco's commercial I went to collect some Tea's and Coffee's during a break and found Prunella Scales just finishing a telephone conversation on her mobile phone by the tea urn. She then stood in silence as if she was waiting for someone or something. This made me feel a touch uncomfortable, so I broke the silence and offered to make her a drink. She turned to check who had asked then ignored me as if I did not exist. As I continued to get the order in for my colleagues a female Assistant Director came into the room, to check on her. She demanded a tea as if it was her birth right. I wasn't even good enough to be her servant.

For Christmas 2001 I secured a lucrative deal advertising MacDonald's, although I was unclear how decorating a Christmas Tree with no trousers on fitted into their campaign to persuade people to eat more junk food.

An ad, for the Gold sub-brand of Kingsmill Bread, was apparently successful as it was apparently recalled by 55% of consumers in a survey. Starring Mel Giedroyc and Sue Perkins as Bakers, who are extolling the virtues of their 'home-made' bread to their customers while almost being rumbled by my arrival to deliver a full load of Kingsmill Bread which is thwarted at the door. It was the first time I had worked with this pair and found them naturally amusing. This advert was repeated extensively, and their gentle humour and good nature sold a lot of bread and earned us all a lot of dough.

Paul's record company were going from strength to strength with their new soulful artist Gabrielle who reached number 1 in the charts with *"Rise."* I felt my career was also heading that way.

I became the mastermind of an attempted £350'000 jewellery heist, an exceptionally large step up from my antics in Redhill Technical College. Fortunately, this was for a BBC docudrama on the attempt to burgle the Millennium Dome exhibition in November 2001

You never knew what you were up against when you arrived on a set, which made it a little exciting at times. I really enjoyed playing a football hooligan in the Bill, throwing rubber bricks, and mock fighting was a fantastic way to spend your day and get paid. At lunch time I spoke to the Assistant Director and said their scene was very unrealistic, and when they asked why I explained that I had been in the middle of these types of events when I followed Chelsea for years. Without any acknowledgement or a thank you new direction was given which fitted with my free advice, and the scene looked very real when broadcast a few weeks later.

One of my favourite two days, but perhaps one of the most exhausting, was for London's Burning where the call was to be on Streatham High Road at the Go-Carting Centre. We were all pleased to be told that our job today was to race each other, keeping near to each other stay in shot. Go-Carting is fun for a couple of hours but then it becomes tough. This turned into an event similar to Le mans 24-hour endurance race. The remarkable thing was that we were getting better and better as drivers, to the point we knew the course so well we were in turn regularly improving the course record.

Paul Heaton had previously arranged a Go-carting day for his birthday in Hull, and when we compared the times, they exactly corresponded to body weight, the lightest being the winner, the knowledge of which makes friendly competition pointless unless it's with weight watchers.

There were also several assignments where there was no filming at all, and these could be incredibly good fun. Every new series of Channel 4's Fifteen to One needed a run through for cameras and lighting before they filmed an entire series back-to-back. So, fifteen of us stand-ins got to play the game as if it was real, before the real contestants arrived.

After the millennium I had a small role as a Policeman in a British Sky Broadcasting surreal production called Strangerers starring Mark Williams. Driving down a deserted racetrack with raised bends in hot blue light pursuit of another car was exciting, and then I was to arrest the alien, also known as the comedian and presenter Jack Docherty.

I fell short of expectations. I had been given some cheap toy hand cuffs props, with no cuff holster, and had to find a way to hide them getting out of the car and then produce them to cuff my suspect alien. However, I couldn't get them around Jacks thick wrists which was probably because they were child sized. So, on the second take we had to fake it, and the planned close-up shot was duly abandoned.

I never got used to the shock of seeing myself in a poster campaign, but a lucrative contract to advertise internet banking for HSBC took things to new heights of embarrassment. They had designed six-foot cardboard cut outs of me holding a surfboard which appeared at every branch across the UK for a few months, along with leaflets and small posters, larger ones started to appear on a few billboards across London. I managed to persuade the Coulsdon Branch not to throw their cardboard me away, and it was not long before I had it home as a souvenir. Unfortunately, Lissa convinced me to dump it. This advertising campaign became an exceptionally large earner.

I was also regularly appearing in newspaper ads and posters, for a diverse range of goods and services, including Teletext,

Jewson's Builders, Danepak, Sainsburys Fish, British Gas, and as previously mentioned Autoglass.

A friend returning from France on holiday told me my face was splattered on large billboards all over the place, with me dressed like as a boy scout, described as looking like Russ Abbott. I had almost forgotten a photoshoot I had done for Scoot.com a new French search engine for the growing internet.

I had never had to consider how far I would have to go down the nudity route, as I had not ever been offered anything like it, but I was offered a photographic for Roo's Roofing where I was warned it might be a little uncomfortable. Stood in a photographic studio in just a pair of shorts, I was then greased up copiously by a shy female make-up artist, which exacerbated my embarrassment, which increased as she tied me Houdini style in chains and padlock.

Strangely I felt more embarrassed when fully clothed in the BBC's the Vice where I played a creepy attendee at an illegal strip joint in a disused warehouse behind Kings Cross Station. It might sound like everyman's dream to watch a young girl strip over, and over again, but I felt degraded and really felt for her doing this on a dirty piece of carpet in such a dirty seedy place amongst her peers. It must have been especially degrading for her.

I was brave enough to audition for a TV commercial that required full nudity but did not expect to have to get my kit off for the casting. Arriving at the studio I found that not only was this required, but I was to be accompanied by a female colleague which heightened both our embarrassment. I was partially relieved at not getting the part given the trauma of the audition.

A large percentage of my work was what could be described as moving wallpaper, whereby you would just fill a space in a crowd, and I did a fair share of these, being thrust aside by Michael Caine's bouncers in *Shiner* as he enters a boxing hall, steering clear of Ian McShane in *Sexy Beast* as he storms down the street, as a journalist scrambling after Toby Stephens in front of Buckingham Palace in James Bond's *Die Another Day*, or simply just walking down a street on the Merchant and Ivory production of *The Golden Bowl*. However, I can say that I have tasted the cuisine of Ismail Merchant who takes on the added role of head chef for the catering on set, which considering the quantity of food prepared was unbelievably good.

Occasionally even with background work you sometimes got a result, such as lying in a bed all day pretending to be sick for BBC's Casualty.

# CHAPTER XX FALLIN'

Up there with the worst calls I undertook was for a fantasy TV series called Dinotopia. Waterfall City, Dinotopia's fictional capital was by far the most impressive set I have ever worked in, it took up five-and-a-half acres of the back lot of Pinewood Studios, with canals, fountains, waterfalls, and beautifully designed imitation buildings. I had a few weeks work booked supplying background and had most of my days been in Waterfall City it would have been enjoyable. However, I was destined to be a peasant farmer and was sent out to a remote outdoor set. As I have said before background artists were often treated like peasants but playing one as well only worsened the experience.

The set was unprotected from the winter elements, and I was wearing the skimpiest of summer wardrobe each day trying not to look freezing in a harsh winter, as I tried along with my colleagues to avoid entering the zones marked out with various coloured ping pong balls on sticks. These showed where the VFX Dinosaurs were to be located, when computerised in in post-production.

There was no escaping the very harsh Hertfordshire weather, no shelter, warm coats too far away to grab up while you waited for the grouchy crew to set up. They were obviously also faced with the same conditions as us except, but they could wear their coats and thermals.

The atmosphere between crew and extras as they liked to call us begun to get somewhat hostile, as they seemed mostly impervious to our condition. At one stage there was even talk of a strike, and at the time I was a committee member of the Film Artist Association but as mobiles were not allowed on set for obvious reasons, I was unable to get advice.

A thoughtful Assistant Director said they would simply hire in a new batch of supporting artists if we went on strike, however I informed him that everyone was complaining to their respective agents, and to each other, and the production was getting a reputation which might make it difficult to re-recruit.

Eventually, our voices were listened to, and arrangements were made to ensure our coats or blankets were at hand, and that we didn't have to spend most of our lunch hour queuing for food.

When the Director Marco Brambilla saw the rushes for the farm sequences we had suffered for, most of it was binned because it was obvious that people do not turn blue with hyperthermia on a tropical island, and as there was no driving rain in the story, so it was hard to explain away the Somme like deep mud that people had to waddle through. Perhaps they should have taken us to a tropical island for a few weeks to film.

After weeks of filming, I was sincerely glad it was over, and when they decided to re-shoot the scenes, I respectfully declined. This was only the third time I had refused work. As mentioned, after refusing to play a perpetrator in the Murder of Stephen Lawrence docudrama, I also refused work to model for a photograph of a suspected paedophile for a wanted poster prop to be used in the TV series the Bill. The public often mistake fiction for reality, but a police poster would re-enforce the belief. I asked the agent how many people he had asked before me, and he replied don't ask.

New channels were starting to appear on TV, and I managed to secure some feature roles with Discovery Fitness, and DIY channels, as well as a UK Gold commercial as a night street cleaner watching TV through a shop window.

I managed to secure work on a TV Drama Longitude starring Jeremy Irons and enjoyed listening to his lecture attentively in the grand surroundings of the University College of London lecture hall. We learned all about John Harrison's efforts to develop a marine chronometer so that ships could navigate the globe with precision. The subject matter was fascinating, and I revelled in being paid to learn something from such a fantastic orator.

I was also the Irish dancing hallucination of Al Murray and Phil Daniels in *Time Gentleman Please* and had walk on parts for *Mr Charity* starring Stephen Tomkinson and Olivia Coleman.

BBC had commissioned a new comedy sketch show Lenny Henry in Pieces. I was sent to a Premier Inn to play the part of a chef and assumed wrongly that I would be filmed in the Kitchen. Upon arrival, we were told that Lenny was an assassin staying at the hotel, but is having difficulty re-assembling his sniper gun, and had called room service for help. We were supposed to help as best we could, gesturing like temperamental chefs do when things go wrong.

This was a difficult scene as although it was one of the larger rooms, it was extremely cramped with the equipment and with four performers it was a little like playing twister, which provided the desired effect on the final cut. Lenny Henry must have taken a shining to the bedroom as he later fronted Premier inn's extensive advertising campaign.

I am sure many British TV programmes get aired in the USA, but I did film one US production in the UK called *Emma Brodie* in which I played a British Social Worker sadly taking custody of a baby.

Perhaps the strangest scene I undertook, and the most ludicrous I have ever been seen on camera was for the BBC's Comedy Drama *Surrealissimo* about the trial Of Salvador Dali starring Stephen Fry.

I was dressed for an oversized 14 stone ballet dancer, and sporting a long fake beard, I performed on stage a few ungracious and incomplete arabesques, and a couple of Échappé's, as Stephen Fry looked on trying to keep a straight face. I never got a call from the Royal Ballet, which was disappointing as had I been able to shed a couple of stone, I might have forged out a new career.

Johnny Vaughan was well known for his presenting skills on Channel 4s Big Breakfast, and in 2001 he penned and stared in his own situation comedy called *"Orrible."* I played one of his dodgy mates in his local pub, but the series was panned by critics for the script and Vaughan's acting inability. Thankfully they didn't mention mine. It achieved incredibly low viewing figures and ran for one series and has never been repeated by the BBC. "Ultimately, it was shit" said Vaughan in a 2004 interview in The Stage.

When I received a call to Kings Cross Station, I was given virtually no details, the nature of the filming was secret, all I knew was the call time and where to report to. I was disappointed that this was a large call with many supporting artists going through wardrobe and make-up together, and although I had been given a character, a wife, and two young children, and some prop luggage I recognised that this was simply background work for another period piece. I managed to glean from others that it was a feature film based on a children's book, and it had only just commenced production.

A classic old red steam train was parked on platform 9 3/4, with old fashioned carriages which would be our holding area for now, but we were to stay with our designated families.

When direction came it was simple, we would walk our families up the platform, find our designated carriage, put our children on the Train and prepare to wave them off. After a full day of filming, which involved multi camera angles, we were treated to the old engine puffing its way out of the Station as we waved a tearful goodbye to our children heading to a School for young Magicians called Hogwarts.

At the time I assumed this meant a school for illusionists, as the phenomena that is Harry Potter had not yet mushroomed into the wider public consciousness. This was one of the first scenes shot of the first film and book *Harry Potter and the Philosopher's Stone*, and I am one of the very few people on earth who has sat on the Hogwarts Express

From my days at Dudley Samuel & Harrison I was familiar with the Grosvenor Chapel on South Audley Street for my early morning call for a new Richard Curtis romantic film in which I would play a guest videoing a Wedding. I had already worked on Bridget Jones Diary the previous year as a drinking guest in the Tate Modern top floor bar overlooking the Thames in an arduously long night shoot brightened up by Sally Phillips for whom I developed a secret crush through the night. I recall the assistant director responsible for the background appeared clueless when giving direction, and although I was able to hit my mark at the correct moment of dialogue, other supporting artists were sent into action without consideration of any appropriate timing. If you watch the scene back you might observe a group of three of my colleagues pass by together three times within seconds of each other.

Upon arrival at the Chapel, I was confused because one of the feature artists Andrew Lincoln also had a video camera. I was apparently booked in error, but the crew made use of me anyway. Dressed in my best wedding suite I followed the action as Keira Knightly and Chiwetel Ejiofor were surprised by Andrew Lincoln's surprise rendition with a brass accompaniment to *All you Need Is Love* for the opening sequence of *Love Actually*.

One of my last films to be involved with was *Finding Neverland*, filming for a couple of weeks in Richmond Theatre, playing a stagehand for Johnny Dep as JM Barrie who was getting his stage play of Peter Pan ready for production.

Dustin Hoffman was in an arm sling throughout and in obvious pain due to an earlier accident he befell off set, and it was admirable how he managed to slip it off when needed and not show any sign of discomfort. Most actors spend their lives trying to look genuinely in pain, but this was an example of his supremacy in world of acting.

I remarked how impressed I was in his ability to disguise the pain, and he joked he wouldn't get paid if he had to drop out. I held Mr Hoffman in awe before meeting him, and while his superstardom was obvious, he was very attentive to everyone around him, and ensured all the cast and crew felt comfortable in the Theatre and had a good array of jokes to share during the many breaks.

I was thrilled to be cast in the TV series for an episode of My Uncle Silas as one of a few friends setting up an outdoor wedding reception for the great Albert Finney. For three days we worked closely together, and he seemed genuinely as interested in me as I was in him, asking about my life and work. He asked the Director if he could give me a couple of lines, but it was respectfully declined, probably as there was no voice coach at hand to teach me an instant old school rural Somerset accent which was needed.

However, given his status, he adlibbed and threw me a line which needed an impromptu response which I delivered and got my small, upgraded pay for the three days much to the annoyance of the Director.

A year later I arrived at the most impressive of sets. After getting through the rigmarole of wardrobe, hair, and make-up, in which my appearance was fundamentally altered, I walked into the chamber of the House of Commons as a1930's MP. If I hadn't been directed to the Conservative side, and if this was real, it would have been a political fantasy come true.

Our direction was to heckle Winston Churchill in his famous speech to the Commons where he described the militarisation of Nazi Germany, and then fall silent when the facts supplied sent a chill through the house. I really enjoyed being boisterous shouting my unscripted but directed *"sit down Winston*" as the actor perused his surroundings. The performance was outstanding, and I wondered where they found this Churchill look alike who combined with the set and crowd convinced me time travel had been invented.

At lunch time I felt compelled to see if I could find out who this Churchill fella was, and approaching the Tea and coffee stand behind the set, he turned to me and said, *"hello Ray, how are you?"* Looking puzzled and somewhat bemused, he added *"It's Albert."* Grinning at me he said he had trouble recognising himself today, as he was quickly whisked off by an Assistant Director who frowned on my fraternisation with her star as it was considered unprofessional. *The Gathering Storm* added three more awards to the Finney collection, and he deserved them all.

I was booked as a stand in for the third series of the game show *My Kind of Music* hosted by Michael Barrymore. His guests were a new band called *Blue* who had a song in the chart called *All Rise.* Rehearsals for the show were not going well, and after the boy band undertook their first run through, they were told that there was no time to run through it again and to get off the stage. A standoff ensued between the respective managements, as it was clearly unreasonable to only allow one run through before a live performance. In front of me Barrymore snapped at his crew *"who's fucking show is this, who do they think they are? Get them off!"*

My admiration for the funny man of British TV declined rapidly, which was worsened soon after when he was arrested with others over the death of Stuart Lubbock who sustained anal injuries at his house party in Essex. Ironically the lyrics to *Blue's All Rise* were prophetic.

*Your honour, please, gotta believe what I say, What I will tell happened just the other day, I must confess, cause I've had about enough, I need your help, gotta make this here thing stop...... You're on the stand, with your back against the wall,*

*Nowhere to run, and nobody you can call (oh no), I just can't wait, now the case is open wide, You'll try to pray, but the jury will decide*

I had a casting for a lucrative photographic shoot to take place in Prague, and I was given to understand from my new modelling agent Mugshots that I was one of two being considered, but unusually it took a while for them to decide. Meanwhile, I was offered a walk on part sitting in a bar in a new Ralph Fiennes movie called *Spider*.

Arriving in suitable time I had the customary breakfast and was taken to wardrobe to get fitted in a 1950's style suit. When the Assistant Director came to take me to hair and makeup, she checked that I was aware that the haircut was going to be very severe. I asked what she meant and she explained I needed to be shaved short back and sides, and that they had confirmed this with my agent.

This was the first I had heard about it and was very conscious that I should not change my hair for the Prague job. I could lose thousands for a couple of hundred at best. I explained my predicament but sensed real annoyance from the Assistant Director. I asked for a few minutes and rang Mugshots for an update, but they had still not had any confirmation of otherwise but would chase it up given the circumstances. I was due on set and the Assistant Director took me into the pub and asked the Director David Cronenberg for advice. Without being told anything I was escorted off set and told to go home as I was no longer needed, and they refused to sign my attendance documents. Half an hour later I got a call from Mugshots that I had not been successful.

I did get paid for the full day eventuality, having gone through the PACT/FAA arbitration route, but this summarised the kind of work security deployed in the TV and film industry.

This was not Mugshot's fault, but I was soon to fall out with them when I was successful in a casting, they sent me to, to model for a poster for Braun, a sponsor of the forthcoming 2002 FIFA World Cup.

I had always considered taking up football refereeing when I retired from playing, something I did in 2021 with the Essex Football Association. This was my chance to try on the kit twenty years in advance.

Dressed in a FIFA Referee's black kit with an extensive false beard, I understood that I was only getting a studio fee, as the way they were presenting the poster and internet campaign I would not be recognisable, and therefore my image rights were waived. The usual studio fee was £100 per hour before tax and agency commission of 20% which left you with about £60. This session went on for three hours, but when I informed Mugshots of the overtime, they told me that they had agreed a standard fee of just £100 gross. I was not happy with this as considering travel time and costs, including for the casting trip, it was not worth doing.

Later, on the set of another production I was congratulated on getting the lucrative Braun contract. They too were one of four of us featured on the various posters and internet advertising associated with the World Cup, and it was being displayed across the world. They had recognised me on a billboard on the Underground. They were also being paid for their image rights in the thousands, but they had a different agent.

I rang Mugshots and asked for an explanation, and it was woeful. They did not agree I could be recognised so that was that, even though it was obvious that I could and the other models with similar shots were all getting global image rights. I was being mugged, and I thought perhaps my agents name derived from being mugged and then shot. I found out in hindsight that the worldwide rights amounted to close to £10'000.

The problem was by complaining I had in effect bitten off a hand that was feeding me. I was very reliant on the occasional windfall of lucrative advertising contracts, but if I was to accept this swindle how could I continue to make ends meet, which would in effect mean biting my own hand off.

In late 2001 I was asked to do background on another version of the film The Four Feathers, filming in an East London Dock this involved hundreds of supporting artists recreating the boarding of cavalry onto a ship to go out to war in the Sudan. It took hours to get through wardrobe given the sheer volume of crowd and it was something of a military organisation to get people into place to ironically to film a military operation. Most of the women were in end of the century garb which severely restricted movement, and it was clear from the very beginning of filming that the many horses being ridden, or pulling carriages were restless and there was an obvious ever-present danger given the congestion that someone might get hurt filming this sequence.

This was an exceptionally large, complex, and dangerous scene, with multiple camera positions as hundreds waved union jacks to cheer on the departing force, and this noise along with the marching military band further unsettled the horses. I felt uncomfortable and eased my way back to the rear of the crowd only to realise others had the same idea and gaps started appearing at the front where the horses were parading just a few feet away, and it was no longer obvious that the riders were sufficiently experienced as horses occasionally reared up, requiring further takes. Assistant Directors tried to encourage the crowd to get tighter, but there was a genuine fear in the air greater than being sacked.

During lunch there were a lot of heated conversations about safety, but it was hoped that the hours break would settle the horses and they may get used to the cheering and music.

We returned to set, and I noted we were a little short in numbers and guessed some people had quit. I joked we should send them some white feathers; A joke I later regretted.

It wasn't long after lunch that the inevitable came to pass.

Without warning, a carriage driver lost control of his horses, and veered into the crowd just fifty yards from me, many of whom were unable to get out of the way, some women restricted by their costumes fell, some others were knocked over by the horses and the attached carriage ran over them. Some brave people managed to grab the reigns of the horses and bring the carriage to a standstill, with the occupants not really understanding what had happened, they got out laughing probably through nerves, but then realised there were bodies in their trail. Some moving slowly, some getting up and looking around in a daze, but some lay motionless. They looked lifeless.

We returned to our holding tents and waited. We then heard that the producers were still considering filming it caused uproar. This is the value placed on supporting artists by some production companies. I didn't know the injured but others did and they were distraught, unsure if they had died, or how severe their injuries were. We heard air ambulances come and go, and we were all released and told to come back tomorrow. I politely declined.

When you budget a $35 million film, human life can be viewed as cheap, and it was clear this American production on British shores were cutting corners with health and safety. All animals on set are usually very well trained, and risk assessments are usually thorough, and any significant risk moderated to a reasonable level. There was little sign this was the case on this day, and with a little Schadenfreude I was pleased the film made a $6 million loss.

I assume the families were paid off with a silencing gag, as little information materialised about the accident in the public domain, but I heard with good authority that three of my working colleagues died that day or soon after from their injuries. They were killed while in the care of the production companies Miramax Films, Jaffilms and High Command Productions Ltd.

I had been living my dream. I was a homeowner again, settled in my community surrounded by family and doing a job I mostly adored. What is more, I had plenty of disposable income to pay for classy designer clothes. However, as this year unfolded, the dream slowly started to turn sour, and become a nightmare. Alicia Keys was in the chart's with

*"Fallin',"* with the lyrics *I keep on fallin', in and out of love, with you.*

Returning home from The Four Feathers, I met an atmosphere, hoping to off load my trauma of the day, Lissa was distant, it was if we were sharing a house, but no longer together.

As Christmas loomed, I confronted Lissa about her mood, and distance, and she told me in a very matter of fact way, that took no account of our thirteen years together, that she wanted me to leave. Of course, it got very heated and a spell went by when we just kept apart, me hoping things would iron out, her not sure what to do about the father of her child who was too young at three to understand anything.

After a few days of unpleasantness, it had been determined that she wanted to stay in the house, so we could not sell it. She even argued I had no right to the house as she paid the mortgage, before I countered that my name was on the deeds with hers, and if we swapped genders, she would not accept the same scenario.

She was obviously getting legal advice from somewhere, and she made an ultimatum. If I didn't move out, she would take Sean to her parents in Stourbridge and I would never see him again.

I agreed to move back into my parents' house, while we negotiated a settlement. I made a cassette copy for my dad of the new Robbie Williams album of Frank Sinatra covers, which he liked being a Sinatra fan. *Somethin' Stupid* with Nicole Kidman became the Christmas number one that year which was ironic given my circumstances.

Eventually I agreed that Lissa could have and stay in the House with Sean, but she would pay me half the equity on the current value of the house which amounted to £14'000 so that I had some cushion to re-establish myself. She had wanted half the equity of Granville, but she dropped this idea when she found out at that time it had negative equity as prices had dropped significantly in Hull. In hindsight I should have added this to the pay-out.

I found this process soul destroying, my world had been torpedoed and the underlying reason eventual emerged when Lissa explained in a way to be hurtful that she was engaged in an affair with a Croydon Solicitor called Gary, who was obviously the person advising her on her every move, while holding down his own large property with his wife and children.

Lissa secured a loan from her dad and step mum, but the money never came to me, so a week later, having not returned my key, I moved back in for a couple of hours until she transferred some of the money.

It was at this moment that I realised the depths Lissa was contemplating. She had gone upstairs for a while to discuss things with someone over the phone and waiting for a long time I decided to see what she was up to. As I approached the open door of her bedroom she was stood in front of a mirror, with a hairbrush gripped tightly in two hands raised to her face. I stopped silently confused at what she was up to, why would you brush your hair at a time like this?

I watched in stunned amazement as she released one side of the wooden hairbrush which cracked into her face. She yelled out in pain, and despite still being terribly angry with her, my immediate sympathy took over, but she shrugged off my attention. I realised that she had deliberately caused herself an injury while we were alone in the house and no doubt this was to be used to portray herself as a victim of domestic violence.

Things had gone too far, and there was no way back, any chance of getting back together was extinguished. The Lissa I knew would never have considered such an action, she was a ferocious supporter of women who were the subject of domestic abuse, and this pathetic stunt undermined everything she believed in. In hindsight I wondered if this Gary had put her up to it to strengthen her negotiation position.

More through being found out and probable guilt she transferred the first instalment of £10’000 of the agreed £14’000 to the bank, as this was the maximum transfer per day, and although my instincts said hang around until after midnight, I agreed to trust that she would transfer the remaining £4000 in the morning. To her credit she never falsely alleged she had been assaulted, but the black eye that emerged on her face allowed people to draw their own conclusions.

Two days passed and she said she had changed her mind as she was being bullied into paying me money she needed for our child. We had yet to agree maintenance it was true but we had not really discussed it yet, and before we could, I got a letter from the infamous Child Support Agency detailing my commitments which if they were not met would result in dire consequences for me. The owed £4000 was not relevant to the CSA, and ironically my intention was to pay far more that the CSA demanded.

She was on a decent income my family were supplying every working day free child-care and I had already paid in thousands of pounds into a child savings account for him.

I decided to take her to Court for the £4000, in which her defence was to try and turn proceedings into a divorce settlement hearing which it was not. The judge sided with her story which I chose not to counter because I understood the Judge had no legal choice but to award the money to me which he did.

During this process it was difficult to concentrate on work, however the BBC employed me to be the Landlord of a he pub in a new comedy written by David Cummings and Paul Whitehouse. Happiness had the plot line around becoming single and was very pertinent to me at the time. It was great to work with a comedy icon in Paul Whitehouse who played the lead. I also appeared in another David Cummings BBC comedy called *World of Pub* as a Newspaper Seller outside Phil Cornwell's pub.

Just before Christmas, I managed to rent a flat above a Chinese take away shop on Old Lodge Lane Purley, a road which if followed for a couple of miles would take you back to where it all begun for me at Betts Mead Parade. It was almost opposite the old ABC Cinema where I had as a toddler enjoyed Saturday Morning Cinema but this large building like so many others had succumbed to becoming a Bingo Hall.

As things settled down Sean spent a lot of time with me, and I enjoyed picking him up from school and dropping into my Parents before returning him to Lissa, and when I was working my mum took over.

Lissa's affair did not work out for her, and it was not long before she gleefully and without warning introduced her new boyfriend to me when I returned Sean one day. It was then that I realised whatever feelings I had ever had for her were gone. I really didn't care anymore and felt happier on my own, spending time with my son and family was all I needed.

I was approaching forty years old and had not ever lived alone before. I was either in the family home, shared accommodation, or living with a partner. I started to revel in the relative freedom. I was determined to stay single for some time to come.

On a warm summer night with my windows open struggling to sleep, I heard the Chinese family below talking in mandarin in their rear garden, and although I never understood a single word, I could feel their warmth and love for each other in their tone and laughter, and the deep respect given to the obvious head of the family business. This was the first time I felt empty and cried myself to sleep, I had not lost my family, it was just fragmented and broken, and would never be fixed.

My dreaded 40$^{th}$ Birthday arrived without ceremony or recognition. I dug out the present Lissa had bought me last year, David Bowie's Hours. I often stood in my second-floor bay window looking out across the valley and listened intently to *Thursday's Child* repeatedly as the lyrics rather than the song title took on a new and very personal meaning to me.

*"All of my life I've tried so hard,*
*Doing my best with what I had,*
*Nothing much happened all the same,*
*Something about me stood apart,*
*A whisper of hope that seemed to fail,*
*Maybe I'm born right out of my time,*
*Breaking my life in two,*
*Throw me tomorrow....* Chorus,
*Seeing my past to let it go,*
*Sometimes I cried my heart to sleep,*
*Shuffling days and lonesome nights,*
*Sometimes my courage fell to my feet."*

My work had suffered with these distractions, I managed to get a feature on a corporate video and play a priest again for a BBC advert promoting their new BBC Talent programme.

I appreciate, but I have never been an enthusiastic fan of Rowan Atkinson, and just do not get Mr Bean. In 2002 I was sent to a large call at St. Albans Cathedral for a new comedy film Johnny English and was dressed as a Catholic Cardinal in the grand crowning ceremony with John Malkovich and Natalie Imbruglia. It was very much like a supporting artist and walk on artist convention, which was convenient as it was a good chance to say farewell to many good friends and colleagues, I had worked with over the years.

The issues with Braun and Spider along with the Four Feathers tragedy had soured my outlook and from careful monitoring of my income, it was obviously significantly on the decline. My pay out from the house was also declining, and my future seemed uncertain.

Paul Heaton had many obsessive admirers, but perhaps his super stalker was a charming American citizen called Christina *Tina* Lyons, who flew around the world to ensure her attendance at every Beautiful South event at great expense to herself. She spent so much time in the UK she had started to develop her own friendships and her own social circle. I often felt my role was to try and do what I could to protect members of the band from unwanted attention, which could involve distraction techniques, coaxing hotel staff to restrict access to the bar, giving false information about meeting up, and sometimes being cruel to be kind, and telling it straight. Tina was too smart to fall for any of these antics, and if there was a way to get where she wanted, she would be there, and she coached younger fans in her dark arts.

Paul Heaton was promoting his new solo album called Mitch under the name Biscuit Boy at the 2002 V-Festivals in Staffordshire and Essex. Having arrived in the secure area of Hyland's Park Chelmsford, it occurred to me that I had never been to this small City before, and I had now spent time in every city in England. It is therefore ironic that in time to come I would settle down in this picturesque capital of Essex, as if I had completed a board game.

Paul's backing band had started playing cricket with a tennis ball behind the JJB Puma Arena Stage, and it reminded me of playing cricket backstage at a festival in Ireland in the famous Pairc Ui Chaoimh Stadium in Ballintemple in Cork, not far from where my grandfather Valentine Sheehan was born, and when it was my turn to bat, I had to face an over of fast in-swingers from Paul who was as good at Cricket Player as he was at Football, and from my experiences playing target cricket in his back garden in Chipstead over many years he usually got me out quickly. Surviving the onslaught from him, I started to enjoy myself getting into a winning rhythm as each less competent band or crew member took their turn to bowl at me, when an exceptionally large security man snatched my cricket bat. Looking around in disbelief he was too large and scary to argue with, and then realised he was clearing the way to ensure the safety of Kylie Minogue who was making her way onto stage.

I looked incredulously at her, but from her shrug and apology it was obvious this was her over-protective management team's decision rather than hers. After she was gone with my concentration broken, I was out first ball.

Band cricket was highly competitive, but was a great distraction between sound checks and performance, and most importantly kept us away from bars and pubs.

The relationship with Lissa had become increasingly difficult, I must look after Sean when it suited her to support her work and lifestyle, but I would have to organise my work around her needs became her self-centred mantra. This arrangement was also causing my mother a great deal of heartache, as Lissa felt it was my mum's duty to look after Sean regardless if I was not available, and my mum was tormented by a sense of guilt when she was busy.

Lissa understood how much I loved Sean and used this as a bargaining chip to get what she wanted. I felt by moving away for my needs, and not being at her disposal it would re-balance things. We agreed to take it in turns to look after him at weekends.

Living in Coulsdon was becoming torturous. Daily, driving past my home that I partly owned, and where my first-born child lived, and where I now needed permission to enter was painful, and became increasingly so. Picking Sean up from my old School I had attended all those years ago, and now must return him to his separate home that I had managed to buy in my home town but could not enjoy, eroded my spirits.

I clearly became depressed, to the point of considering ending it all. Being self-employed, and with work wilting I had too much time to stew and feel sorry for myself. There were too many triggers in my neighbourhood, and I had to get out, but where?

I thought back to the dart throwing in Paul's back garden back in 1982 and took comfort that sometimes taking the risk of just upping sticks can shake things up for the better. I loved the song Billericay Dickie by Ian Dury and the Blockheads and was amused by the name of Braintree in Essex. I considered Southend as it was by the sea, but remember it was on the Thames Estuary, much like Hull. I was able to secure some freelance work in Social Research as this would give me the flexibility to work from anywhere.

I started to apply for work away from Coulsdon and Purley.

A new housing development on the old Marconi Factory site in Chelmsford, where radar was first invented and developed, were advertising new flats to let which extended over the former home of Chelmsford City Football Club who had moved to Melbourne Park. I didn't have a lot of things to move and managed it in a small, hired transit van. However, by the time I had off loaded into the second floor flat I felt too exhausted to drive back to pick up my car, so I slumbered on a mattress amongst the unopened boxes and dismantled Ikea furniture.

In the morning, I woke to the sounds of a building site, Crompton Street was full of bull dozers, and hard hatted men going about their business. The Estate was far from complete. I still had an escape plan to move back to Coulsdon where my family resided if things didn't work out, but I felt free, and the misery of rejection started to decline, as I was no longer confronted by the regular triggers that set off my depression, as the place where I grew up and had felt safe and secure had become infected with misery. From here I could spend quality time with my growing son and start a fresh.

The next day I drove the transit van back to the hire company and picked up my car and drove away from Surrey back towards my new life in Essex.

A couple of weeks later, when picking Sean up from my new flat, Lissa asked me to move back in with her again. She had betrayed me twice and I no longer had any trust love or affection for her left. To be kind I said I would think about it, but I was intoxicated with my new adventure, close enough to Sean to be part of his life, but far enough way not to be at the beckoning and call of Lissa, and all the negative triggers of the trauma of the separation. My home town had become toxic, and I felt I had to look after myself. Furthermore, she had betrayed me a second time. There was no trust left.

Looking back, moving to Chelmsford looks like a strange decision at the time. If I could have moved Hull within commuting distance of Coulsdon, then I would have undoubtedly relocated there, where I undoubtedly had ample friends for support.

However, the world had moved on, internet technology was accelerating in leaps and bounds, keeping in touch was no longer necessarily about distance, and I could work from anywhere undertaking social research. Chelmsford provided just the right amount of contact and distance to my son.

As I complete this autobiography, I have been settled in Chelmsford for two decades now, and it is a place I have grown to love, as it provided the platform for my renewal, and where I was able to restart my borrowed life again.

## PROLOGUE

Upon completing this autobiography late in 2021, it became apparent that many of my teenage friends from our Reigate days have had incredible success in their lives. Paul Heaton, after an extensive career fronting the Housemartins, and then the Beautiful South, is still writing, performing, and charting as a duet with Jacqui Abbott, and as I write, are about to tour the United Kingdom again with his 21st studio album. Gus Gregory recently co-hosted the TV show Flippin' Bangers and is a professional photographer held in high esteem. Chris Lang has become a successful Television Producer and Writer with countless credits including Unforgotten, Dark Heart, Undeniable, Innocent, A Mother's Son, Torn, and Amnesia. All this after a successful acting career appearing in Drop The Dead Donkey, Outside Edge, A Dance To The Music of Time, Shadow Of The Noose, and All Along The Watchtower. Steve Musham had success with a few bands, the Corn Dollies, Lockjaw, Repetition, Rhythm of Space, and the Escalators. Quinton Cook who changed his name to Norman during a short successful outing with the Housemartins, formed Beats International and then shot to international superstardom as DJ Fat Boy Slim. John Laurenson is currently a BBC Radio 4 Journalist.

Despite its taste, there must have been something magical in the beer served up at the now demolished Railway Hotel, and the boxing day PORAJ team of the early 80's if reformed would certainly now be regarded as a celebrity team.

Stan Cullimore went on to write over 120 children's books and appeared in the Bopps for the Nickelodeon Junior Channel as well as becoming a free-lance journalist.

On a sad note, I learned that Susan Oliver née Lillywhite "Silly" after emigrating to New Zealand and marrying Malcolm Stuart and bearing two children Joe and Kate has since passed away. Christina "Tina" Lyons, the person who introduced me to my wife has also passed away, both leaving this world prematurely.

Sue Oliver (Silly)1963 -2015

Christina Lyons (Tina) 1964-2014

## Ode to Raymond

When Teddy Boy was no longer hot
But mod was getting real warm
In April 1962
A baby child was born

That Russian dog had travelled in space
But man hadn't reached the moon
Meanwhile down in Coulsdon
They were suffering a baby boom

The 50's had brought Denise
Followed by Viv and Des
The 60's Raymond William Barry
Or so the Certificate says

Yes, the swinging 60's
And what that era brought
From Comrades Club to Golf Club
Raymond's parents would cavort

On then through the 70's
Through flower power and glam
Through General Strikes and Power Cuts
And being a Chelsea fan

Through It's A Knockout, Crackerjack
And Generation Game
Through feather cuts and tight-knit perms
Ray's parting stayed the same

Then September 78
This month that us two met
The meeting place-refectory
The college – Redhill Tech

Like punk had never happened
Line dancing not just yet
There we sat two fashion gods
Blue jeans and black V-neck

Already too old for new romantic
No rhythm for rhythm and blues
That day we forged a friendship
Based on football, crisps, and booze

We took to regions pubs and clubs
We took to floor with ease
Me a slightly Dirtier Dancing
Ray a greaser Grease

Onwards to the 80's
We went to Hull and back
On the dole in Grafton Street
In red but never black

And those New Years spent in Germany
Dietkirchen uber alles
Sabine, Alfred, George, and Berndt
But who the fuck was Alice?

On then to the 90's
And new priorities born
My number one "A Little Time"
And Ray's a little Sean

Finally, to the noughties
And Raymond settled down
Nights spent in, cuddling up (bottle of wine)
But far from his home town

But the reason that he's far from home
The reason he's right here
Is he met the girl who gave him more
than football crisps and beer

And now we've both turned 43
Some say over the hill
But I've got Golden Linda
And Ray's got diamond Gill

So let those memories touched upon
Stay Raymond's and stay mine
But let that Gold take hold
And let the Diamond Shine.

# Family

The Barry & Sheehan Family on a Ferry to Ireland 1963
Aunty Patsy, Denise, Me, Mum, Desmond, Dad, Vivien,
Nancy & Valentine

Mum & Dad at my wedding 2005

# My Siblings

Denise, Vivien, Desmond

## The Reigations

Paul Heaton, Chris Lang, Norman Cook,
Gus Gregory, John Laurenson, Steve Musham

## New Family

Jessica, Charlie & Gillian

# My Portfolio

Danepak, Autoglass/Chelsea FC, HSBC Internet Banking, Proo's Roofing

Jewson's, Teletext

Sainsbury, Sony

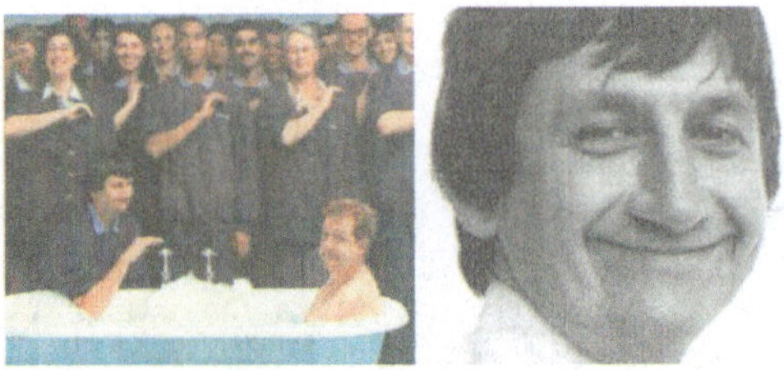

British Gas, Telewest Cable TV.

# FILMS

JOHNNY ENGLISH

loveactually
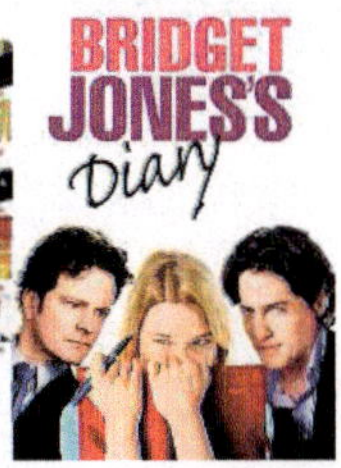
BRIDGET JONES'S
Diary

Harry Potter

FINDING NEVERLAND

FOUR FEATHERS

Printed in Great Britain
by Amazon

83224353R10163